DATE DUE

S

622 mm
12 . 10 . 21

# Perception, Learning and the Self

# Perception, Learning and the Self

## Essays in the Philosophy of Psychology

### D. W. Hamlyn

Professor of Philosophy,
Birkbeck College, University of London

ROUTLEDGE & KEGAN PAUL

London, Boston, Melbourne and Henley

This collection first published in 1983
by Routledge & Kegan Paul Ltd
39 Store Street, London WC1E 7DD,
9 Park Street, Boston, Mass. 02108, USA,
296 Beaconsfield Parade, Middle Park,
Melbourne, 3206, Australia, and
Broadway House, Newtown Road,
Henley-on-Thames, Oxon RG9 1EN
Set in IBM Press Roman by
Columns, Reading
and printed in Great Britain by
Page Brothers Ltd, Norwich, Norfolk

ISBN 0-7100-9264-4

# CONTENTS

# Contents

# PREFACE AND ACKNOWLEDGMENTS

Over the last ten to fifteen years I have been concerned with a number of issues which have to do, explicitly or implicitly, with the philosophy of psychology. The papers which have emerged from this concern have not in every case been conceived as having a direct bearing on each other. It has now become apparent to me, however, that they do have such a bearing and that it might be useful for them to be seen together. Hence the present volume. I have divided the papers into three sections, but there is considerable overlap between the sections, and I believe that the papers as a whole present a certain view of issues arising in and from cognitive psychology. That indeed is the case even where they contain reflections upon other parts of psychology, upon epistemology and upon the philosophy of mind. I am grateful to the various people who made the original papers possible.

The original sources of the papers are given below. I acknowledge with thanks the permission of the editors and publishers of the journals and books from which the papers are taken to reprint the papers in this book.

1 'Unconscious inference and judgment in perception' from *Images, Perception and Knowledge*, ed. J.M. Nicholas, Dordrecht, D. Reidel, 1977, pp. 195-212.
2 'The concept of information in Gibson's theory of perception' from *Journal for the Theory of Social Behaviour*, vol. 7, no. 1, 1977, pp. 5-16.
3 'Perception and agency' from *The Monist*, vol. 61, no. 7, 1978, pp. 536-47.

4 'Perception, information and attention' not previously published, but presented orally to the British Psychological Society, December 1980.

5 'The logical and psychological aspects of learning' from *The Concept of Education*, ed. R.S. Peters, London, Routledge & Kegan Paul, 1967, pp. 24-43.

6 'Conditioning and behaviour' from *Explanation in the Behavioural Sciences*, eds R. Borger and F. Cioffi, Cambridge University Press, 1970, pp. 139-52.

7 'Epistemology and conceptual development' from *Cognitive Development and Epistemology*, ed. T. Mischel, New York and London, Academic Press, 1971, pp. 3-24.

8 'Human learning' from *Philosophy of Psychology*, ed. S.C. Brown, London, Macmillan, 1974, pp. 139-57.

9 'The concept of development' from *Proceedings of the Philosophy of Education Society of Great Britain*, vol. 9, 1975, pp. 26-39.

10 'What exactly is social about the origins of understanding?' from *Social Cognition*, eds G. Butterworth and P. Light, Brighton, Harvester Press, 1982, pp 17-31.

11 'Unconscious intentions' from *Philosophy*, vol. 46, no. 175, 1971, pp. 12-22.

12 'Self-deception' from *Proceedings of the Aristotelian Society*, supp. vol. 44, 1971, pp. 45-60.

13 'Person-perception and our understanding of others' from *Understanding Other Persons*, ed. T. Mischel, Oxford, Blackwell, 1974, pp. 1-36 (less passage pp. 30-2).

14 'Self-knowledge' from *The Self*, ed. T. Mischel, Oxford, Blackwell, 1977, pp. 170-200 (less appendix, pp. 197-9).

15 'The phenomena of love and hate' from *Philosophy*, vol. 53, no. 203, 1978, pp. 5-20.

16 'Learning to love', not previously published.

# INTRODUCTION

If there is one underlying implication in the following essays it is the inadequacy of the information-processing model for cognitive psychology. That may seem a bold claim, since it is taken as axiomatic in many quarters that the theoretical structure of cognitive psychology must be expressed in terms of the notion of cognitive systems with varying functional roles, but which together serve to receive and process the information about the world that the senses provide. It is also sometimes said that the sense of 'information' that this view presupposes is a technical one which has only a remote connection with our ordinary notions of information, whatever these are. Moreover, it is claimed that it is the notion of information-processing systems which makes possible a satisfactory link between psychology and physiology; whatever the exact nature of physiological purposes, they have to be construed for psychological processes in terms of the functional roles that systems of such processes perform, and from the point of view of cognitive psychology those roles are the receipt and processing of information.

I do not myself believe that the notion of information presupposed in such a theory is so remote from our ordinary notion of information. Certainly it is parasitical upon that ordinary notion (something that I believe to be true even of the sense of 'information' implied in so-called 'information theory'). To speak of the receipt and processing of information in this context is in fact another, more technical, way of speaking of our perception of the world and the significance that this has for our beliefs and knowledge of the world, as well as for subsequent action. (Some of this is spelled out in relation to the views of James Gibson in the second of these essays.)

1

As I have said, the main negative conclusion to be derived from these essays is the inadequacy of this story about information processing for cognitive psychology. It is important that those last words 'for cognitive psychology' be included. It might be held that no story about information receipt and processing tells the whole truth about perception, for example, simply because there is more to perception than the strictly epistemic factors (expressible in terms of our seeing that such and such is the case or possibly in terms of seeing things as such and such) that the connection between perception and belief implies. There is, as the first and some subsequent essays suggest a sensory, aesthetic aspect to perception such that no account of perception is complete without reference to it. A cognitive psychologist might, however, reply by saying that, whatever truth there is in that claim, it is irrelevant to his purposes. He is interested only in those aspects of psychological processes which involve or reflect upon cognition.

I am not entirely sure that that would be an adequate reply. 'Seeing-as' may presuppose, for example, as Wittgenstein in effect emphasized, certain aspects of the imagination which are not easily construable in information-processing terms. The same applies to the role of attention, as is brought out in the fourth essay. A final point in this regard is that the information-processing model suggests, even if it does not positively assert, that for cognition the organism can be construed as a system the relation of which to the environment can be described as a passive one only. That is to say that cognition is construed simply in terms of reactions, however processed by internal mechanisms, to the environment that impinges on the senses. In the philosophical literature there are to be found occasional references to the idea that anything that can perceive must also be capable of action (in a strong sense of that word), but just why that is so has not always been spelled out clearly. Some psychologists too, notably Jean Piaget (and, to an extent, James Gibson), have emphasized the role of activity in perception and in the general acquisition and growth of knowledge and understanding of the world. Once again, however, the exact role of activity in this respect has not always been made clear, and what *is* said about it suggests that its role is taken to be a limited one. If I am right in what I say in the third essay, the role of agency and activity is more fundamental than that and no adequate account of perception can be given which does not recognize that a perceiver must be an agent. How is the fact of agency to be incorporated within an information-processing model?

2

It might be thought that the straight answer to that question must be 'Not at all'. However, as I have already said, one of the strongest motivations for accepting the information-processing model is the thought that it fits well with some, at least, of the known facts about physiology. (Neural and brain processes can well be thought of as involving coding of information.) If one insists, as I think that one should, that perception must be seen in a context which presupposes that a perceiver must also be an agent, the problem immediately arises how the psychological facts are to be accommodated to the neural and other physiological facts. How in particular is activity to be construed in physiological terms? That question raises immense problems which would not be nearly so apparent if perception could be thought of simply in terms of the acquisition of information.

Or so it might seem at first sight. There are, however, additional problems, which are in effect brought out by the essays in my second section. These have to do largely with learning and with what Piaget calls 'genetic epistemology' (which ought, I think, to be taken as concerned with the question 'How is the growth of knowledge and understanding possible?'). The papers are also concerned with themes which are worked out more systematically in my *Experience and the Growth of Understanding* (London: Routledge & Kegan Paul, 1978), even if they also add to that. The central problem is how we are to understand as possible the growth of knowledge and understanding in the individual, or, in other words, how we are to understand the possibility of learning viewed as the acquisition of new knowledge or understanding (or at least as something dependent on that) as a result of an interaction between old knowledge or understanding and experience. It might be thought tendentious to view learning in that light. Have not behaviourists, for example, classically dealt with learning in terms of such notions as conditioning and habit formation? The sixth essay brings forward fundamental criticisms of the whole notion of conditioning and thereby of the kind of view of learning that has been put forward by psychologists such as B.F. Skinner. It is suggested, among other things, that many of the phenomena that have been discussed under the heading of 'conditioning' involve perceptual considerations, involve seeing things in certain ways, something that cannot be elucidated in terms of notions such as that of conditioning.

Moreover, to see something in a certain way in effect involves bringing it under a concept. To see $X$ as $F$ is possible only if the perceiver knows something of what it is for something to be $F$ (and that is what having the concept of $F$ essentially involves). Hence the acquisition of knowledge of the world presupposes some kind of interaction between conceptual understanding and experience. How then does that conceptual understanding grow? More crucially, how does it even start if conceptual understanding of the world depends upon experience but if experience itself links up with conceptual understanding only if it itself is, like perception in general, concept-dependent? Some of the answers to those questions are spelled out in the eighth and tenth essays, along with some answers to what are perhaps even more basic questions, to which I shall return.

Nevertheless, any attempt to lay down any general rules about conceptual growth in the individual (*not* development, despite the existence of what is called 'developmental psychology', as is indicated in the ninth essay) must face the question how much of what is constant and universal is due to logical considerations and how much is merely psychological (if that 'merely' can be forgiven). That is in effect the theme of the fifth and seventh essays. Just as in the first section there is one psychologist occupying the centre of the stage — James Gibson — so here it is Jean Piaget (both of whom died quite recently). Piaget comes under criticism for insufficiently distinguishing the epistemological from the psychological, despite his advocacy of a subject to be termed 'genetic epistemology' and his distinction of it from developmental psychology. Some have found the criticisms unjust, if not misconceived, but the distinctions on which the criticisms are based — those between the logical and the psychological and between the epistemological (or philosophical in general) and the psychological — still seem to me valid ones. Indeed, both Piaget and Gibson can be accused of not doing sufficient justice to epistemological considerations (see the second essay for criticisms of Gibson along those lines), but the accusation is merited for different reasons in each case. Gibson simply fails to take account of certain epistemological considerations, e.g. the role of belief and concepts in perception; Piaget takes a quite different view of epistemology from that taken of it by modern Anglo-Saxon philosophers, and he has not altogether learnt the lesson provided by their critique of the Kantian-Hegelian tradition within which he works. In consequence Piaget does not offer a clear account of what he supposes genetic epistemology to be — which is *not* of course to say that there is no such subject (see the tenth essay).

Piaget himself seems to believe that learning can be construed in

terms which are more or less biological or alternatively in terms implying organization of structures. Despite his emphasis at times on activity
on the part of the individual such an account is not far from that
implied by the information-processing model. It is at any rate compatible with it just as it is compatible in some respects with ideas implicit
in thinking concerning artificial intelligence. It is sometimes said, however, (and is said by me in the fifth essay) that Piaget takes insufficient
account of social considerations in his account of the growth of understanding. That criticism can be understood in two ways: (1) that Piaget
is too much preoccupied with the individual and does not take sufficient account of the fact that individuals live in societies which pro-
foundly influence them, and (2) that a social existence is a very
precondition of understanding itself.

The first criticism is sometimes countered by saying that Piaget did
after all recognize the influence of social factors. Other people are,
after all, as much part of the environment with which the individual
interacts (by means of what Piaget calls accommodation and assimilation) as anything else; hence socialization might be viewed in much the
same terms as interaction with anything else. Whatever might be
thought of that, the second form of the criticism presents a much
greater difficulty for Piaget. It is that knowledge and anything that
presupposes it (including perception) is possible only for a being that
has an appreciation, however minimal, of what it is for things to be so
and not so, of what it is to be right or correct and wrong or incorrect.
The argument for that thesis is given in schematic form in the tenth
essay, and it is represented there that this in turn is possible only in
beings who stand in something like a social relationship to others who
can serve as correctors. Such social relationships cannot be entirely
epistemic but must be based on feeling or whatever it is of that kind
that we find in a personal relationship. (It is not claimed that all
knowers must stand in a personal relationship, but that knowledge can
be attributed to a being only to the extent that he/she/it can be taken
to approximate to that.)

Hence, just as perceivers must also be agents, so they, *qua* knowers,
must have feelings and must be capable of standing in relations to
others which are dependent on such feelings. (That and its converse
are spelled out also in the sixteenth essay.) That must be taken to mean
what it says. In consequence it would make no sense to speak of
information receipt and processing except in a context where the
individuals concerned are agents and have feelings which can be directed

to others. That implies that the framework within which cognition is to be viewed from a psychological point of view cannot be restricted simply to the individual considered as a system supplied with input and leading to output, within which various functionally determined subsystems bring about whatever connection there is beween input and output, all of which to be construed in information-processing terms. The framework required is an essentially social one within which individuals are to be seen as the kind of beings that can participate in social relationships, i.e. they are agents and have feelings.

The essays in the third section were in some cases originally written for other purposes and with a view to other considerations than those so far indicated. It has however been borne in upon me that they are not only consistent with what I have already said, but even add to it along the same lines. Thus the essay on self-deception (the twelfth essay), which takes further some of the considerations raised in the eleventh essay about unconscious intention, also emphasizes the point that it is important to see deception, whether of oneself or of others, in a context of relationships. Whether someone is deceiving another cannot be discovered simply from what he says and from the consideration whether what he says is true or false; we must know also how he stands to that other. Similar considerations apply to self-deception. Analogously the thirteenth essay (on understanding others) emphasizes the point that for full knowledge and understanding of another it is necessary to stand in a relation to that other (and various forms of that principle are investigated). The principle is, however, quite general and does not apply only to knowledge of persons. One who knows anything must stand in some relation to that thing. Once again a knower must be capable of attitudes. The fourteenth essay on self-knowledge applies that consideration to knowledge of oneself, and emphasizes the extent to which self-knowledge in the full sense involves a kind of commitment and decision. Self-knowledge is in a way practical; it involves agency, relationships with others, and once again it cannot be viewed as merely epistemic. Hence the dependence of the epistemic on other factors is brought out here also.

Nevertheless, these essays can be viewed as having a status of their own. They are not designed simply to stress the limitations of cognitive psychology as generally viewed by its practitioners. They are meant cast light on certain features of social and individual psychology of a non-cognitive kind. All the same, their concern with knowledge and error makes clear their concern with the epistemology of such matters.

If Gibson and Piaget were the dominant psychologists of the first two sections, the psychologist who gets pride of place here is Freud, if only in a negative way. (I emphasize, for example, how little Freud had self-knowledge in mind as one of the aims of psychoanalysis.)

The fifteenth and sixteenth essays deal with one very important emotion for social relationships — love (and its counterpart, hate). The fifteenth essay insists that love can be non-epistemic, i.e. that it is possible for it to exist without there being any beliefs about the beloved other than that he/she/it is the beloved; it also insists that it could not always be like that. Hence this essay and the one that follows it move towards the converse of the theses presented earlier. Then it was said that the epistemic presupposes the non-epistemic; now it is said that, while love can exist without epistemic considerations applying in any determinate form, love in the mature, full sense, without which a life would not have much sense, implies epistemic attitudes on the part of the lover towards whatever he/she loves. Hence in any full life which involves others there must be a blend of the epistemic and the non-epistemic in a significant way. Moreover, the considerations which were the concern of the second section (the growth of knowledge and understanding) depend on that.

There is thus in the end a close relationship between the papers in all three sections. Although some of them had originally different aims from that of others, they fit together within a general framework of understanding. For cognitive psychology there is the moral with which I started — that no account of cognitive processes which restricts itself to the receipt and flow of information alone is adequate to those processes. The information-processing model is at best an over-simplification and at worst a distortion of what is at stake. Moreover, the thought that it is in some sense more scientific is an illusion. It fits in with physiology only by taking a simplistic view of what a physiological system itself is. It thus involves trying to fly before we can even crawl. On the other side, there is the moral that the psychology of attitudes and social psychology in general must at some stage take account of purely epistemic considerations.

One way of putting that would be to say that both for cognitive psychology and for certain aspects of social psychology it is important to reckon with the fact that the individuals who in the end make up the subject matter of those studies are persons or selves. One cannot fully understand perception, learning or cognitive matters generally without appreciating what it is to be a person or self. That is why the term 'self' appears in my title. It is not merely a reflection of the fact that two of the individual essays have the word 'self' in *their* title. It is also an indication of something that must be taken into account if the different aspects of psychology with which I am concerned are themselves fully to be understood. Even if it is true that animals perceive things, and that animals (or some of them) can learn, it is in terms of what holds good of human persons, with reflexive consciousness, that a full understanding of perception and learning is to be gained. How that fits in with the fact that both human persons and animals have physiological systems that work (as far as we can tell) on structural principles (that, as Daniel Dennett has put it, the brain is a syntactic engine) is one of the supremely difficult questions to answer, and I for one have no clear idea as to how it is to be answered. That, however, makes it no less true that to adopt a model because it fits, or does so superficially, such facts as we know about physiological systems is to put an obstacle in the way of understanding some of the central parts of psychology.

# PART I

# PERCEPTION

# 1

# UNCONSCIOUS INFERENCE
# AND JUDGMENT IN
# PERCEPTION

The notion of unconscious inference and the suggestion that it has a part to play in perception is, I suppose, mainly associated with the name of Helmholtz. He used it to explain those cases where the way in which we perceive things deviates from what would be expected on the basis of the pattern of stimulation alone – in connection, for example, with the phenomena of colour contrast, or size perception. Though I put it in this way – in terms of the pattern of stimulation – this is in fact not quite correct. For, why should not the phenomena of colour contrast, for example, be explained entirely in terms of the pattern of stimulation on the retina, or if not there in the cortex, as long as interaction between areas of excitation is allowed? Why should it not be the case that a grey patch looks different when set alongside or in the context of an area of red from the way it looks when set in a neutral context? And what prevents our explaining this, at any rate partially, by reference to the effects that the stimulation of one area of the retina has on the effects in another area produced by accompanying or parallel stimulation, wherever in the nervous system the final integrating mechanism is to be found? (I make this last qualification for reasons that will appear directly.)

Helmholtz's need to invoke another factor in such cases must therefore be due to his embracing a theory which ruled out such explanations as I have mentioned. And this is indeed the case. For he embraced what has become best known through the criticisms of the Gestalt psychologists as the 'constancy hypothesis' – that there should, unless other factors intervene, always be a constant relation between how we perceive things and the pattern of stimulation. I suspect that the constancy hypothesis has at its back another doctrine — that of 'specific nervous energies' — put forward by Johannes Müller in the 1830s, although he himself acknowledged its source in another physiologist named Bell. On this theory each nerve has its own function and cannot take over another function. It was inferred from this that the excitation of any given nerve attached to a sense-organ produces its own experience. Such a theory is naturally associated with and could be used to bolster up, firstly, a sensory atomism — the thesis that in vision, for example, excitation of the eye produces a mosaic of discrete and atomic visual experiences. Secondly, it could be used to provide the backing of the constancy hypothesis to which I have already referred, since the hypothesis of discrete neural functioning naturally has as a corollary the thesis that what takes place at the level of nerve-endings must be repeated at the level of resulting experience. And if the neural functioning at the level of nerve-endings is discrete so must be the array of experiences which result. Discrete functioning rules out interactive processes. One can see from this why the Gestaltists, who were so opposed to the idea of discrete functioning in the nervous system, were equally opposed to the constancy hypothesis. But the thesis of isomorphism — that there is an identity or complete similarity of structure between the phenomenal (how things appear) and the cortical (how things are in the brain) — is nevertheless a theory in the same line of country. For it assumes that there is a correspondence between how things appear and the pattern of neural excitation, even if it rejects the idea that the correspondence must be at the level of what happens at nerve-endings.

Helmholtz thought that the deviations of perceptual experience from what is to be expected on the basis of the constancy hypothesis are to be explained not in terms of anything further in the process of stimulation of sense-organs (for how could it be on the assumptions in question?) but in terms of 'intellectual processes' carried out by the perceiver. In particular the perceiver makes some kind of judgment or carries out some kind of inference, which, since he is not aware of it, must therefore be unconscious. The role that this might play is most obvious in the case of space-perception where the sizes and shapes that things seem to have often deviate from what might be expected from a consideration of the pattern of stimulation on the retina alone. Helmholtz also used the idea in connection with such phenomena as colour contrast. The Helmholtz three-cone theory of colour vision allows a deviation from the thesis of one experience — one kind of nerve being stimulated, in that it allows that some experiences, the perception of yellow, for example, may be the product of the excitation of more than one kind of cone simultaneously in a given proportion. But it does not allow for interactive processes between areas of the retina stimulated in the ordinary way. That is to say that a set of cones being stimulated by light of a certain frequency should produce a definite experience whatever might be going on in adjacent areas of the retina. But this does not seem to be the case. Hence it has to be explained, given these presuppositions, in a quite different way. It is assumed that a grey patch seen in the middle of a red area will tend to look green because the perceiver makes an inference about the colour of the inset patch. That is to say that there is a tendency to infer that the inset colour must be opposed to the colour of the surrounding area, and this inference sometimes overrides the given facts of sensory experience. Helmholtz thought that it does this because we have the tendency to take the inset patch as seen *through* the surrounding colour.

My phrase 'the given facts of sensory experience' is important because it reveals that there is presupposed in all this a thesis about the relationship of sensation to perception. The constancy hypothesis in fact assumes that, at least over the range of phenomena where it applies, perception is just a matter of sensation. Thus where the hypothesis cannot get application the deviations that are apparent cannot be due to anything sensory and must therefore be explained by reference to processes that are not sensory.[1] In fact the rejection of the constancy hypothesis by the Gestalt psychologists and its replacement by the thesis of isomorphism is, despite first appearances, a kind of reinstatement of the role of the sensory in perception, except that it is recognised that the nature and structure of the sensory is not determined simply by what happens at the level of nerve endings. At all events it rejects the idea that anything non-sensory or intellectual plays a part in perception, the gap between what might be expected on the basis of what happens at the level of nerve-endings and what appears to be the case from a consideration of the phenomenal being closed by appeal simply to further or different causal physiological processes. It is perhaps of some interest in this connection that J.J. Gibson claimed in his *The Perception of the Visual World* to be resuscitating the constancy hypothesis by providing a more comprehensive account of what must be taken as happening at the level of the retina; he thereby ruled out any role for anything like unconscious inference.

13

He also claimed that his theory was a psychophysical one. In his more recent book *The Senses Considered as Perceptual Systems*, which in many ways extends the account of the earlier book, he makes an explicit rejection of the notion of sensation as having any part to play in a theory of perception, as well as a rejection of any intellectual processes such as those involved in conception and belief. Yet in most ways the theory of the later book is just an extension of that of the earlier. How can he in that case reject the notion of the sensory in an account of perception?

The answer to this question lies, I think, in the tradition of thinking against which the psychology of perception has developed. For while it is natural perhaps to think that the stimulation of a sensory organ must eventually result in a sensation or group of sensations, it is not so clear exactly what a sensation is; and for that there is a whole epistemological tradition to fall back on. When I say that it is not clear exactly what a sensation is, I mean that this is not clear in the case of the majority of the senses. The suggestion that the stimulation of one kind of nerve ending may produce a sensation of pain is relatively unproblematic. But what counts as analogous to this in the case of, say, vision? The empiricist tradition in epistemology has generally had recourse to the notion of sense-impressions or sense-data as what is given in perception. It is thus natural, once given this notion, to suppose that these sense-impressions are what are caused by the stimulation of our senses – and the term 'sense-impression' is such that its very etymology supports that idea. Any suggestion that what we perceive and how we perceive it must be a function of construction or other activity on our part correspondingly undermines the view that perception is ultimately a matter of things being given via sense-impressions. And that is how it is with Gibson. I say nothing here about the rightness or wrongness of his view; I wish merely to make clear its ancestry and general character.

I have tried elsewhere, particularly in my *Sensation and Perception*, to make clear the role of sensation within perception. It may be enough now to say that what I have described above as natural – that it is sense-impressions that are the result of the direct stimulation of our sense-organs – is, when one comes to think about it, not natural at all. The supposal that it *is* comes from the pervasiveness of a tradition, and the way in which the psychology of perception has emerged out of a long course of philosophizing about perception with epistemological problems in mind. Though I find it an increasingly unpopular view

14

these days, I am still of the opinion that distinguishing philosophical from psychological questions is a desirable prolegomenon to any fruitful thinking in this and other areas. Progress does not always come from everybody trying to tackle the same issues in the same way, without distinction of function, and without, to mention a more important point, getting clear what the problems are. Co-operation between philosophers and psychologists may be more fruitful if it comes from delimitation of function rather than an attempt to answer any question that presents itself without first sorting out what kind of question it is. However that may be, the question whether there is anything given in perception is the question whether the use of our senses provides us with any knowledge which is both incorrigible and independent of any knowledge of any other and prior kind. The empiricist who wishes to claim that knowledge is in the end totally dependent on the use of our senses must claim that there is knowledge of this kind. And such knowledge must not be concept-dependent in the sense that it presupposes, whether simply logically or also temporally, any conceptual understanding in terms of which what the senses provide is to be construed. For such conceptual understanding would involve a form of knowledge − a knowledge of how what is provided by the senses is to be construed, or, to put it in another way, what it is to be construed *as*. And in that case what the senses provide could not constitute a 'given'.

The issues here are about the foundations of knowledge and whether there are such foundations and if so where they are to be sought. The empiricist view that such foundations are to be sought in sense-impressions or sense-data does not necessarily have as a corollary that these must be *caused* by the stimulation of our senses, however natural it is to think that this must be the case. For one thing, there are alternative theories, however plausible or implausible they may seem, e.g. the view put forward by Berkeley that sensory ideas can only be caused by spirits. Such a view would be absolutely excluded if the thesis that sense-impressions are caused by the stimulation of our sense-organs was a necessary corollary of the thesis that sense-impressions provide the foundations of our knowledge. If it is natural to look in such a connection to the stimulation of our sense-organs, it is because a causal process of this kind seems to exclude the possibility of its results presupposing the application of knowledge derived from any other source. It remains however a question whether those results can be construed as knowledge at all, and if they cannot they are of no use in providing the

15

foundations of knowledge. There would in that event be a gap between the causal story and the epistemological pursuits. In fact the ramification of these factors and the kinds of philosophical influences that have come to bear on psychological theories of perception have been very complicated; but basically the issues turn in the end on considerations of the kind that I have mentioned.

If we return to the constancy hypothesis, it is worth noting that what is supposed to be constant is the relation between the pattern of stimulation and the resulting pattern of sensations; yet those sensations must be thought to constitute forms of perception. For, anyone who embraces the constancy hypothesis ought to suppose that how we see the world can be explained ultimately in terms of perceptions corresponding to the sensations brought about by strictly sensory processes, and any other factors that are introduced simply build on the foundations of the original perceptions. The Helmholtzian notion of unconscious inference in a way makes this clear, for inference must take place from what is known or believed; hence if the inference is to be the explanation why we do not see things as the constancy hypothesis suggests it must work by moving from what is known or believed as a result of the processes that the constancy hypothesis supposes hold good. In other words the stimulation of the senses must on that account produce a form of perception which involves knowledge or belief. Yet neither that knowledge or belief nor the process of inference from it to the perception that finally results are such that the perceiver is in any way aware of them.

It might be objected that the process of stimulation itself need not be thought of as producing knowledge or belief but that the perceiver has to regard whatever it does produce in such a way as to make inference from it. That is to say that the perceiver has to believe something about whatever the stimulation of the senses produces as a basis for subsequent inference, but that the product of the process of stimulation does not itself have to be a belief. It sometimes happens that we infer things from what are in a genuine sense sensations. We may for example infer from the quality of a bodily sensation something about the identity of whatever is causing it, e.g. that the prick is being caused by a prickle or splinter. Such inferences, which need not be in any way unconscious, depend however on further knowledge, presumably acquired through experience, about the kinds of sensations that certain kinds of thing produce when they affect our bodies. Given this knowledge the inference to the identity or nature of the thing causing the

16

sensation may be a genuine inference in every way. But the Helmholtzian situation is not like that (although it is perhaps worth noting that the local-sign theory about the location of sensations – a theory that Helmholtz also embraced – may involve something of this kind). Consider the Helmholtzian theory of colour contrast, which depends, as I have already noted, on the thesis that we tend to make an inference about the colour of an inset area from that of the surrounding area on the basis that we are seeing the inset area through the surrounding area. The principle of inference here must presumably be that seeing something through an area of a given colour must inevitably make the something look more like the colour of the surrounding area than it would otherwise have done. The situation would be supposedly like seeing things through coloured spectacles. But a grey patch set in the middle of a red area does not look reddish. Hence what we must infer is that its real colour is not plain grey but of a colour that is shifted more towards the opposite of red. Hence it looks greenish.

There are several points of interest in this, and a discussion of them will bring out certain general considerations about the relation between how things look and any putative intellectual processes that are involved in perception. The first thing to note is that in the story that I have given a reference to how things look appears twice. There is, first, the suggestion that something seen through another colour must inevitably look tinged with that colour. There is, second, the final report about how the thing in question actually looks, and it in fact looks different from how it would look on the first hypothesis. There is, in fact, of course the same deviation in looking at things through coloured spectacles, in that as a matter of fact things look or at least come to look more like their actual colours than one might expect at first sight. The explanation clearly lies in certain features of context. Hence the principle that is supposed to give rise to the inference is not itself founded on any confirmed law about the looks of things in these circumstances. It is based on an *a priori* belief that seeing things through a coloured medium must make them look tinged with that colour. I say that this is an *a priori* belief to indicate that it cannot in the circumstances be based on any exact empirical findings. Wearing rose-tinged spectacles may well alter our view of the world in various subtle ways but it may not make things actually look rose-coloured. Whether it *will* probably depends on a number of other factors, including how long we have been wearing the spectacles. What will undoubtedly be the case is that the wave-lengths of light reaching the eyes will be affected by wearing spectacles of this kind. If we believe that this must necessarily affect how things look, it must be because we think that there is a uniform correlation between the look of a thing and the wave-length of light which reaches our eyes from it. And such a belief is manifestly falsified by the empirical facts. Hence if we retain the belief we must do so on *a priori* grounds, and one ground of this kind is provided by the constancy hypothesis, or, to put it in other ways, by the hypothesis that how things look must be a function of the sensations that we receive, unless that look is somehow corrected by other factors.

But how can these other factors correct the look by way of *inference*, unless there is a belief connected in some way with the look? I do not mean to suggest by this that when one infers $q$ from $p$, one infers $q$ from the belief that $p$, although it is undoubtedly true that one comes to believe $q$ from the belief that $p$, if one *has* the belief that $p$. The last qualification is necessary because the inference may be entirely hypothetical and need not lead to any unqualified beliefs. To infer $q$ from $p$, $p$ must be taken as a datum, i.e. as something either taken as true or assumed as true for the sake of argument.[2] Either way, it would be impossible for the inference to take place unless beliefs came into the picture in some way. The pattern of inference in the case that I am considering could only be at best: 'It looks grey. But it could look grey in these circumstances, i.e. when seen through red, only if it were in fact greenish. So it is greenish.' And then somehow it looks greenish. Here one moves from the belief about how it looks, together with the belief about its actual colour. The inference is from its look in these circumstances to its actual colour. And that is then supposed to determine its final look. If the inference is unconscious, so must presumably be the beliefs on which it is founded. Hence the first look is not one that is ever made explicit to himself by the perceiver. It is difficult to think such a view coherent.

It might be objected that the look of the thing – the final look on the previous account – is inferred not from a previous look but from the sensations that the perceiver is having. This would be like the case that I mentioned earlier, in which one infers something about the cause of the sensations from their character together with a belief that sensations of this kind are produced by things of a certain kind in turn. The inference need not of course be from the sensations to their cause; it might be from the sensations to the character of the circumstances in which they occur, without these being taken as the cause in a strict sense. Thus perhaps one might infer from the fact that one has pins and needles in one's arm that one's arm is in an awkward position. Nevertheless the form of the inference in the case before us will still be: 'I am having such and such sensations. I would have those sensations only in such and such circumstances. So the circumstances must be such and such, i.e. I must be looking at something of such and such a colour.' And then it somehow looks of that colour. In the case in question the sensations would have to be such as to be produced by light of a greyish hue in the context of light being emitted from the surroundings of a reddish hue. One would, if the inference is to be unconscious, have to believe or know this without being aware of it. If such a view is not incoherent it is at least extravagant as a possible account of what happens.

I have in all this omitted consideration of what is perhaps an even more difficult point, although it must have been evident in what I have said. This is that the inference to the real character of the object has also to determine how it finally looks. In fact in the case that I have been considering the conclusion of the inference when taken as revealing the real colour of the object is in fact false. This need not be so in all cases where unconscious inference has been invoked, e.g. distance perception where there is yet again a deviation from what might be expected on the constancy hypothesis. One sees the size of distant objects as more nearly correct than would be predicted on that hypothesis. There are no doubt cases in which how one comes to see a thing's correct size is genuinely a matter of inference. That is to say that in those cases one actually works out the size of the object from other data that are available, including perhaps an estimate of the distance or a correct view of the size of neighbouring objects. But that is not the kind of case that we are now considering, when concerned with unconscious inference; it is rather assumed that in cases in which there is no evident sign of any inference of this kind there is nevertheless inference all the same. It might well be said that even without relating this to the question of the thing's look this account of the matter is too coldly intellectual. Our ability to see things as more or less of their right size might be put down as a kind of skill. The analysis of skill is not to be carried out in terms of inferences from data. Someone who is good at estimating, say, the weight of things by looking at them need not be making any inferences from clues that he can observe, even if those clues exist. The notorious case of the chicken-sexer is crucial here; there may be clues which would tell the sexer what the sex of a

19

chicken was if he knew about them. But there is no obvious sense in which the chicken-sexer does know them, since he has not been taught to observe such clues and go by them, and he makes no obvious inferences.

The main point on which I wish to concentrate, however, is the relation of these intellectual or quasi-intellectual processes to the look of the thing perceived; for this is the most Pickwickian element perhaps in the story that I have reviewed. I said, for example, that when the perceiver has gone through the inference, unconsciously, to the conclusion 'So it is greenish', then somehow it looks greenish. Why should it? In order to get a proper view of this question we need, I suggest, to consider the different kind of factor that may affect the look of a thing and how they do so affect it.[3] One might put the Helmholtzian position that I have been considering by saying that according to it perception and how things look is a function either of the sensations that we have when our sense-organs are stimulated or of judgment, inference, or similar intellectual processes based on sensations. Since neither the inferences nor their bases are evident to the perceiver in at least the majority of cases they have to be put down as unconscious. If I am critical of this last move it is not because I have a general objection to the notion of unconscious intellectual processes of this sort. It might, for example, be necessary to appeal to unconscious inference in order to explain certain cases of mathematical insight. It is not in any case uncommon to want to say of someone that he must have inferred a certain conclusion from the data available to him without being aware that he had done so. It is in such terms that we might explain the fact that the person in question holds a certain belief when that person can give no account of how he has come to the belief. I am not saying that such an explanation must necessarily be correct; but there does not seem to be anything outrageous or logically incoherent about it. Equally there may be cases when it is reasonable to say that someone has formed a judgment on a certain matter without being aware that he has done so. Hence unconscious mental processes of this sort are not objectionable in themselves. The question at issue is whether they can be properly invoked in the case before us, in the sense that they can be the necessary explanatory work.

That there is a need to make a distinction between at least two forms of perception – the epistemic and non-epistemic – and a similar distinction between the looks or appearances of things is now relatively common-place among philosophers. (One might mention Roderick

Chisholm's *Perceiving* and Fred Dretske's *Seeing and Knowing* in this connection, though I might say that an acceptance of the distinction does not commit one to agreement upon all the uses to which the distinction has been or may be put.[4]) I have spoken of the distinction as one between two forms of perception, though this may not be the best way to put the point, which can be expressed simply by saying that in some cases to see something in a certain way, or for it to look a certain way, implies a belief to that effect on the part of the perceiver, while in other cases this is not so. The distinction is perhaps most evidently applicable in the case of illusions. In those illusions which are sometimes called 'sensory', e.g. the Müller-Lyer illusion, the illusion may hold good whatever our beliefs or knowledge about the real state of things, and the illusion may not be a function of any beliefs on the part of the perceiver; it may be explicable if at all in quite different ways. (I put the matter in this rather hesitant and delicate way in order not to step on any empirical toes. I do not wish to trespass on ground reserved for empirical investigators. If the Müller-Lyer illusion is explicable in other ways, so be it; but to my knowledge the illusion is put by many psychologists in the class that I have roughly delimited as sensory. The findings of Piaget and his associates as recorded in the *Mechanisms of Perception* that the illusion is at its maximum at the youngest investigable age are not without relevance here.) There are certainly other illusions which are the product of beliefs on the part of the perceiver. In some, if not all, of these cases the illusion can be explained by saying that the thing looks that way because for it so to look is simply, or at least in part, for the perceiver to believe it to be so, and the perceiver does have that belief. Thus, if it is true to say of a child that his father looks to him the biggest human being in the world, this may be so because he believes this and to say that his father so looks to him is in part at least to refer to that belief. In one sense he sees his father as the biggest human being in the world while in another sense perhaps he sees him as the same size as a lot of other human beings. I say that this may be true in some, if not all, cases where how the thing looks is produced by beliefs on the part of the perceiver, because there may be cases in which while the illusion or whatever has beliefs in its causal ancestry it itself is not to be unpacked in terms of beliefs. Such cases cannot be ruled out *a priori*.

Unfortunately, however, this qualification does not end the complexities of the situation. There are other factors apart from beliefs and purely sensory factors that may determine or help to determine

21

how something looks. As I write this paper I can see out of the window in the distance a number of objects that look like sea-gulls. I do not know whether they are sea-gulls, and in saying that they look like sea-gulls I am not saying that I believe that they are sea-gulls; I am not even saying that I believe that they are *like* sea-gulls. But they could not look like sea-gulls if I did not know in some way what sea-gulls looked like (though it has to be admitted that someone else might say of me that the objects looked like sea-gulls to me, on the strength of a description offered by me which amounted to a description of sea-gulls, without my knowing that that was what the description amounted to). In other words the way in which we understand the world, its objects and their properties and relations may well affect how we see things and how they look to us. So much so that there is a sense in which something cannot look to us in a certain way if we have no understanding or knowledge of that way or of anything that is relevant to its being characterized in that way. In ambiguous figures like the wife and mother-in-law picture or in the duck-rabbit which, thanks to Wittgenstein, has become so popular among philosophers, there may be a variety of factors which make the picture look one way rather than the other, but it will not be seen in one way or the other if the perceiver has no idea of what a duck or rabbit looks like or perhaps if he does not know at least something of the stereotypes about wives and mother-in-laws in western society and culture. The perceiver who lacks those concepts may see the picture in some way or ways, but not in those ways in particular.

The case of ambiguous figures may also draw our attention to another factor which may play a part in the determination of how things look — attention itself. It is clear that sometimes when our attention is drawn to some feature of an object or to some part of it that object may, often suddenly, come to look to us as it has not done before. Wittgenstein devotes considerable consideration to this kind of dawning of an aspect in section xi of Part II of the *Philosophical Investigations*. Where the figure is not overtly ambiguous, as the duck-rabbit figure is, it may still be possible to see a figure like that of a simple triangle in a variety of ways, e.g. as lying down, standing up, as suspended from the apex, and so on.[5] In doing so one is of course putting the figure into something of an imaginary context, and one may be enabled to do this in a variety of ways by paying selective attention to different features of the figure. To the extent that one does this one is, as it were, making the figure ambiguous, even if it is not obviously ambiguous in itself, and the whole thing is necessarily something of an imaginative feat. It is probably for this kind of reason that Wittgenstein says that the concept of an aspect is like that of an image (op. cit. 213). This remark has sometimes been taken as casting light on the notion of an image, but I think it is meant to be taken the other way round. Thus there is also a genuine sense in which an exercise of the imagination may contribute to and partly determine the look of a thing. It was argued by Kant in his discussion of the 'schematism' and it has been argued more recently by Strawson[6] that perception always involves the imagination in some way as a link between the abstract and formal understanding involved in having a concept and the concrete experience that sense perception brings. If that is so, the consideration is relevant to the point that I was making earlier – the fact that the look of things is influenced by our understanding of the kinds of thing that they are. The kind of use of the imagination that may influence the dawning of an aspect is, I think, different[7], though it may depend on the former.

So far, I have considered factors on the side of the perceiver that may influence the way things look to him – his beliefs, his knowledge and understanding, the way in which his attention is directed, and his imaginativeness. There are of course additional factors on the side of the object or its context. A shift in what is literally a point of view may make an object look entirely different from how it has done hitherto, as may equally a change of context; it is in effect the latter which the Gestaltists emphasized so much, often to the exclusion of other factors which may in certain circumstances be just as important. What sort of account, however, can we give of the way in which these factors influence the look of a thing, when by 'look' we do not mean to imply anything about the beliefs of the perceiver with regard to the object? With this question we can go back to the kind of example that I instanced at the beginning in connection with Helmholtz. What sort of explanation should we look for in attempting to explain the facts of colour contrast? The answer may seem obvious. This is a phenomenon where context is obviously important, and we might well look for the explanation in the facts of sensory stimulation and the background physiology. That is to say that in this case the phenomenology has its basis in the interaction of neurological processes, given the way in which stimulation of the retina takes place when one coloured area is surrounded by another. It is conceivable (I say no more) that a similar reference to physiological processes will serve to account for any illusions which

23

may be categorized as 'sensory', e.g. the Müller-Lyer illusion of it is a phenomenon of that kind.

But in the case of the Müller-Lyer illusion (and I do not know how far this applies also to other 'sensory' illusions) one can, given practice, sophistication, and determination, perhaps by directing one's attention to certain features of the figure, make the illusion disappear; the lines may be seen as of equal length. It is this kind of fact that raises in a crucial way the relation between sensory and 'intellectual' processes in perception. Helmholtz recognized this kind of point and declared categorically that where a process could be overriden by intellectual processes or by learning that process could not be a sensory one. For this reason he said that 'only qualities are sensational, whilst almost all *spatial* attributes are results of habit and experience.'[8] Such a position demands a hard and firm distinction between the sensory and intellectual in perception; that is to say that it implies that some perceptual phenomena can be classified under the heading of sensation simply, while others cannot. Those that cannot do not involve a suppression of sensations, nor strictly speaking their modification; the sensations are still there but we cease to be aware of them. To put the matter in the way in which I put it earlier in my discussion, we somehow become unaware of the fact that the area of grey inset in a red expanse looks grey in making an inference from this to the fact that it must be green. If that account was incoherent so it must be if put in terms of having sensations unconsciously and making inferences from them equally unconsciously.

I suggested earlier that instead of attempting to construe our perception of the world in terms of the ideas of data and inference or judgment, one might better invoke the notion of skill. Thus our perceiving things correctly might be thought of as the exercise or perhaps the results of the exercise of skills on our part, skills which may of course sometimes break down or be misapplied. What I have said just now about practice, sophistication and determination would be in line with this suggestion and the direction of one's attention to certain features of the objects of perception might then be thought of as devices used in the exercise of skill. What, however, is the skill a skill at? It will not do to say that the skill is one in arriving at correct judgments about the character of things. When one is successful in seeing the lines in the Müller-Lyer illusion as of equal length one has not simply come to a correct judgment about the lines; one's *judgment* may well have been correct already. One has come to *see* them correctly; they *look* as they really are, and that look is not to be analysed simply in terms of belief. Analogously, if it is true that we have to learn to see and become good at seeing distant objects as of more or less the size and shape that they are, is it the case also that we thereby become good at estimating or judging their size and shape? There are of course occasions when we do estimate and judge these things, and there may well be devices that we can use to this end. But in such cases when we have reached a correct estimate of a thing's size we may still not be able to *see* it that way. What else is involved in *that*? Isn't it *that* that we become good at and which we learn to do as part of what is involved in learning about the world. What is it?

This seems to me an immensely difficult question, one that is this, I suspect, just because the experience is one of those, which, as Wittgenstein said, is so ordinary that we really do not find it puzzling enough. I have already referred to Strawson's discussion of the link provided by the imagination between formal understanding and experience in the phenomenon of seeing something as such and such. But whereas it is possible to understand how the imagination plays a role in enabling us to see, say, a figure in ways that we might justly call imaginative it is less clear what work a reference to the imagination plays in gaining an understanding of ordinary 'seeing-as'. It might be better to look at a very simple case of the phenomenon which is my present concern. In conclusion, I wish to do just this and it seems to me best to consider a case of touch, if only for the reason that touch being (a) a contact sense and (b) fairly simple in structure it does not bring in the complications of the distance senses at least.

In putting one's hand on something, and perhaps moving it over the object to some extent, one may get a variety of sensations or feelings in one's finger-tips. If one attends to those sensations under the circumstances noted one may come to find out something of their nature — whether, for example, they are closest to a tickle, or more akin to an irritation. (Unfortunately our phenomenological vocabulary is fairly restricted here, perhaps because we have little interest in this kind of operation in the ordinary way, and perhaps because there is not all that much to find out.) What happens when we come to realize or recognize that what we are feeling is, say, a fur fabric, what is it to feel it as furry, as distinct from merely having the sensations in our finger tips that I have already mentioned? What I shall offer in reply to these questions will be at the level of description only, but it may be as well to draw attention to some simple facts. First, to feel the object as furry one must have one's attention drawn to it rather than to the sensations. Do the sensations cease to exist when that happens? It seems to me difficult to believe that they do, although they do not exist as such *for* the perceiver, since they are not within his attention. (I am aware that this raises large issues, but I must leave the matter there.) Second, one must know what it is for an object to be furry, and this I take it involves knowing also in some part what it is for an object to feel furry; one might say that it involves knowing what it is for an object to be furry under the aspect 'feeling', and that one must have come to know about furriness in that way as well as in others. To know this one must have learnt what furry objects feel like. Third, one must be aware of the object and that it feels of this kind. In this the knowledge that I have mentioned under my second heading is somehow made explicit in application to the particular object to which one is attending. But the awareness is not detached from the medium by which it is mediated. It is mediated by the fingers and through the fact that the fingers are sensitive — if you like through the fact that one is having the sensations that one is having. What all this amounts to is simply the point that the form of awareness in question must be tactual, though I doubt whether this means any more than what I have already said. But there need be no beliefs about the real nature of the object or about whether it is actually as it feels. On the other hand if one does believe that it is a certain kind of object this may itself influence how it feels, perhaps because one's attention will then be directed in a way that it would not otherwise have been. For this to be possible the experience must be complex enough to admit of differences of emphasis or perspective. Hence, when I said that one must have learnt what it is for objects to feel furry, there must be presupposed in this at least the possibility of descriptions of other kinds being applied to the object in applying this one. This is a point of some importance.

I suspect that there is much else to be said here, and that what I have actually said might not add up to all that much. Some morals may however be drawn. First, whatever role sensations play in all this it is not as a basis for judgment or inference to any of the properties of the object. What might be said is that they give a kind of character to the form of awareness of the object even when one's attention is not directed to them. If one runs one's fingers over an unevenly textured object there may indeed be a kind of vacillation of attention depending on whether it is features of the object or aspects of the sensations in one's fingers that loom the larger. But when it is the features of the object that grip our awareness and attention that awareness is still coloured, as it were, by the sensations that may so easily come before our attention. Second, feeling something as such and such is in an important sense an application and manifestation of knowledge; for to feel it in this way presupposes knowledge of what it is for something to be such and such under the aspect of feeling. Yet, in order to feel it in this way it is not enough just to have that knowledge, since there are cases in which while we know very well what the object is or what it is like, we are unable to feel it as such. There may be something lacking on the sensory side, or perhaps a lack of fit between that sensory side and the knowledge that we have. The latter is the case where, as in a puzzle picture, we may know exactly what the face to be found there looks like but just cannot see it in the picture. This may be for various reasons, such as an attention to the wrong things, and the picture may, so to speak, suddenly click into place. Sometimes there may be nothing that we can do, no steps that we can actively take, to bring about that result. But when it comes about, it is the dawning of a phenomenon which in less particular circumstances is with us all the time whenever we see something in a certain way. In some cases, as in illusions, it is in a certain sense a misapplication of knowledge, but that does not alter the general nature of the phenomenon. And if it is an application of knowledge it is not one that necessarily issues in knowledge or belief itself. That depends on whether the sensory or the epistemic side looms larger. Given this, it would be wrong to say that perception is always a matter of getting information or that we come to be able to do when we come to be able to see something in a certain way is to be able to get information about the world. The story about perception which, *à la* Gibson, links it with information-getting, is at best only one side of the whole story.

Yet, third, feeling, seeing or in general perceiving something in a certain way may, nevertheless, be a source of knowledge about the world, to the extent that in so perceiving we are concentrating on or attending to the way things are or may be rather than their more aesthetic aspects on how they feel or look, in the senses of these words that I have been emphasizing. It is natural that one who is concerned with the part that perception plays in biological functioning in general should emphasize that aspect of the matter, and that epistemologists should do likewise for their own reasons, but it should not be taken for granted that that is all that there is to it. At the same time, however, while the aesthetic attitude is always possible, in theory at least, and

27

sometimes looms largest in practice, it is always theoretically possible for it to be dropped in favour of what one might call the epistemic attitude. This involves at least a shift in attention in the way that I have indicated is possible in the case of some illusions like the Müller-Lyer. And just as a belief about an object may cause it to feel or look in a certain way, so may the way a thing feels or looks cause us to believe certain things about it; there is however, no necessary connection either way. Thus to the extent that we do make judgments or inferences in perceptual contexts these have no necessary implications for how things look, feel, etc., nor vice versa. (I have in the foregoing deserted the case of feeling *simpliciter*; how far considerations about feeling apply to the other senses will depend on whether there are crucial differences between those other senses and touch. There *are* differences, it is clear, but I suspect that it is a case of *mutatis mutandis*.)

Finally, a general remark about what I have been concerned with. Whatever one thinks of Helmholtz's theory of perceptual phenomena, it is clear that he worked with a very simple dichotomy of sensation versus intellectual processes. And the same applies to many other workers in this field, if with varying emphases. One thing that I have been anxious to indicate is that this is *too* simple a dichotomy. Both intellectual processes and sensations play a role in perception, but so do other things. Moreover it is sometimes the case that seeing something in a certain way is simply a matter of its looking this to us. Whatever else is to be said about this 'looking' it cannot be simply broken down or analysed into sensations, or intellectual processes like judgment, inference or belief, nor into any ordinary combination of these. If one wants to understand perception that is a point that should be faced.


## NOTES

1 Helmholtz stated this as an explicit principle. See the discussion in William James, *Principles of Psychology*, vol. 2, New York, Dover, 1950, pp. 17ff, 218, 242ff.
2 See D.G. Brown, *Analysis*, 15, 1955, pp. 135-44.
3 Jerry Fodor has put to me the point that since I, as will appear, allow that beliefs may have a causal role in the production of looks, there is no logical objection to invoking causality in the present case. I agree. But in that case there is no need for all the complexities of the story about unconscious inference to explain, via causal factors,

the greenish look of the thing.

4 See also the papers by J.W. Roxbee-Cox and F. Sibley in *Perception*, ed. Sibley, London, Methuen, 1971.

5 Wittgenstein, *Philosophical Investigations*, Oxford, Blackwell, 1958, p. 200.

6 See his contribution to Foster and Swanson, ed. Experience and Theory, Amherst, University of Mass. Press, 1970.

7 See Wilkerson *Mind*, **82**, 1973, pp. 481-96.

8 As noted in James (1950), vol. II, p. 218. James goes on to point out justifiably that Helmholtz was scarcely consistent over qualities and this must be evident from his treatment of colour contrast.

# 2

# THE CONCEPT OF INFORMATION IN GIBSON'S THEORY OF PERCEPTION

When James Gibson's *The Senses Considered as Perceptual Systems* appeared in 1966 I reviewed it in the *Philosophical Review*, and in the course of the review I said that it seemed to me the best book in psychology to appear for many years. Given the wide range of issues that psychology covers this may seem an extravagant claim; it still seems to me, however, a fascinating book and I have a great admiration for Gibson's work. If I seem critical in what I have to say here, I hope that my criticisms will be taken against the background of these remarks. Gibson's work in the field of perception seems to me of the greatest importance for our understanding of that phenomenon. I wrote something about Gibson's earlier book *The Perception of the Visual World* (1950) in chapter 5 of my *The Psychology of Perception* (1957) and in 1969 I added an appendix to that book, in which I included a few brief remarks about Gibson's later book (remarks written in 1967). What I have to say now will be to some extent an amplification of those remarks.

Let me first rehearse the development of Gibson's views about perception as I see it. In the earlier book Gibson put the contrast between his theory of visual perception and that of earlier and still current theorists by saying that he was putting forward a 'ground theory' as opposed to an 'air theory'. In effect this was to say that in trying to get at the factors involved in our perception of objects from a visual point of view we ought to consider those objects set against the ground which constitutes their environment, and not consider them as it were stuck up in mid-air. The retinal stimulation produced by light from objects in their environment will inevitably be structured; in

30

particular the pattern of excitation will involve gradients which are a function of the fact that, for example, the projection of nearby parts of our visual environment takes up a larger part of the retina than that of more distant parts. This has a phenomenological counterpart in our experience if we view the world not as we ordinarily do but as, for example, painters are supposed to do when trying to see things in perspective. (It may help to get this view of things if we half close our eyes. It sometimes manifests itself dramatically in photographs.) Gibson distinguished what we see in this way from what we see in the ordinary way by calling the former the 'visual field' and the latter the 'visual world'; the distinction, he said, was his substitute for the old distinction between sensation and perception. The parallel between the structural properties of the retinal stimulation and those of the visual field implied a resuscitation of what used to be called the 'constancy hypothesis' (the hypothesis of a constant relation between how we see things and the properties of stimuli) in a new dress; it gets application in relation to the visual field but not to the visual world.

On this view there is, however, still a relation between the pattern of retinal stimulation and our perception of the visual world. The visual field differs from the visual world in being bounded, unstable, lacking in depth and subject to deformation when we move. We have already seen that the property of depth which is evident in the visual world has its counterpart in certain structural gradients in the visual field and therefore also in similar gradients in the pattern of stimulation. The other factors, and in particular the stability of the visual world, have their counterpart in invariants on the ordinal patterning of stimulation, particularly over time. Hence all the factors necessary for the perception of the visual world are present in some way in the pattern of retinal stimulation. Every feature of the visual world, one might say, has its counterpart in the visual field, and for that reason also a counterpart in the pattern of stimulation. Gibson could therefore call his theory a 'psychophysical theory'. It is, however, a different sort of psychophysical theory from some that have been called that. In it there is a constant relation between stimuli and the visual field, but a more complex relation between stimuli and the visual world. The pattern of stimuli do not *determine* how we see the world; there may be many other factors that have a part to play in that — e.g., attention, learning and background experience, even personality factors. But the pattern of stimuli do provide one extremely important set of necessary conditions for seeing the world. To the extent that Gibson suggested more

31

than that — and the reference to a psychophysical theory did suggest more than that — the philosophical position implicit in his view at that time is the traditional causal theory of perception. At the best the visual world is a kind of construct out of the visual field, and the latter is a straightforward function of stimulation.

I know little of the course of Gibson's thought in the sixteen years between *The Perception of the Visual World* and the appearance of *The Senses Considered as Perceptual Systems*. But in that latter book reference to the visual field has been more or less dropped; there is a rejection of the idea of a psychophysical theory of perception and of the idea that the concept of sensation has any role in a theory of perception; the concept of information is now the central concept and the senses are thought of as systems for getting such information about the world, with a consequent emphasis on the extent to which perception involves activity. There is in this new theory, not only an aspect of generalization from the old theory in that it is meant to cover other senses apart from vision, but also important differences from the old theory. Yet in a sense a certain continuity from the old theory can be detected. Gibson has claimed more recently[1] that his theory provides new reasons for accepting realism as a philosophical theory of perception. I agree with Hintikka[2] that this claim involves a certain misconception about the questions that lie behind such philosophical theories. No psychological theory could provide reasons for answering those questions in one way rather than another; it could not, in Hintikka's words, deal with *de jure* questions of epistemology, since it must be concerned with how we see things not with whether we are justified in supposing ourselves to see anything at all. Nevertheless, Gibson's new theory in certainly *consistent* with the point of view inherent in philosophical realism, and in many people's eyes that is a very big point in its favour — in mine too, I might add.

I said just now that there is between the new and the old theories a certain continuity. One way in which to put it — although it would not be quite accurate — would be to say that the new theory is the old one minus all the stuff about the visual field, and then generalized over other senses. The dropping of the idea of the visual field certainly makes it impossible to characterize the theory any longer as a psychophysical one; for it has the consequence that there is no direct connection between properties of the pattern of stimulation and anything else. I also said of the old theory that it provided by reference to the pattern of stimulation one extremely important set of necessary conditions for

seeing the world. If I had said that the pattern of stimulation constituted the information necessary for seeing the world, I should have
been wrong, both in relation to Gibson and in general. It was not part
of his older theory that the pattern of stimulation provides information
which we can rely on in gaining knowledge about the world. The role
of the pattern of stimulation in that theory is causal only. It seems
extremely implausible in any case, to say the least, that we get to the
features of the real world through the features of the pattern of stimulation; this would imply that we always make some form of inference
in perceiving the world, and it is most unclear that any such thing takes
place or how it would work if it did so.[3] The same is evident from
what Gibson says in the earlier theory about the visual field which is
the correlate of the pattern of stimulation. Perception of the visual field
is not the norm in perception; it is not a constituent part of perception
of the world, for it requires that we adopt a special attitude. In that
case, is it not logical to drop any reference to it in a theory of how
perception of the world takes place?

Gibson seems to believe that it *is* so logical, and that is why no place
is given to the notion of the visual field in the new theory. He is equally
positive that the parallel concept of sensation has no place in a theory
of perception; it is not that sensations do not exist or occur, it is rather
that perception takes place in spite of them, or at any rate does so
normally. I make the latter proviso because in discussing cases of incomplete phenomenal constancy in his book (pp. 306-8) he does speak
of sensations obtruding on perception and he makes in that context a
rare reference to the visual field. So it is not that these ideas have no
content; it is that that they have no place in a theory of normal perception. There are, however, difficulties about this, and indeed about my
original question, which I wish to investigate. In doing so I hope that
we shall get closer to the concept of information which is so central
to Gibson's theory.

Gibson is quite clear that the concept of information on which he
relies is not the one employed within information theory, which has to
do with the functioning of signal systems. Perception is not a matter
simply of the reception of signals from the world which the brain has to
interpret. The brain and the receptors constitute systems for the
obtaining of information through the relation of the animal to its
environment – a relation which is constantly changing and may be
varied as part of the process of information pick-up. It is a matter of
the detection of invariants of one kind or another in the process of

33

stimulation. It is not of course in any way controversial that we and other animals use our senses to, among other things, get information about the world. Our behaviour in the world is largely based on such information. I say that we use our senses to this end *among other things*. For human beings, at any rate, sometimes use their sense for aesthetic ends also — to enjoy the beauty or ugliness of certain things. This is not easily to be expressed in terms of information pick-up, nor has it the same relevance to behaviour. However, it is easy to see why a psychologist should concentrate on the use of the senses to gain information. None of this is, as I have said, controversial, or need be so. What the ordinary man would expect of a psychologist is an account of *how* it happens. It is here that Gibson's theory of ecological optics comes in. His answer lies presumably in the invariants of the ambient array to which the senses as perceptual systems are tuned. My difficulty is over how Gibson knows this to be the case, given his own principles.

Ecological optics, as I understand that notion, has no reference to any aspects of experience. It is, Gibson says (*The Senses* . . ., pp. 221-2), 'put together from parts of physical optics, illuminating engineering, ecology and perspective geometry'. It involves the idea of points of observation for which there are invariant structures in the changing optic array. It thus 'concerns light that is *relevant* to the eye, leaving aside radiation that is *irrelevant*'. It is clear that all this could be explored without reference to any form of perceptual experience; it would involve exploring the properties of a system that involved light as a stimulus. The idea involves the assumption, however, that the sense-organs are naturally adapted to such a system, that they do naturally function in this way. It is of course a natural assumption that they do, but the question remains how we know that they do. The assumption has indeed been denied. If I understand correctly the theory that Piaget puts forward in his *Mechanisms of Perception*, his idea, based on a welter of experiments on so-called sensory illusions, is that the visual system is naturally distorting and requires the use of intelligence to correct it through a process of decentration. I do not refer to this idea to suggest in any way that it is the truth; I am sure that it strikes most of us, prima facie at any rate, as rather odd. It is just that it is a suggestion that runs counter to the assumption that I find in Gibson's theory. It is, moreover, of interest to look at the way in which Piaget comes to his conclusion and to consider its relevance to Gibson.

Piaget's theory is based on the results of a vast number of experiments on so-called sensory illusions, such as the Müller-Lyer, in which it is presumed that how we see things is not a function of knowledge or beliefs that we have. The illusions were found to decrease with age, from which it is inferred that vision is most distorting at the youngest age at which it is functional. Let me emphasize again the point that I am putting no weight whatsoever on the truth of these claims, merely their intelligibility. The point that is important for present purposes is that the intelligibility of the findings depends upon an acceptance of reports of subjects' experiences, how they see one thing in relation to another. In Gibsonian terms, Piaget is claiming that young children naturally get the wrong information because that is the way in which unadjusted senses naturally function. I am aware that Gibson himself has an explanation of the Müller-Lyer illusion in terms of the information to be got from the drawings when seen as constituting the edges of three-dimensional objects. Personally I am not much inclined to think that I see the drawings in that way, but I take it that in any case it was Piaget's intention to rule out such a possibility by taking very young children as subjects. However that may be, all these views presuppose some conception of how things *look* to people — and that is the important point, since it in turn presupposes something about people's experiences.

It is after all important for Gibson's original (1950) findings about the gradients involved in depth perception that, e.g., a series of tiles *can* look the way that they do when seen according to the instructions for perceiving the visual field. It is not that they *must* look that way; it is indeed important for perception of the world that we can see them as all of the same size. It is, however, equally important that we can see them as conforming to a gradient of sizes, for it is that fact that gives the structure of the stimulation the relevance that it has. Suppose that we were quite unable to see a series of tiles receding from us as anything other than the same size. In such circumstances the gradient formed by the pattern of ambient light would be thought to have no relevance to information pick-up. The same would be true if the senses were naturally so distorting in their functioning that the natural way to see the tiles was with a gradient in the opposite direction to the normal.

The point of all this, as I meant to suggest by my emphasis of the word 'can' above, is not that having visual experiences of the kind described by Gibson in his initial account of the visual field is a constituent part of perceiving the world. That suggestion would be akin to the suggestion that we receive certain basic sense-data experiences

35

which are then modified in some way. I agree with Gibson that there is every reason to reject such a suggestion. The trouble is that there is a tendency, if not a whole-hearted one, in Gibson's later thinking to throw out the baby with the bath-water. The point might be put by saying that vision is not just a system for obtaining information about the world but a system for obtaining *visual* information about it. The trouble is to cash that word 'visual' in that context. The suggestion in what Gibson says about ecological optics is that the meaning of the word can be cashed in terms of the function of light as a stimulus for the optical system. I do not think that this is enough. If it were enough there could be no question of sensations obtruding on perception.

It might be said on the latter point that there is no need for Gibson to speak in that way. It would be sufficient for him to say, as he also does, that the compromise that takes place in cases of incomplete perceptual constancy is between two alternative kinds of attention, between perhaps two ways of seeing things. I would be sympathetic to that suggestion but it would not affect my underlying point. The two forms of attention would still be forms of *visual* attention and it would be necessary to ask what that is. My suggestion is that it is impossible to answer that question without some account of the way in which perception involves experience. Hence I agree entirely with Gibson about the wrongness of supposing that we are given information in basic sensations which is then modified in subsequent experience. But I also think that the concept of sensation is not necessarily identical with that of sense-data, as the view of basic sensations seems to suppose. I have discussed this elsewhere;[4] the situation seems clearest in connection with touch where the experience of the texture of a surface seems to be mediated by sensations in our finger tips. I have spoken of the feeling of the texture being 'coloured' by those sensations. I shall not say more about that here. Suffice it to say in the present context that it does not seem to me that a sufficient account of what it is to see an object as it is in its context has been given when it is said that we have obtained correct information about it through the operation of the sense of vision considered as a system for getting such information. A further but connected point is the one I made before — that such a view does not allow for the aesthetic role that the senses may play.

So far what I have said amounts to some doubts as to whether the use of the concept of information in this context constitutes quite enough for the purpose. I want now to raise some points in the opposite direction — to ask whether Gibson does not put too great a weight on the notion. He begins his book with a quotation from Thomas Reid, the eighteenth-century Scottish philosopher, in which Reid distinguishes perception from sensation by saying that the latter involves, as the former does not, conception and belief. (It is incidentally an extremely important point about Reid that by 'sensations' he does not mean anything like sense-data; they play no epistemological role in his theory. Gibson pays no attention, however, to Reid's claim that we never find perception and sensation disjoined. Reid might have said to Gibson that even if it is a function of the senses to make us perceive, i.e. to give us information about the world, the information would not be *perceptual* without those sensations. This is the same point as the one that I was making just now.) Gibson goes on, however, to say that there is no need for the reference to 'conception and belief', and he adds that when the senses operate as perceptual systems they can obtain information about objects in the world 'without the intervention of an intellectual process'. Later in the book (pp. 275-7) and elsewhere (e.g. *J. Psych.* 1966) he puts similar strictures on memory.

Let us take the latter point first. It seems to me that Gibson is quite right to object to the thesis that we cannot perceive sequences of events in time. The claim that we can perceive only the momentary present is an old and hoary fallacy, and it is as much a fallacy about the notion of the present as it is one about perception. There is certainly a sense in which I can see what is taking place (a continuous series of events); there is also a sense in which I can see what has been taking place or what is about to happen. Moreover, Gibson seems to me absolutely right to insist that learning need not involve remembering anything. There is, however, a sense in which Gibson, like the queen in Hamlet, as it seems to me, 'protests too much'. There is, first, the phenomenon of suddenly seeing something in a certain way because of a recollection of something in the past; as a consequence, perhaps, it is all seen as fitting in. Gibson might say that such a feature of perception is incidental only; such recollections are not an essential part of perceiving things. I would agree with this, if only to add that nevertheless such phenomena ought to be taken up into the theory. More important, however, is the point that the ability to perceive a sequence of events as a sequence certainly presupposes an ability to keep in mind some members of that sequence as past. One could not perceive a sequence in time without some concept of the past (and equally the future), and this is in a broad sense a memory phenomenon, as Kant saw.[5]

If Gibson were to admit this, and I do not know whether he would, he would already be committed to the view that perception presupposes concepts, despite his objections to Reid. I shall come back to that directly, but first a few words about belief. The extent to which perception must involve belief has been much discussed by philosophers in recent years. There are few of them who would want to deny that seeing is sometimes believing or that what we believe may sometimes determine or partly determine how we see things. Moreover, it is one of the important features of the later chapters of Dretske's book, *Seeing and Knowing*, that he shows how wide is the range of things of which we can properly be said to see that they are such and such. And in seeing that they are such and such we come to believe that they are this. However, while it is agreed by most philosophers that seeing sometimes involves believing it is not by any means agreed that it always does so. This is not the place for reviewing that issue in general or in detail; let us take it that while belief may be a common feature of perception it is by no means essential to it. There remains the point about concepts.

Gibson claims, as I have already noted, that in so far as the senses operate as perceptual systems they can obtain information about objects in the world without the intervention of an intellectual process. One might indeed object to the suggestion that it is the senses that obtain information at all, just as one might object to the parallel suggestion that the senses hunt for stimuli in order to get information. Surely it is rather the case that we or the animal do this by means of the systems that the senses consist of. Information is not information if it is not such *for* someone or something — and something that is capable of receiving it as information. Of course various things have to be the case for this to be possible. Gibson is quite right to insist that it is not sufficient for this purpose that we consider the brain as a mere analyser or interpreter of the stimuli received. That in effect was one thing that was wrong with the older theory, which emphasized only *some* conditions necessary for seeing the world as it is; it did not explain how those conditions could function as information-providing. For this purpose there has to be at least considerable interaction between the animal and its environment; hence the importance of the reference to ecology.

Mere reference to such interaction, however, does not sufficiently explain how information-provision comes about from it. It is clearly possible to set out or give some indication of the possibilities for sequential relationships that an animal may have with its environment. This will show that the possibilities exist within the general contexts of stimulation for it to get information about the world, *provided it is an information-getter*. It is this, I think, that is implied by Gibson's emphasis on perceptual *systems*. But the proviso is important, and it might be objected to Gibson that he has said little or nothing about it — i.e. what it is that makes it possible for something to take advantage of the possibilities that these kinds of system provide.

It might be replied that I am in one sense asking for too much here. Surely the answer is to be provided only by a complete account of what kind of physiological system is capable of responding to such possibilities — and we know very little about that at present. In another sense, however, the question 'What is it for something to be an information getter?' is not to be answered in terms of the 'mechanics' that makes it possible, but in terms of the concepts through which the notion of 'information-getting' is to be understood. I said earlier that information is only information to or for somebody or something. To speak of information in this context is not just to say something about the structure of stimulation or the structure of the system within which stimulation takes place; it is to say something about the significance for the perceiver of the objects that produce this stimulation. To put the matter in other words, when an object in a given context affects a perceptual system in such a way that information is derived about it because of the structure of stimulation, the perceiver is enabled to see the object in a certain way, *as a such and such*. It is impossible for something to see something as X unless it has some idea of what it is for something to be an X. To say this is to say that it must have in some way, and to some extent, the concept of X. Thus to speak of it as obtaining information is not in fact to rule out as unnecessary any reference to concepts. (I also think that, since to have the concept of X is to be explained in terms of knowing what it is for something to be X, this reference to concepts implies that the perceiver must have some form of knowledge. This, however, raises large issues, including genetic ones, that it would not be profitable to go into here.)

Whether or not Gibson would count what I have said as a reference to an 'intellectual process' I am not sure. The general point that I am making, however, is that it is not right to say that it is possible to obtain information about the world without such things, since the concept of 'information' itself can have no application where such things are not presupposed. Since ecological optics makes no reference to such things it is *ipso facto* insufficient as a comprehensive account of how we see things. It might be argued that this problem can be taken care of by reference to the notion of a perceptual system. For this implies that the stimulation available to the perceiver is not simply received by the sense-organs and then interpreted by the brain; rather the stimulation is made use of and it is this that makes possible the obtaining of information from the stimulation. Gibson's emphasis on this point is very important. What I have insisted on about concepts, therefore, could be explained in terms of properties of a perceptual system which make possible a given kind of use of the stimulation available to it at a given time; such properties might change as a result of learning and the like. I feel sure that if one were to seek the properties of the physiological system that make concept-use and therefore information-getting possible it would be in this direction that one would have to look. On the other hand it seems to me that it would be foolish to deny that we know very little of what this amounts to. To that extent too it seems to me that Gibson's notions of 'perceptual systems' and 'information' conceal a large amount of obscurity — obscurity, that is, if we are really interested in the question of how it all happens.

If, however, we are interested only in some of the details of what makes it possible to happen and in how we are to construe this, then what Gibson says about information and perceptual systems is a vast improvement on the view against which he is reacting. Moreover, his later views provide an important and illuminating extension from what was there in the earlier book, even apart from the shift of theoretical point of view. It should be apparent, however, that I think that he puts too much weight on his central theoretical concepts and that in doing so he excludes too much. In this paper I have concentrated on two such exclusions — sensations and concepts. They are not, however, entirely parallel. For one thing Gibson excludes concepts altogether but this is not true of sensations, which still have a marginal, if somewhat disruptive, place in his view of perception. I would argue that in effect the role of concepts receives a covert recognition, despite his denial of it, within the concepts of information and perceptual systems. This is not true of the notion of sensation. In the first place Gibson does give a subsidiary role to that concept, particularly in connection with certain illusions; he is more concerned to insist that perception does not *necessitate* them — there are indeed cases of 'sensationless perception'. Second, as I would argue, the subsidiary role that sensations do play on occasion are not really taken up into the theory as a whole; one needs a clearer account for example of how sensations can obtrude on perception. What, that is to say, is the exact relation between sensation and information-getting?

I have hinted at one sort of answer to this question in what I have said about the necessity of something like the concept of sensation in connection with vision in order to explain the sense in which the information obtained by the use of the eyes can be said to be 'visual'. That, however, it is clear, is not the sort of thing that Gibson has in mind. One of the phenomena that he adduces in this connection is that of perceptual occlusion, the perception of one thing behind another. He says that this takes place without sense-impressions, meaning presumably that there cannot be any such thing as a sense-impression of something behind another. I agree with this; there are indeed other examples that philosophers have adduced (particularly Wittgenstein in his discussion of 'seeing–as' in *Philosophical Investigations*, II, xi), e.g. certain cases of 'figure-ground' perception, where it is implausible to explain the fact that we see something in a certain way by reference to anything about sense-impressions or sense-data. If we see the figure constituted by a Maltese cross drawn in a square sometimes as that and sometimes as the diagonal cross formed by the gaps between the arms of the Maltese cross, there is nothing in what could be given in sense-impressions that could by itself explain that difference. And there are very many cases in which we see more than could be so given — and of these Gibson's occlusion case is an example. I agree too that there need be no awareness on the part of the perceiver about how he has the information that the senses provide. I have no desire in all this to defend the thesis that a place must be given in a theory of perception to sense-impressions in this sense — even in the cases where Gibson tentatively does give them such a place, i.e. certain illusions. All that I ask is that I be told what makes certain information visual, auditory or what have you.

It is not sufficient for such purposes that the information is acquired by means of the relevant perceptual system. Seeing that something is so is not the same as just knowing that it is so, even when it is added that the knowledge comes about through the mediation of a perceptual system. This is the point that can be taken care of, as it seems to me, only by some reference to experience, and this is excluded by Gibson's theory. However, I would like to add that, as it seems to me, there is no need for it to be so excluded; that is why I said earlier that Gibson seems to have thrown out the baby with the bath-water. My main

41

criticism of Gibson's theory is that it is not complete in the way that Gibson seems to think it is. That, however, is not to say that it is wrong in its essentials, and I would like to end as I began — with a tribute to one of the best pieces of psychological theorizing for many years.

## NOTES

1 'New Reasons for Realism', *Synthese*, 17, 1967, pp. 162-72.
2 See J. Hintikka, 'Information, Causality and the Logic of Perception', in *The Intentions of Intentionality and Other New Models for Modalities* (Reidel, 1975), pp. 59-75.
3 For some difficulties see my 'Unconscious Inference and Judgment in Perception', (this volume, pp. 11-29).
4 *Ibid.*
5 See too my *Theory of Knowledge*, New York, Doubleday, 1970; London, Macmillan, 1971, p. 200.

# 3

# PERCEPTION AND AGENCY

The traditional empiricist view of perception (though to represent it in this way may well be a caricature of any actual philosopher) is that in perception we receive information through the senses of the so-called external world. This idea is reflected in the notions of the 'given' and of 'data' which have figured so largely in theories of perception. Even if philosophers of this persuasion have gone on to say something about what we do with the data, it remains true that at rock bottom and in the last resort perception is thought of as something passive. I have tried to chart the historical issues elsewhere,[1] and I shall not repeat anything about them here. That is not my concern. I am interested here in the question whether the notion of a purely passive perceiver makes any sense in itself. That it does not has been suggested by philosophers on occasion. There are some brief remarks to that effect in G.E.M. Anscombe's *Intention* (p. 67); and Stuart Hampshire's *Thought and Action* lays great weight on action in connection with our awareness of the world, although I do not myself believe that the exact nature of the connection is clearly worked out by him. Some aspects of his views, however, have been taken up by Campbell Garnett with explicit reference to perception in his *The Perceptual Process*, with a resulting theory that bears more than a superficial resemblance to that of Maine de Biran.[2]

Certain psychologists too have reacted against the purely passive view of perception. There is, for example, a considerable emphasis on activity in the writings of Piaget, although largely in the context of a view of what the intellect has to do in order to counteract the purely passive and often distorting functioning of sensory systems. I say 'often

43

distorting', but if I read him aright it is a feature of the theory that Piaget expounds in his *Mechanisms of Perception*[3] that perception is of itself necessarily distorting and leads to knowledge only via processes of decentration that are due to the intellect. Without going to this extreme, there has been an emphasis on constructional processes in the writings of other cognitive psychologists, e.g. Neisser.[4] Moreover, Jerome Bruner has stressed the role of activity on our part both in perception and in thought, and has developed a whole educational philosophy on this basis, involving in particular the idea that learning about the world is best achieved through the active participation of the learners in the educational process.[5] James Gibson too has come in his *The Senses Considered as Perceptual Systems*[6] to put great weight on the fact that animals (or, as he sometimes puts it, the senses) hunt for stimuli and that this is very important for the business of information-getting. I might finally mention in this context the often-quoted experiment of Held and Hein,[7] on the basis of which a contrast was made between the ability of kittens to learn about their environment when (a) allowed to explore it and (b) offered a view of it while being towed around in a box that made them unable to move of their own will; the perhaps not very surprising result was that only the former kittens learnt much about their environment, although this still leaves open different possible explanations of that fact.

With the possible exception of Piaget, the psychologists to whom I have referred seem to assume that perception involves certain passive processes which are at any rate the preconditions for the supervenient active processes that make adequate knowledge of the world possible. Bruner expresses that point well when he speaks of going 'beyond the information given'. Even if the growth of our knowledge about the world depends on our so going beyond the information given and would be impossible if we did not do so, there is still information *given*. For Gibson too there is still all the information necessary for perception of the world given in the stimulus array, even if activity on our part is required for the acquisition of maximum information, since a passive perceiver is necessarily limited in his points of view. Piaget, as I have said, is a curious exception to the rule in all this, in view of his idea that sensory mechanisms are distorting. It is natural to think of his being a *curious* exception to the rule, because it is difficult to see how the intellect could build up a picture of the world unless it based itself on something — and how is that possible if the basis is a distortion? An appeal to the structuring function of the intellect is not in itself a justification of claims to its objectivity. One can assume only that Piaget thinks that even if there are distorting elements in the process of perception (due to what he calls centration) the process is not absolutely distorting; there is something there for the intellect to work on. The model that he puts forward, obscure though it is, suggests just this with its references to 'encounters' between elements of the sensory receptors and elements of what is perceived, together with 'couplings' between the respective elements. Nevertheless, what the intellect works on according to this model is merely a set of causal processes, and even if it remains obscure how it does this, it seems that Piaget does not really think of information being given in perception. His philosophical allegiances are not, strictly speaking, empiricist.

Even among those whose philosophical allegiances *are* empiricist, however, there does not seem to be a single motivation for the reference to activity. It is, for example, one thing to insist that to go beyond the information given we need certain active processes of construction or that perception involves putting forward hypotheses to explain the sensory data;[8] it is another to say, as Gibson does, that activity is necessary to make possible an adequate flow of sensory information. Indeed, Gibson seems to think that if we take his notion of information seriously we shall not need any reference to further intellectual processes in perception;[9] so that it is not a question of going beyond the information given but of making sure that adequate information is in fact given. It is clear that if we once accept the idea of the given there is more than one way in which activity can be invoked in relation to it in a theory of the acquisition and growth of information about the world.

There are, however, sound objections to the notion of the given itself and to the empiricist theory of knowledge that goes with it.[10] In the end an adequate theory of perception must show how causal processes, sensory experience, conceptual understanding, attention and other active intellectual processes, belief and truth come together. That obviously entails a very complicated story which I cannot attempt to tell here.[11] It should be noted, however, that I did not include in the list any reference to overt activity. It is not that I think that it does not belong there, but that it raises issues which are different from those raised by the other items. Nevertheless, reflection on the issues that it does raise may in the end lead to conclusions that have implications for the way in which some at least of the other issues are to be seen.

Let me start from the classical, Berkeleyan argument concerning distance perception. Berkeley was an empiricist, over perception at least, since he maintained that all that we are given is sensations; these sensations were, however, sensations *of* things — of heat, colour, etc. Hence, on this view, in having a sensation I am thereby given information. Berkeley's argument with respect to distance perception was fundamentally that the eye, being a two-dimensional surface, can provide information only about two-dimensional aspects of things. The argument is thus one from the causal conditions of visual perception, or certain aspects of them, to a thesis about what can be perceived by its means alone. The argument has nothing to do with phenomenology. Indeed, it is difficult, if not impossible, to state in an intelligible way what would be supposed, on this theory, to be the phenomenology of the situation. What would it be for things to appear to us to present a two-dimensional manifold? In his first book, *The Perception of the Visual World*,[12] Gibson thought that he could do something about an answer to this question by attempting to describe the result of looking at things with the eyes half-closed and with a lack of attention to the actual nature of the things perceived. This Gibson called the 'visual field', but maintained that it was a secondary phenomenon, dependent on perception of the visual world and not its foundation. (The notion of a visual field plays a much smaller part in Gibson's later writings, but survives to some extent in connection with cases where, as he puts it, sensation obtrudes on perception.) This idea plays no part in Berkeley's argument, however, since he was arguing, without respect to phenomenology, about how things must be, given the causal conditions of visual perception. Berkeley argued, in consequence of these supposed facts, that the perception of distance can come only through touch, and certain visual sensations come, in effect through learning, to suggest ideas of tactual properties. The tactual properties in question are not just texture and the like, but what we can find out about bodies by feeling them and their relative positions. Hence the use of touch that is in question is one that in effect involves movement.

The question that immediately suggests itself, especially given other things that I have said, is whether passive movement would be enough for these purposes. Suppose for example that we never made any active movements, but that we were continually being carried around in a passive sort of way. This supposition inevitably brings to mind the experiments with kittens that I mentioned earlier. Those experiments, however, have only an indirect relevance to the present question. If the facts about the kittens are as they are represented, they do not determine whether the kittens which were subsequently unable to find their way round their environment were unable to do so because they had no idea of distance or because, for example, they had been given no reason for attending to features of their environment. (Something of the same problem arises over the visual perception of people born blind who have their sight restored. How far is their visual perception influenced by their previous dependence on touch and by the techniques for finding their way round the environment that they have developed through touch?) It is, however, fairly clear that Berkeley has in mind, given his terms of reference, that we originally find out about the distance of things by active movements involving exploration. And, given again those terms of reference, that would be quite right. For we would surely get no idea of distance from passive movement unless we knew that we were being moved, and that would presuppose a prior idea of different positions in space. We could not find out the distance of things unless we had some idea of distance, while even with it dependence on passive movements would be unreliable. We get more information from active exploration. Of course, in a way, as far as Berkeley is concerned, active movement is in no better position; one could not get the idea of distance by its means unless we already knew something of what it is for things to be at a distance. For the active movement in question is presumably intentional, and this implies that to some extent at least we know what we are doing. Nevertheless, it can be seen that active movement can in principle provide more information about the distance of things than would otherwise be possible, in that the access to relevant information is thereby more under our control.

As far as concerns the acquisition of the very idea of distance, what Berkeley seems to have in mind is that there are not the same objections to its possibility in the case of touch as there are in the case of sight. For the possibility of moving through space makes access to a third dimension possible in a way that it is not possible for sight alone. Gibson in effect argued in his first book that the premise was mistaken. There is available, he thought, within the pattern of stimulation, as revealed by the details of the visual field, all the information necessary for perception of the visual world with things at varying distances from us. It is things at varying distances that we come to perceive, and we learn how things look at varying distances; it is not that distance is something that we just add on to the other perceptible properties of things. This will be true whatever the nature of the eye; the fact that the retina is a two-dimensional surface cannot be used as an argument for the impossibility of direct visual perception of distance. In one way perhaps this Gibsonian argument involves an *ignoratio elenchi*. For Berkeley does not deny that certain visual features of things may suggest spatial properties; he simply argues that this 'suggestion' can operate only if other conditions are satisfied — the tactual movement in question. Gibson's argument at this point holds good only if it is assumed that what is the case with the pattern of stimulation is sufficient for the corresponding perception — or, to put the matter in other words, that it is enough that information should be available for it actually to be received. This assumption is part of Gibson's acceptance at this time of a version of the so-called 'constancy hypothesis' and of a psychophysical theory of perception. A three-dimensional array will of course project on to a two-dimensional surface; but that fact does not in itself explain how we can see the array *as* three-dimensional. Gibson's subsequent emphasis on the part played by movement through space and the hunting for stimuli is a partial admission of the inadequacy of the older account in this respect.

The main difficulties in all this arise from Berkeley's empiricist assumption that any idea must be derived from some aspect of experience. The argument is that the idea of distance must in consequence be derived from something in our sensations. But, it is claimed, there are reasons for thinking that there can be nothing in our visual sensations which answers to that description. Yet, if one were to accept the thesis that all ideas must be derived from some experience, it might still be argued that in fact the idea of distance comes from our visual perception of distance. The only remaining problem would then be what makes it possible for us to see things at a distance when the retina of the eye is a two-dimensional surface. Berkeley answers that nothing makes that possible unless we bring in other factors — those involved in touch; Gibson answers that the results of projection on to a two-dimensional surface make it possible — but such factors are clearly insufficient. One is not thereby left in Berkeley's camp, however. One can and should reject his empiricist assumption about ideas being derived from experience; it is clear that the concept of distance is *presupposed* in seeing things at a distance. Nevertheless, there will still be a story to tell about the relationship between the having of that concept of distance and its embodiment in experience. It is as such a story that the early Gibsonian account is insufficient (and in this respect the later theory is no improvement). It indicates some of the causal conditions that are necessary for this purpose; it is inadequate in making clear what would be sufficient. Nor does it do enough to undermine Berkeley's argument from the two-dimensional character of the retina. What we have to see is that that consideration is irrelevant. It could be to the point only if there were reasons for believing that the features of the perceived world must correspond fairly exactly to the features of the retina. Gibson does not deal adequately with the claim that there are such reasons, even if he denies the conclusion, concerning himself with correlations between the two sets of features, not similarities.

If we now ask whether all this is in itself sufficient to rule out the possibility of a purely passive distance perceiver, the answer seems to be that it is not. It nevertheless remains *unclear* how there could be such a thing — how we are to *conceive* of its possibility. But the situation is in this respect no better with regard to an active distance perceiver unless we can explain why activity in itself makes a difference. It will not be enough if the activity merely produces a changing succession of static visual experiences. The activity, that is, must not merely multiply experiences of the kind that could be had by a purely passive perceiver, to the extent that we can give sense to that. Such a qualification is necessary because in speaking of a succession of static visual experiences we may have in mind that we now see things in such and such relations and then see them in other relations. But under these assumptions it is the whole idea of seeing things in relation, let alone in differing relations, that is in question. Could indeed a purely passive perceiver see things as such at all? To answer that question we must look to some extent at the way our understanding of the world depends on our relationships with it, as embodied persons, and as persons who can thereby act physically.

It seems prima facie clear that there are many aspects of things that we could have no idea of if we could not manipulate either those things or things that are in some way like them. One such aspect is the property that, according to some, Locke mistakenly included in his list of primary qualities — impenetrability. The supposal that it was a mistake on Locke's part presumably derives from the consideration that, while we can see or feel the shape of a thing just like that, this is impossible with impenetrability — the discovery of which requires something like an experiment. That may be true, but it is really the very point with which I am concerned. There is clearly a connection between the impenetrability of two bodies and their ability to exert causal effects on each other — in the way in which two billiard balls may repel each other or at least stop or modify to some extent each other's movement. But the possibility of seeing bodies in this way presupposes some understanding of identity. Notions like that of the identity of bodies and causal notions such as that of impenetrability are closely connected; for the identity of bodies is preserved under certain causal conditions which may vary with the kind of thing in question.[13]

Piaget's conservation studies can well be construed as studies of the child's appreciation of this kind of thing and of the conditions under which it may break down or fail to manifest itself. Bruner has said,[14] 'Perhaps the psychology of conservation, indeed, all forms of invariance, involve the recognition that the same thing can take many guises and still be the same thing'; and he comments in the same context on the effect of combining manipulation of an object and the labelling of it, e.g. as fatter or longer, on the ability to appreciate such things (the combination having more effect than either process taken separately). It is surely not just a matter of doing that simply. For the objects of which all this is seen to be true are *physical* objects (in the experiments on which the conclusions are based, lumps of plasticine); so that what the child learns in such cases is not just, as it might be put, the principle of identity in difference, but some of the principles underlying *physical* identity and its relation to appearance. What the child in these circumstances has to come to appreciate is that *plasticine* can be transformed into different shapes while remaining the same amount of plasticine; and this involves an understanding of some of the causal properties of plasticine. After all it is not true of all things that they remain the same thing under varying transformations. What is true in this case and in the various Piagetian investigations that have generated the issue is that lumps or dollops of certain kinds of stuff remain the same amount of stuff and the same kind of stuff under varying transformations; learning that is certainly learning something about physics.

Suppose that, by contrast with the studies so far noted, one is confronted with a shape of a certain area that is transformed into another shape of the same area by some means. To judge by the Piagetian studies it might well be the case that a very young child would say that a tall thin shape is bigger than a low broad one of the same area. One might speculate about the reasons for this. A child who learns the errors of his ways in this respect would learn that tall thin shapes are not necessarily bigger in area than low broad ones, but he would not have learnt in this anything about the identity of objects. The same

would be true even if the child were shown one shape being transformed into the other by some continuous process that preserved
constancy of area. The only principle to be derived from that would be
that constancy of area is not a direct function of shape; and that is not
a principle about the identity of *things*, even if it is a geometrical
principle about the identity of area. It could have application to
physical things only if some idea of physical identity is separately
presupposed.

The same kind of comment could be made about Michotte's studies
on the perception of causality, substantiality and permanence.[15]
Michotte claims that as a matter of phenomenology we can just see
something pushing another, without this being a function of learning.
But in his experiments nothing as a matter of fact pushes anything
else, since he presents moving shapes in varying conjunctions and
circumstances, not real objects; his interest would in any case be in the
phenomenology of the situation, not the situation itself. At one level
the studies can be interpreted as showing the conditions under which
a very good illusion of causality, etc. can be produced so that there is
no inclination to say that the look of a thing depends on an inference
from anything else, even if it is caused by certain features of what is
presented. The studies can even be represented perhaps as something of
a demonstration of the existence of non-epistemic perception. But for
X to be seen as causing some effect in Y (e.g., pushing it along), X and
Y must be seen as having a certain kind of identity which fits in with
the kind of causality in question. This cannot be put down to purely
configurational aspects of the figures presented. For these to be seen in
terms, say, of one thing pushing another, some idea of physical identity
and its connection with causality must again be presupposed.

Given all this, the question at issue is whether a purely passive perceiver could acquire such an idea. It has sometimes been claimed that
our idea of causality is one that we get from the experience of our own
agency, and that the idea of one physical thing acting upon another is
one that is parasitical upon what we know of our own agency. This
suggestion has also, perhaps as often, been denied, but it is important
to be clear about what is at stake. What cannot be true is that we get
the idea of causality from the experience of agency as such. For one
thing the concepts of causality and agency are not the same; but, more
fundamentally, to experience ourselves as agents we need some understanding of what it is to be an agent. I do not mean by this to suggest
that we need this understanding if we are to *be* agents; but to experi-

51

ence ourselves as agents we need to be aware in some way of at least the distinction between me and not-me and of what it is for one to act on something else. It has been argued by D.G. Brown[16] that this in turn presupposes an understanding of the way in which bodily causality is involved in it all (or at least this is, I think, a fair implication of what he has to say). Whether or not that is true of all agency (what, for example, of mental activity?), it is surely necessary for any being that is recognizably human, and it would be difficult to think of the possibility of our having a concept of agency that did not at least have this background. Given this, it would seem that our experience of agency presupposes too much, including some idea of bodily causality, to make it plausible to think that our idea of causality in general is founded on *it*.

This however, does not make it unintelligible that agency should figure somewhere in the story about what makes appreciation of causality possible, and with it the possibility also of an appreciation of physical identities and the conditions for the changes that they may undergo. The crucial point lies in the sort of thing that I said earlier about the notion of impenetrability — that its discovery requires something like an experiment. The reciprocal relation between bodily identity and causality makes it impossible that one of these factors should be presumed and then treated as the basis for the attribution of the other. That is what is wrong with the conclusions that Michotte draws from his experiments. In effect identity is presumed by the subjects in how they see what is presented to them, so that they then see one thing causing effects in another in a certain way. If they had been in the position to see causality of a different kind in operation, they might have identified objects in a different way too; if they did not do this it must be because they were already disposed to see the world in terms of persisting objects in a web of causal relations and subject to causal conditions. What makes this possible?

An answer to this question may be possible through a recognition of the continuing validity of Kant's point that our ability to experience things in this way is correlative with the recognition of oneself as something with an identity (the central feature perhaps of the 'transcendental deduction'). That identity is not dependent on the same conditions that make bodily identity possible, although its recognition is no doubt mediated by the fact that we have bodies to which as such the same conditions apply as for other bodies.[17] To break into the web of identity and causality that I have spoken of a basis is necessary, and that basis is provided by the self-identity in question; for it is in relation to a continuing self that application can be given to identity in general. But this will work only if there is an interaction between the self and the rest of the world, via of course the body that makes causal interaction possible.

It must, however, be *inter*action that goes on. Part of the discovery of what bodies are and are capable of is the discovery of what one's own body is and is capable of. That would not be possible unless we were agents and not merely passive receivers of causal effects. For the discovery of what our bodies are *capable* of involves interaction with other bodies in a genuine sense of 'interaction'. Thus learning what impenetrability amounts to is dependent on learning what limits there are to our agency through the interaction between our bodies and other bodies. That is what the 'experiment' that I have referred to comes to. It is not a genuine experiment which presupposes a question put to nature. It is rather that the idea with which we are concerned emerges and can only emerge in the context of our manipulation of things. It would be quite wrong to think of the young child as a little scientist experimenting with his environment; for the conditions of presupposed fact and theory which make a genuine experiment are necessarily missing. Nevertheless, it can be seen that the conception of physical bodies and what they are capable of begins from and emerges out of our active interchanges with the environment. Through this the child learns not just these things but also and correlatively what he or she is and is capable of. But that learning is not possible unless the child *has* a persistent and distinct identity and a form of consciousness that goes with this, so that the knowledge gained is in relation to a persisting self.[18] Recognition of *this* identity by the individual himself cannot be thought of as conditional simply upon the criteria of identity that are brought to bear on bodies, even if it involves the body in the ways that I have suggested as requisite for agency in any adequate sense. It has often been pointed out, as something learnt from Wittgenstein, that there are self-ascriptions that are made without reference to criteria, whereas the same does not apply to ascription to others; not that all self-ascriptions must be of this kind but that some must be. But the very possibility of self-ascription presupposes the recognition of one's identity, in some way and to some degree at least. If I ascribe a feeling to myself it is a single 'I' that is involved with a persistence through time. Such an identity cannot be thought of as merely conventional or dependent on the application to the world of a system of concepts. It is *presupposed* by anything of that kind; and at least an implicit recognition of it is presupposed in any awareness of anything that deserves to be called a 'world'. But this, I have argued, implies that the 'I' has to be an agent too; it is through that agency, mediated by the body, that interaction with the world comes about and it is on that basis alone that there can arise an understanding and perception of the world as physical.

Once given this there is, no doubt, much else of our understanding of the world that comes about in the course of our agency in relation to it. That would be true, for example, of those properties of objects that are in a genuine sense physical. Thus even our appreciation of distance — the feature that Berkeley was so much concerned with — brings with it considerations of what things we can effect and what things, the very distant ones, we cannot. (Distance is to that extent not merely a formal aspect of things in our environment.) But it would be wrong to think that this must apply to all properties of things or to think that physical objects are for us just objects of manipulation (or that they are for us the internal objects of touch, as sounds are for hearing). The perception of the colour of things, for example, need not depend in any direct way on agency on our part. Nevertheless, colours are properties of physical things and are seen as a feature of their surfaces, so that we should not have our present concept of colour if we did not have a concept of physical things. (Someone brought up somehow in an environment of coloured light, but not objects, if that were possible, would have a quite different conception of colour from that which *we* have.) On the other hand, the fact that we need agency and what that involves in order to have a conception of physical things by no means entails that the conception of those physical things is simply the conception of an object of manipulation or anything like that. It is important to distinguish the factors that make possible a given concept from the features of the concept which result from this.

It is equally important, however, to distinguish in all this between what must be so and what may generally be so as a matter of fact. I suspect that as a matter of fact the role of agency extends far beyond the sorts of considerations that I have mentioned; but there is no necessity that it should do so. As many of the thinkers that I have mentioned earlier have emphasized, we are in fact active creatures in all sorts of ways, and we should not get very far in acquiring knowledge of the world if that were not so. But as far as concerns the question with which I started — whether the idea of a purely passive perceiver makes sense — the answer is, I think, the one that I have given. That is to say that such a conception could get no initial purchase. Once given, however, that a creature is a perceiver (and presuming the point that it must therefore be an agent also to the extent that I have emphasized) the relative importance that must be attached to activity and passivity respectively is an empirical matter. In some cases more is to be achieved by making oneself receptive than by taking an active role; in other cases the reverse is true. Which case is which is a matter for experiment, empirical inquiry, and, sometimes, thought as to what is involved. Moreover, the sort of emphasis that I have put on activity even in the field of perception has no implications for educational ideology. It neither follows nor does not follow from what I have said that educationalists should put a premium on activity on the part of those being educated. On the other hand, what I have said may well have implications for an understanding of the way in which learning processes get a purchase in the first instance — for, that is, the theory of genetic epistemology; it is in this that the importance or otherwise of what I have had to say lies.

## NOTES

1 See my *Sensation and Perception*, London, Routledge & Kegan Paul, 1961.
2 See G.E.M. Anscombe, *Intention*, Oxford, Blackwell, 1957; S.N. Hampshire, *Thought and Action*, London, Chatto & Windus, 1959; A. Campbell Garnett, *The Perceptual Process*, Madison, Univ. of Wisconsin Press, 1956. For Maine de Biran see the bibliography in F.C.T. Moore, *The Psychology of Maine de Biran*, Oxford, Clarendon Press, 1970.
3 J. Piaget, *The Mechanisms of Perception*, London, Routledge & Kegan Paul, 1969.
4 See, e.g. U. Neisser, *Cognition and Reality*, San Francisco, W.H. Freeman, 1976.
5 See J. Bruner, *Beyond the Information Given*, ed. J.M. Anglin, London, Allen and Unwin, 1974.
6 J.J. Gibson, *The Senses Considered as Perceptual Systems*, Boston, Houghton Mifflin, 1966.
7 R. Held and A. Hein, *J. Comp. Physiology*, 56, 1963, pp. 872-6.
8 Cf. Richard Gregory's theory that a perception is itself a hypothesis based on sensory data. See e.g. his 'Choosing a Paradigm for Perception' in E.C. Carterette and M.P. Friedman (eds), *Handbook of Perception*, vol. I, New York and London, Academic Press, 1974, pp. 255-83.

9   On which see my 'The Concept of Information in Gibson's Theory of Perception', *Journal for the Theory of Social Behaviour*, vol. 7, 1977, pp. 5-16, (this volume, pp. 30-42).

10  For some of the objections see my *The Theory of Knowledge*, New York, Doubleday, 1970; London, Macmillan, 1971, ch. 6.

11  I have tried to tell some parts of it elsewhere. See, e.g., my 'Unconscious Inference and Judgment in Perception' in *Images, Perception and Knowledge*, ed. J.M. Nicholas, Dordrecht, Reidel, 1977, pp. 195-218, (this volume, pp. 11-29) and my *Experience and the Growth of Understanding*, London, Routledge & Kegan Paul, 1977. One might view that I am trying to do here as another chapter in what I have tried to do in that book.

12  J.J. Gibson, *The Perception of the Visual World*, Boston, Houghton Mifflin, 1950.

13  Cf. Kant's 'Third Analogy'.

14  J. Bruner, *Beyond the Information Given*, p. 323.

15  A. Michotte, *La perception de la causalité*, Louvain, Publications Universitaires de Louvain, 2nd edn, 1954; *Causalité, permanence et réalité phénoménales*, Louvain, Publications Universitaires Belgium, 1962. In the latter work Michotte suggests that preservation of identity may be a function of the *number* of attributes of objects that are changed.

16  D.G. Brown, *Action*, Toronto, Univ. of Toronto Press; London, Allen & Unwin, 1968, ch. 2.

17  Cf. on this the views of M. Merleau-Ponty on the role of the body, in particular those put forward in his *Phenomenology of Perception*, trans. C. Smith, London, Routledge & Kegan Paul, 1962. How far Merleau-Ponty goes with the other views that I am putting forward is not clear to me, despite what I owe by way of elucidation to my colleague David Murray.

18  For it to be *knowledge* the child must also accept public standards of truth and thus share in a public form of life. That, however, is another part of the story that I cannot tell here. I have tried to tell it in my *Experience and the Growth of Understanding*.

# 4

# PERCEPTION, INFORMATION
# AND ATTENTION

It seems to me that one of the remarkable things about perception, and something that makes it difficult to understand and categorize, is that it provides a point of convergence, a focus, for a number of quite different things that may hold good for human beings and, to some extent, animals. This fact makes it impossible to analyse perception into these other factors in such a way as to be able to say: 'Perception is this, that or the other thing.' What I have in mind are such factors as sensory stimulation, information reception and processing, belief and/or knowledge, concepts, attention, imagination, action, sensory experience and other forms of consciousness, and so on. In one case or another of perception all or any of these factors may be involved. And yet I do not think that perception can be exhaustively analysed in their terms. Perhaps I might describe my aim on this occasion as to remind you of some such facts, which must in any case be very well known.

It is natural these days for a psychologist to think of perception largely in terms of the reception and processing of information. Whatever happens at the level of the stimulation of nerve-endings must, if perception is thereby to take place, be such that action eventually performed as a result must be capable of being characterized as done in the light of information thus received. It is also natural to suppose that if what happens is to function as information it must be fitted into previously existing schemata, to use the term originally introduced in this context by F.C. Bartlett, and resuscitated more recently by, among others, Ulric Neisser.[1] Or, to put the matter in quite other terms, but which I believe to come very much the same thing, what is

57

perceived will not be perceived *as* anything unless the perceiver has prior concepts, knowledge and beliefs.

There is of course one eminent psychologist, the late James Gibson, who has thought otherwise, claiming that in vision, for example, the ambient optical array provides enough information in itself to make it quite unnecessary to make reference to anything that goes on inside the perceiver. Although I believe that Gibson has done immense service to the subject in pointing out how complex an amount of information is available to the perceiver in the optical array itself, and particularly in what is invariant in the transformations that this undergoes, the suggestion that we do not need to refer to anything inside the perceiver in order to explain his perception of the environment seems to me an absurd exaggeration. Worse than that, it seems to me that as Gibson has used the term 'information' he is not entitled to the supposition that the features of the environment on which he has concentrated provide or constitute information except as information *to* the perceiver; and something cannot constitute information *to* a perceiver unless something holds good of the perceiver that makes it possible.[2] When Gibson speaks, as he did to a great extent in his later writings of 'affordances', that term ought to be taken seriously in terms of its natural meaning. There are various things about the environment which in relation to a perceiver afford information about that environment; and Gibson has done wonders in pointing them out. It remains true that even if such things afford information, that information need not be received as such, and it will not be received as such unless certain things hold good of the perceiver that makes that possible. In the terms in which I prefer to think of these things, perception is concept-dependent, to say the least, and the environment will not be perceived in any way, let alone as it is, unless the perceiver has the relevant concepts.

That, however, applies to any kind of acquisition of beliefs, to any form of information pick-up, and it is not peculiar to perception. If one were to ask what makes a given form of information pick-up perceptual, a natural first move by way of an answer would be to speak of the information pick-up being mediated by the senses. There are, however, difficulties about what exactly constitutes a sense. It will not do, for example, to specify it in terms of some anatomically differentiated organ. It is the *function* of the organ which is in point here and the whole problem lies in how that function is to be defined. Gibson, it will be remembered, speaks of the senses as perceptual systems. It will not do, however, to say that a sense is a system of information pick-up associated with a given organ. If the stimulation of a certain organ characteristically produced, in given circumstances, beliefs about the environment to the extent that we might say that information pick-up had occurred, but in a way such that the acquisition of the beliefs had no experiential aspect, would we be willing to speak of perception? Or if we were, would we be willing also to speak of sense perception?

It is at least logically conceivable (and more than that if the findings of Weiskrantz and others on 'blind sight' are correct[3]), that the stimulation of the retina of the eye might result in a given organism in beliefs, whether correct or not, about the immediate environment to the extent that it was optically suited to it, without anything that constituted the experience of seeing. In such a case, if the possibility that the experience is there but subliminal can be ruled out, it would not be right, I suggest, to speak of sense perception or to say that the retina in such circumstances had the function of a sense or part of that function. (Indeed in the cases empirically investigated the phenomena arises because the perceptual system as a whole is not functional because of cortical damage.) The function of a sense is not just to make possible information pick-up but to do so in a characteristic way. What that characteristic way is is difficult to spell out or define, but it is worth noting that any account of it should provide not only for the epistemic factors that are involved in information pick-up but also for the more aesthetic aspects of experience.

I have suggested elsewhere[4] that it is impossible to take account of that without bringing in something like the notion of sensations, meaning by that not the sense-data which have been the stock in trade of numerous philosophers and some psychologists, but something analogous in the case of, say, vision to what occurs in bodily sensation. I shall not elaborate further on that precise suggestion here, but I should like to go back to an example that I have invoked in that connection, because morals may be derivable from it additional to those which I have derived so far. It is the example of what happens in tactual perception when one moves one's hand over some textured object. I have pointed out elsewhere[5], what may seem obvious, that as far as our awareness is concerned, there may be a vacillation between our being aware of the feelings in our finger-tips and our being aware or more aware of the details of the texture of the object. It is of course possible for us to concentrate our attention on one or the other, but it also happens that our attention may be *drawn* to one or the other by varying aspects of the relationship between our hand and the surface. Since, however, all this is under any circumstance a function of attention, and since it seems to me implausible to suggest that sensations, the feelings in our finger-tips, come into existence only when we attend to them (and if they did what would be the 'them'?), I have suggested that it is those feelings which, even when our attention is drawn to the texture of the object, give the specific character that it has to the awareness of the texture in these circumstances. They 'colour' the awareness, so to speak, if I may use a metaphor.

Whether people find that suggestion plausible is not so important in the present context as the recognition that the phenomenon that gives rise to the suggestion exists — the vacillation of attention between sensation and the perceived texture of the surface. When I first referred to it at a conference in Canada, someone in the audience said in the course of the discussion that it was customary for panel-beaters involved in car repairs to place a cloth between their fingers and the surface of the body-work when trying to make sure that the surface was completely smooth. I hope that it is true that they do, but it perhaps does not matter too much whether it is or not. At the time I did not see the point of the observation, but having thought about it since I have come to the conclusion that the point is that the function of the cloth is to divert attention from what is happening in the finger-tips so as to concentrate on the properties of the surface.[6] If you like, a more accurate perception of the tactual properties of an object is possible only where the risk of one's attention being drawn to something else, i.e. the state of one's fingers, is reduced. I believe that this conclusion is generalizable so as to apply to other senses too, but I should like to approach that suggestion through another consideration.

One way of putting the point about the cloth might be to say that it, the cloth, constitutes a medium for the sense in question. It has been clear to people since Aristotle that distance-senses such as sight and hearing depend for their functioning on a medium such as light in the case of sight and something like air or some body in the case of hearing. The forms of energy emission from bodies in question depend for the possibility of their stimulation of the relevant sense-organs on the existence of a medium that makes possible the transmission of the energy. Senses vary somewhat in the way that this takes place, but even in the case of something that is relatively a contact sense, like taste, something of the kind obtains. It does not seem obviously the case with touch, and Aristotle, who believed that any sense must depend on a medium for its functioning (pointing out that when an object is put directly on the eye it is not seen!), drew the conclusion that the organ of touch cannot be the flesh, but something within (say the heart) for which the flesh functions as the medium. Aristotle did not of course know much if anything about the nervous system, and for us who know about nerve endings in the skin his conclusion must seem ludicrously implausible, if it does not do so for any other reason.

It is not, however, implausible to say that the cloth in the example that I have quoted performs that role. The question that next arises, however, is exactly what is that role. It is surely a fact of nature that the nerve endings in the retina are sensitive to light and that light has certain physical properties and is due to certain physical processes which affect its transmission. Is it not a similar fact of nature that the nerve endings in the skin are subject to pressure from objects or to the temperature of objects which are in direct contact, and for this no question of *transmission* of energy arises that is at all akin to that which arises in the case of sight? Yes, but the properties of objects which are specifically visual depend for their perceptibility and the forms of their perceptibility on those facts about the way in which the eye functions and the physical processes which enable it so to function. (Note that I do not say that the visual properties of objects, their colour and so on, depend for their *existence* on that; it is the form of their perceptibility that so depends. Things would have colours whether or not there were eyes of specific kinds; the same would not be true, obviously, of how those colours were seen.) Hence how things are seen depends crucially on features of those conditions which make vision as we understand it possible at all. And one of those conditions is the existence of a medium.

The very possibility of tactual perception of the textures of surfaces is not similarly dependent on the existence of a medium. We can feel the texture of a surface without anything between our fingers and the surface. Variation in the pattern of stimulation of nerve endings which is brought about by movement of the hand over a surface is, of course, something that helps the tactual recognition of the properties of the surface because of the, in Gibson's language, invariances that this affords. But that is a respect in which sight and touch are similar. It remains true that they are different in that a medium is not physically necessary in the case of touch. I am not claiming otherwise; touch *is* a contact sense. It may still be the case that, where the circumstances of the stimulation bring about too much concentration on the immediate

61

results of that, tactual perception as such may be inhibited. The same applies to sight in a way; too intense a stimulation for example, so producing a dazzle, in effect brings about too much concentration on the direct results of the stimulation rather than on whatever is its source. Even so that may still seem a different case from that of the cloth between our fingers and the surface; there it is, or so it may seem, not just a matter of a less intense stimulus, although it is clear enough that the more intense the stimulus the more likely it is that we shall concentrate on its effects, i.e. the feelings in our finger-tips.

On the whole, I think that that conclusion is right. The effect of the cloth is not necessarily to cut down on the general intensity of the stimulation; that will in any case depend on the pressure that we exert on the surface. The effect of the cloth is rather to cut down on the *variation* of the pressure, the contingencies of stimulation as one might put it, so that imperfections in the surface stand out. This has as its first effect the making possible of the detection of invariants in Gibson's sense, a task which is made easier when minor and contingent variations are cut down. What is important, however, is that that is the general *perceptual* function of a medium. That is to say that while a medium may be physically necessary for certain forms of perception for physical reasons associated with the form of energy in question it also has a functional role for perception considered as such. The general dampening effect on stimulation which is exerted by a medium plays a role in making possible the detection of invariance even though the stimulation in question would not occur at all in the case of most of the senses without a medium or not in such a way as to produce a genuine response to the properties of the source of stimulation. (What I have in mind by the latter qualification is that, for example, a sound emitting object if applied direct to the nerves of the ear or the tympanum would produce feelings of vibration not the hearing of sounds.)

There is a sense in all this in which it might be said that in the process of perception, the total amount of information available in the environment is too great if adequate perception is to occur; there is redundancy of information in that sense, and indeed too much of it for adequate perception to occur without some dampening down process. This process is a natural part of the workings of the distance senses, and can be introduced with effect in the case of a contact sense. At the same time, while it can enhance perception by making information pick-up of a relevant kind easier, it is that same thing which may give rise to misperception or at least is one of the causes of that. The senses conceived as perceptual systems in Gibson's sense are thus a kind of compromise and function adequately only because they are that. Democritus, the ancient Greek atomist, is reported to have said that if it were not for the air we could see an ant crawling on the sky. One might reply that if it were not for the air or something like it one would not see anything, both because it is the physical condition of the relevant stimulation of our eyes and because the dampening down of that stimulation makes the detection of invariances easier. Yet while all this is so, it is not the only effect of cutting down variation of stimulation. Too much variation of stimulation brings about an inability to make sense of what produces it, an inability to detect invariants, and that in turn produces a concentration on its effects — the feelings rather than what produces them.

I have, in what I have said so far, moved easily from speaking of what takes place in the process of stimulation to speaking of this in terms of information. Some might object to that, and it obviously involves a bit of a jump given my earlier strictures on speaking of information when it is not information to or for someone or something. In any event in the tactual case where there is a vacillation between feeling the sensations in our finger tips and feeling the details of the surface texture, it has to be noted that the information is about different things in the two cases while the stimulation presumably remains the same or can do so. Or to put the matter semi-paradoxically, in the information theory sense the amount of information is the same, while in the Gibsonian sense or in the information processing sense the information in the two cases is different; for it is about different things. Given a general ability to receive information in this latter sense, and given the fact that the process of stimulation is the same in the two cases, the fact that the information is different cannot be a function of the process of stimulation itself, but of something else.

That fact ought to be no surprise to those who think of information reception as having information *processing* as a necessary part. But the difference in the case that I am considering can scarcely, or at any rate not illuminatingly, be construed in terms of pre-existent schemata. There are no doubt differences in the structuring of the nervous system between the case in which we are aware of the feelings in our finger-tips and that in which we are aware of the tactual properties of an object. Hence if by 'schemata' were meant simply structures the issue would be decided easily enough. But that would be at the least un-

63

illuminating, since there must surely be differences in structure of that kind for *any* differences of cognitive state. In any case, it is far from obvious that the feeling of, say, a tingle in our finger-tips requires any pre-existent structure of the kind that would be completely pertinent for the perception of something as rough. For the latter presupposes some concept of roughness, an understanding in some way and to some extent (something that as a matter of degree can be very variable) of what it is for something to be rough. That has to be acquired, it has to be learnt, and is thus in a genuine sense pre-existent if something is to be perceived as a result in its terms.

I spoke earlier of the difference between the two cases in terms of differences in the direction of attention. But that too may be misleading, since when in the ordinary way we attend to one thing rather than another that presupposes some form of awareness of that thing as a suitable object of attention. That is not really the case when we are aware of the feelings in our finger-tips. It is not that we are aware of them *as* feelings and that our attention to them is as such. It is just that we *have* them rather than feeling through them, as I would have it, to the properties of the object which produce them. And of course this latter process does presuppose attention in a positive sense. So it might be better to say in this case that either our attention is drawn to the properties of the object or it isn't; and leave it at that. Nevertheless, attention does seem to be an ingredient in the *perceptual* process somehow; and when, for whatever reason, we become aware of the feelings in our finger-tips rather than the texture of the object it is certainly the case that our attention is no longer on the properties of the object.

The reason why I hesitate to speak of a switching of attention in such a case is that that might, as I think improperly, suggest that the case should be assimilated to the phenomenon of selective attention on which so much psychological work has been done (e.g. Treisman, etc.). That phenomenon, as I understand it, involves selection between, and in that sense attention to, alternative sets of information available in the process of stimulation. Selective mechanisms might make that possible wherever in the process of perception they are to be located. The same might be true of that rather curious switching of attention that may occur when there is an oscillation in how we perceive ambiguous figures; where attention to one aspect of the figure may enable us to see the figure in one way rather than another. Both these phenomena might, I take it, be construed in terms of the idea of selective attention, although in the former the selection is between sets of items of information while in the latter the selection is between, for example, the roles played in the representational process of some aspect of the figure so that the figure is seen in one way rather than another. I think that it would be implausible to think that the selective mechanisms were the same in the two cases, but speaking of selective mechanisms remains appropriate. I do not think that the same is true of my 'feelings in the fingers' case. For there the switching of attention, if that is what it is, is not between perceptible features of the environment, however construed, but between a feature of the environment and something which is not that. To put the matter in the terms which I mentioned earlier, we are either aware of the surface of the object as, say, rough, or we are aware of feelings in our finger-tips, but not necessarily in such a way as to be aware of them *as* anything. (That is not to say that we *could* not be aware of the feelings as such and such, but that would demand a more refined consciousness, a higher-order form of awareness which we do not necessarily have to have to have feelings at all.)

So, while it is true that we either attend to the features of the surface or to the feelings in our finger-tips, it is also true that while in attending to the surface we are aware of it as such and such, in attending to the feelings we are not necessarily aware of them *as* anything. There is, therefore, a difference between this case and those of selective attention, which could be put by saying that in the latter cases the selection is between available information, between perceiving things in one way rather than another, while in the fingers case the selection, if it is right to put it that way, is between having information and not having it. If that involves attention there is involved a concept of attention which is more basic than that involved in speaking of selective attention, such that attention is involved whenever we are aware of anything. It is a *precondition* of information reception rather than a constituent or aspect of it. It follows that it cannot be explained in information-processing terms. What my example suggests, however, is that too much complexity in the information providing process may lead to a switching off of attention to the environment, bringing about a concentration on what is surely more basic — the effects of the information bearing stimulation on our bodies. I describe it as more basic simply because, in the nature of things, there could be effects on our bodies without information reception but not, surely, vice versa. That is why I think (though I find that others do not always find my view totally persuasive) that the effects on our bodies, considered as, so to speak psychical, i.e. in terms of feeling or sensation, must equally condition or colour the information reception process itself in such a way that perception is to be regarded as more than the reception of information *simpliciter*, but as reception of information *in a perceptual way*. When the process of information reception or processing breaks down for some reason the *perceptual way* can attain more importance than the information processing itself. So our attention is drawn to that — to the feelings or sensations as we may now call them — rather than the relevant features of the environment; our attention is drawn to the results of the stimulation rather than to the information available in its source. I have no idea what sort of mechanism makes that possible. Perhaps the matter ought to be investigated; I offer the suggestion of the project free and gratis to anyone who is interested!

I would like in closing to look at the matter from another side. There has been a certain amount of discussion among philosophers in recent years as to whether there is such a thing as non-epistemic perception. The supposition that all perception is epistemic is, roughly, the supposition that all perception is a matter of belief, that all seeing is seeing-that, seeing that something is the case. It is possible to introduce various refinements upon that construal of the issue, but I shall not go into them here. The thesis that all perception is epistemic is roughly equivalent to the thesis that all perception is to be construed in terms of information reception and processing. The thesis that there does exist non-epistemic perception would amount at its extreme to the thesis that some cases of perception cannot be construed in information terms. The thesis need not however be taken at its extreme. For example, it is my belief that in illusions, such as the Müller-Lyer, how we see the lines is not a direct function of belief in the sense that we may see the lines as of different length no matter what we believe about them. Whether or not that is true I should be the last to claim that belief does not enter into the picture in *any* way. It may well be the case for example that only believers, only those who have some beliefs or other, perhaps only those who have beliefs about what it is for lines to have length, could be subject to the illusion. If that were right, the proper thing to say about perception would be that its normal function was to mediate information reception, but that *within that context* perception might occur without there being any conveying of information in a strict sense. To put the matter in another way, perception can only be understood as such to the extent that it has some connection with the acquisition of beliefs about the world; nothing could be conceived of as a form of perception if it did not have that connection. It does not follow from that that whenever we perceive we acquire some belief. Hence I think that perception can be non-epistemic in that, possibly boring, sense.

I think, however, that it works the other way round as well — that an information receiving device could not be thought of as a perceptual device unless non-epistemic perception was possible by its means, unless it was possible to perceive something in a certain way without this implying the acquisition of a belief on the part of the perceiver. This in turn implies that there is more to perception than mere receipt of information. It is really only at that point that what I have been saying earlier has any direct contact with the issue about epistemic and non-epistemic perception. But it does have a contact all the same. It is not very easy to provide an analysis of those cases where we see something in a certain way without this implying any belief; it is not easy, that is, to say what is going on other than by saying that we see whatever it is in that way, or that that is how it looks to us. When we see the lines in the Müller-Lyer illusion as of different lengths there occurs an application of the concepts of line, length and difference, but the application takes place under the condition that, as we might say, that is how we experience it. The problem is what *that* means. I think that it at least means that we have a mediated consciousness of what is there as something suitable for the application of the concepts in question (mediated because it is made possible only by certain processes of stimulation). What is there is, in the terms that I used earlier, an object of attention — not the selective attention to which I have already referred, but the more basic form.

What I have been suggesting is that when the mediation becomes too complex, when there is too much information, attention can fail so that what we become conscious of is not the features of the object that we are confronted with but the results of the process of stimulation itself. Whether or not we think of that as a switching of attention, it does imply that attention must be involved in the ordinary processes of perception. When that attains a greater importance than the information reception that it makes possible there results a form of perception which is non-epistemic. There are finally the processes of mediation themselves, the conditions of stimulation with their resulting forms of consciousness, which I believe colour the awareness of the world we have in perceptual attention to it; and they become obvious only when attention shifts for the sort of reason that I have been discussing. All in all there is more to perception than can be expressed in terms of information alone.

So, to return finally to Gibson, I should like to say again that despite the immense debt that I think we owe to him for pointing out the rich variety of information 'affordances' that the environment in itself provides, the theory of perception that he has offered is essentially flawed. It does not take into account all that is involved in perception as such.[7] Whether his theory is any worse in that respect than any other current theory is not really for me to judge, but, if I may hazard a guess, I doubt it. We still have a considerable way to go to understand perception.

## NOTES

1 U. Neisser, *Cognition and Reality*, San Francisco, W.H. Freeman, 1976.
2 Cf. my 'The concept of information in Gibson's Theory of Perception', *Journal for the Theory of Social Behaviour*, vol. 7, no. 1, 1977, pp. 5-16 (this volume, pp. 30-42).
3 See e.g. L. Weiskrantz, *British Journal of Psychology*, vol. 68, 1977, pp. 431-45.
4 e.g. *ibid.*, or in 'Unconscious inference and judgment in perception' in J.M. Nicholas (ed.) *Images, Perception and Knowledge*, Dordrecht, Reidel, 1977, pp. 195-218 (this volume, pp. 11-29).
5 In 'Unconscious inference and judgment in perception', *ibid.*
6 I once put this to Gibson. He didn't seem much impressed!
7 Also, although I haven't previously said so, I do not think that Gibson himself ever speaks of the affordance *of information*, even if he does say that 'the affordance of things for an observer are specified in stimulus information', (*The Ecological Approach to Visual Perception*, Boston, Houghton Mifflin, 1979, p. 140). Why he does not is an interesting question. I am inclined to think that the pragmatist tendencies implicit in his general theory of affordances is at variance with the realism presupposed in his account of information as 'simply available'. But that is not something into which I can go now.

# PART II

# LEARNING AND
# GENETIC ISSUES

# 5

# THE LOGICAL AND PSYCHOLOGICAL ASPECTS OF LEARNING

It is, I suppose, obvious enough that some children learn better when there is a smile on the face of the teacher, just as it is conceivable that others may learn better when it is all done in time to music. Some learn better when they are happy, others perhaps when the conditions are austere or comfortable enough not to be distracting. The study of such individual differences is clearly a matter for psychology, since it will be a study of the psychological processes which bear on the facility with which individuals learn. It is even possible in principle to produce generalizations in this field, statements which may apply to people in general, although it may be doubted whether these will in fact amount to more than platitudes — that people learn better in general when encouraged or rewarded, when they are given opportunities for practice, when they are given material in digestible amounts, and so on. Nevertheless, these would certainly be *psychological* generalizations if not very exciting ones. But there are questions about learning which are not psychological questions — questions such as what learning is and what is implied when it is said that someone has learnt something. To answer such questions we have to clarify the concepts which we employ in this sphere, something that requires both reflection and some familiarity with the subject matter to which those concepts apply. Investigations of this kind are not so much a matter for the psychologist as for the philosopher.

What, then, is it to learn something? In fact, this is a question which I shall, in effect, shelve for the time being, and it may be that I shall have nothing very illuminating to say about it directly. But I shelve it quite deliberately. One might of course say that to learn something is to acquire knowledge of it through experience; but this, although correct as far as it goes, is not likely to be enlightening because, apart from other vaguenesses in the formulation, much depends on the 'something' in question. To learn a list of words or a set of formulae, to learn to play the piano or to ride a bicycle, to learn a language or a technique, and to learn a subject or a discipline are all very different things. Although they all involve the acquisition of knowledge, that knowledge is of quite different forms. To learn a list of words, simple rote-learning, as it is called, is nothing more than to memorize that list, and the knowledge involved is merely the knowledge of the words in their appropriate order. In skills such as that involved in riding a bicycle 'knowing how' comes to play a role, and the acquisition of such skills may involve practice as much as does rote-learning, even if in a different way. But here too other things begin to emerge; for few skills could be acquired by practice alone in the most rudimentary sense of that word, and few are in any way independent of some understanding of the issues involved. You could not play the piano without some such understanding, and practice in this case, if it deserves the name, must be intelligent practice. The existence of such understanding may indeed be implied whenever we speak of knowing how to do something, and this, among other things, distinguishes knowing how to do something from merely being able to do it. When we come to learning a language or a technique, and even more so with learning a subject, the appreciation and understanding of the subject and its principles comes to the fore. With the understanding of principles goes the ability to use certain concepts. If there is a distinction to be made between my two last categories, it is that learning a language or a technique is inevitably a practical matter in a way that learning a subject is not so obviously so. But this is a matter of emphasis only; technique and intellectual understanding, theory and practice cannot be completely divorced from each other.

What I have said so far is meant to show the complexities involved in any general discussion of learning. Fortunately, for educational purposes, it is surely unnecessary to go into all this. Rote-learning and simple practice may or may not be adequate tools for educational purposes, but they cannot in any way constitute anything in the way of the essence of education. This last, I suggest, is nothing unless it brings with it understanding and appreciation of principles, their relevance and their interconnections. Understanding, moreover, involves and presupposes the acquisition and use of concepts. One can understand nothing of a subject unless one has the concepts in which that understanding is to be expressed. Hence, the process of learning a subject goes hand in hand with the process of acquiring the relevant concepts, the concepts in terms of which the subject matter and its principles are to be formulated. I shall try to say something by way of elucidation of this in the following. But my main concern will be with two points, both of which seem to me comparatively simple. They are as follows:

(1) The subjects into which knowledge is conveniently divided are not block-entities laid out, as it were, in a Platonic realm. There is an inclination, I believe, to think that there exists objectively something called, to take one example, mathematics, and that it is the aim of education to bring the learner to a confrontation with it. Subjects are, on this account, ideal entities available for contemplation. Given this, one can then argue about the best way of bringing about this contemplation, since the subjects are too complicated to grasp all at once. Is it better to concentrate on those parts of a subject which are somehow logically prior to others or on those which are psychologically easiest to grasp? The snag about this is that it is not immediately clear what the question means, what the distinction amounts to. Certainly, I think, the question of what is easy to grasp is not a matter for psychology. On the other hand, the notion of logical priority is perhaps obscure and it has different implications according to the ways in which it is interpreted. I shall enlarge on these points directly.

(2) No one could be said to have come to understand a subject, to have learned it, without some appreciation of general principles, some idea of what it is all about. But knowing and understanding general principles is not just a matter of being able to recite the relevant general propositions. Nothing is contributed by way of understanding when people are made to recite general propositions, even if these are fundamental to a subject. Thus, to present a very young child with, say, the general principles of number theory or algebra would be a futile business; for, he must be capable of cashing such general principles in terms which mean something to *him*, if understanding is to follow. There is in the growth of understanding of any subject an intimate connection between principles and their applications or instances. Principles must always be seen cashed in there instances, but instances must themselves be seen as cases to

73

which principles are relevant.Thus an appreciation of general principles implies in the full sense an appreciation of how they are to be applied. My point is analogous to one which could equally well be made about concepts; it may be expressed in Kant's famous or notorious slogan that 'thoughts without content are empty, intuitions without concepts are blind' (where by 'intuitions' Kant means something like the reference to instances). To present a child with little bits of information without reference to general principles at all is a sure way of preventing the development of understanding; such a child would be intellectually blind. But to go to the other extreme and concentrate on principles alone is another way of producing an equally unsatisfactory end-product; the child's thought, if this could be brought about, would be empty — without reference to any particular cases through which the general principles could mean something to him. There must always be a delicate balance between principles and cases; but since there are degrees of generality it is clear that the attainment of full understanding at one level of generality must presuppose something of a balance attained at a lower level of generality, a balance between an understanding of principles in general terms and an understanding of their relevance to particular cases. Otherwise, there is little hope of the relevance of the more general principles being seen. What is the point of presenting to children the principles of set-theory if they are not capable of understanding what it is for something to be a set? This has an obvious relevance to any discussion of Piaget's 'stages', especially to the distinction between concrete and abstract operations. Indeed, I suspect that Piaget is an essentially Kantian thinker in many respects.

I shall discuss my two points in turn. They are not of course unconnected. I have said that it is a superstition to think that subjects exist as block-entities, the contemplation of which should be the goal of the learner. I do not mean by this that there are no differences between, for example, history and physics. The historian may be distinguished from the physicist by, among other things, his interests, his methodology and the concepts which he brings to his subject matter and in terms of which he thinks about it. There are also differences between the modes of explanation which the two employ — between historical and scientific theories. All these differences — and no doubt there are others — are important. But to suppose that the real difference is that there is one body of knowledge, expressible as a set of facts, called 'history' and another called 'physics', which the two are out to discover betrays a quite erroneous conception of learning. It is to suppose that learning consists merely in the acquisition of knowledge of a set of facts, the contemplation of a set of propositions. At its lowest, it reduces learning to simple rote-learning. But it cannot be anything like that in fact. Even at the simplest level the acquisition of knowledge of facts goes hand in hand with understanding. Even in rote-learning it is essential to understand what is going on, and in higher forms of learning understanding is much more important still. Thus words like 'history', 'physics' and 'mathematics' are not just the names of bodies of knowledge, in the sense of sets of true propositions; they are, if anything, the names of approaches to facts of generally different kinds. At a certain level, perhaps, we cannot even say that; distinctions between subjects tend to break down, they become an administrative matter only, or a question merely of the differences in the background of interests on the part of those who are concerned with them.

I may be thought to be labouring the obvious. Surely, it may be said, no one really thinks that subjects exist in *that* sense. Perhaps so, but I detect suggestions of this sort in certain discussions which imply that learning should start from what is logically prior in a subject, and even perhaps in those who deny this and insist that psychological priorities are everything. Let me explain what I mean – and the best way to do this is to indicate and explain one sense of the words 'logically prior', a sense which I shall directly come to repudiate in this context.

Explanatory theories, e.g. scientific theories, have a logical structure in the sense that the propositions of which the theory is constituted can be arranged in a certain order, so that certain propositions can be derived from others. It is indeed the fact that from general laws and statements of initial conditions it is possible to derive conclusions – the facts to be explained – that provides the basis of scientific, and no doubt other kinds of, explanation. We thus expect that with the help of reference to the general we shall be able to deduce the particular. It is because of logical relationships of this kind – relationships of entailment – that we can speak of the theory having a structure, and we may say, as Aristotle said, that the general is logically prior to the particular. The same sort of thing applies in mathematics. Insofar as it is true to say that set-theory provides the basis of arithmetic it is because arithmetic can be explained in terms of set-theory. Set-theory furnishes the more general point of view under which arithmetic can be

75

subsumed. Hence, we might say that the notion of a set is logically prior to that of, say, a number, because the latter can be explained in terms of the former, but not vice versa. The direction in which explanation must proceed, and the logical relationships which go with it, thus determine what is logically prior within a discipline.

This, however, only applies where the discipline in question constitutes a theory — to parts of science, the foundations of mathematics and so on. Where questions of explanation do not arise and do not have a place, then this sort of consideration has no place either. It is difficult to see how large parts of history or literature could be said to have a structure in this sense. But even where it could be said that this is so — where a subject admits of the formulation of a theory of it — this could have few implications for education. Even if there is *a* sense in which someone could not be said *fully* to understand arithmetic without understanding set-theory, this is only in the sense in which it might be said that someone could not fully understand, say, the movements of billiard balls without understanding the principles of sub-atomic physics. And no one, I take it, would suggest that children should be introduced to physics *by that route*. The most fundamental concepts of a subject, from the point of view of explanation, are not likely to be the most familiar. To concentrate on such concepts may hinder the understanding of how the more familiar concepts are to be applied — a matter which is just as important for complete understanding. But, to repeat the remark which I made earlier, there are subjects for which none of this makes sense, since questions of explanation do not arise within them, or do so only to a minor extent.

If this is accepted, it may be suggested that the only remaining position is that, as far as learning is concerned, the only priorities are psychological priorities. For, from the point of view of learning, the priorities that the structure of explanation provides are not relevant. That is to say that the only possible procedure for an educationalist is to find out empirically what parts of a subject are the easiest to learn and to insist that learning should start from there. For there is now no question, it might be thought, of having to start from those elements which are logically necessary if anything else in the subject matter is to be seen as it is. There is no question of having to see the subject arranged in its proper logical order. There are no logical conditions for a proper understanding of a subject; there are only psychological conditions, e.g. that no one could grasp the difficult parts before grasping the easy ones. So it might be said. To come to this conclusion would, I think, be far too quick a deduction from what has already been established, but there is in any case something very odd about the suggestion that the easiness or difficulty of a subject or a part of a subject is a matter for psychology. It is clearly enough a matter for psychology that something is easier for one person to learn than another; for, the question why this is so could be answered only by an investigation into the people concerned. The conditions under which individuals learn something more easily is also clearly a matter for psychology, as I indicated at the beginning of this paper. It is not so clear that the same thing holds good of the question why one subject or part of a subject is easier than others.

In what ways might one subject be more difficult than another? It might demand knowledge of more facts (so I have heard it said about psychology in comparison with philosophy). It might be more abstract (so I have heard it said about philosophy in comparison with psychology). It might demand knowledge of skills, procedures or ways of thinking not demanded by the other, and it might even presuppose the other in one way or another. Factors like abstractness and complexity loom large here, although these factors may arise in many more ways than one, and I would not claim that these are the only factors at stake. However, abstractness and complexity are obviously very important and I shall concentrate on them in what follows. It may be thought that these factors are relevant because of the truth of psychological generalizations such as that people generally find the abstract and the complicated more difficult to understand or grasp than the specific and the simple. But is this just a psychological generalization? *Could* a man find the abstract easier to grasp than the specific, and the complicated easier to grasp than the simple? Would this indeed make any sense? If not, then we are confronted here, not just with empirical psychological generalizations, but with some sort of *a priori* or necessary truth. That is to say that in that event abstractness and complexity will be *criteria* of difficulty; if one subject is more abstract and complex than another then it will follow necessarily that the one is more difficult than the other. I do not claim that it is always obvious whether some branch of a subject *is* more abstract or complicated than another, and to discover the truth on the matter may require investigation of a kind. The way in which this might be done is by turning what I have said on its head. Given that people *normally* find X more difficult than Y, this will be a reason for saying that X may be more complicated or abstract than Y (depending on the exact nature of the difficulties reported). The idea of what is normal is very important here, and I shall return to it later in an analogous context. The point is that if a subject is difficult people may be expected normally to find it so — just as, if something is red, it is to be expected that people will normally see it so. When I say 'normally', I do not mean 'generally'; I mean 'in normal conditions'. It is this notion of what is normal which provides the link between what something is and how it appears to people or how they find it. Thus, if abstractness and complexity are criteria of difficulty we may expect that people will normally find the abstract and complicated difficult; and conversely, if people normally find something difficult, this will be an indication of its abstractness or complexity.

We need, however, to look further at the idea that there is some kind of necessary connection between the notion of difficulty and those of complexity and abstractness. Can we even conceive of a man finding the complicated or abstract easier than the simple or specific? There are of course people who feel more at home with the complicated than the simple — people of whom we say that they cannot see the wood for the trees; and there may be people who are similarly more at home with the abstract than the specific, people who fail to bring issues down to earth. But this indicates something about their habits or qualities of mind; it indicates nothing directly about the comparative easiness of the subject matter. The man who cannot see the wood for the trees may indeed find the simple too easy for his taste. It may come to be that the simplicity of a thing constitutes an obstacle to his understanding, just because of his cast of mind; we might perhaps say that for some reason he shuts his eyes to the simple. But his case provides no grounds for denying that the complicated is normally more difficult for people than the simple. Indeed, the special explanation that is required indicates that the case is not normal. The indications, then, are that we should expect people normally to find the complex difficult. Indeed, the connection between complexity and difficulty seems to turn on certain things about the concept of understanding. The complicated may, in fact, be described as that which puts a certain kind of demand on the understanding. To grasp a complicated whole is to grasp the simpler components in their relationship with each other; hence this kind of understanding presupposes the understanding of the simpler; and where a man appears not to find it easy to take in the simple by itself, we need a special explanation of the fact. The same is true of the relation between the abstract and the concrete or specific, although this raises considerations to which I have already referred under my second heading and to which I shall return later. I conclude, however, that factors like complexity and abstractness are in fact criteria of difficulty, and that it is thus not just a psychological truth that people find the complicated and abstract difficult.

These considerations, however, open up once again the question whether there are any priorities in a learner's approach to a subject which are more than psychological. (And that there *are* psychological considerations I have no wish to deny, since, for example, personality differences between people may make one way of putting over a subject more rewarding in one man's case than in another's. Factors relative to the learning of something on specific occasions and by specific individuals are always psychologically relevant.) Now, I think that there *are* priorities in learning which are more than psychological, and they might be described as epistemological, or logical in another sense from the one already discussed. In the growth of knowledge, certain things must be done before others. Not only is it the case that certain facts must sometimes be known if one is going on to make sense of others, but it is also the case that sometimes certain things must be understood, certain concepts grasped, before progress can be made at all. For example, in arithmetic it is essential that one should understand the notion of an ordinary integer if one is to understand that of a fraction. This is quite apart from such general considerations as the priority of the simple to the complicated, to which reference has already been made. The appreciation of certain subjects demands a certain order for knowledge. That this must be so is indicated by the existence of general principles for the establishment of curricula, and if it were not so any suggestion that programmes could be laid down for teaching machines would be impossible. What I am now saying is that such programmes, such principles of order, could be established only by decisions on what is the appropriate order for the development of the knowledge and understanding of a subject. To reach such decisions demands that very knowledge and understanding of the subject itself, plus an ability and willingness to reflect upon the exact relationships between the concepts presupposed within it. This is not a matter for psychology. I would emphasize this point.

Let us consider in some detail an example which brings out the kind of consideration which I have in mind. As is perhaps well enough known, Piaget and his associates have carried out a number of studies, which have beocme known as 'conservation studies', concerned with the child's appreciation of such general principles as the conservation of matter, size and weight. It has been brought out that children at a certain age do not always appreciate such principles and even appear to apply them inconsistently. Moreover, they do not come to accept them all at the same time. There appears to be a general assumption in Piaget's approach that they perhaps *should* do so, and that it is surprising that they do not. There is also perhaps a sense of surprise that children should fail at all to accept the principles, despite the fact that in the actual history of thought some of these principles were not formally established until comparatively recently, at any rate during the last three or four hundred years. These studies might be represented as concerned with the understanding of concepts which fall within the general field of physics, and may thus be described as studies in the child's understanding of elementary physics. The question that arises is what could be discovered about the situations under investigation merely by reflecting about them. Let us take a specific and simple case of a Piagetian type: we have, let us suppose, a definite quantity of liquid of a specific colour, which can be poured from a wide transparent container into a similar narrow one. When the liquid is poured from the wide container into the narrow one, a child at a certain stage of intellectual development might well say, because of the comparative depth of the liquid in the containers, that there is more liquid in the narrow one. This may be so even though he sees the liquid being poured from the one container into the other. What are we to suppose has gone on here — what concepts employed and how?

Many sorts of consideration are relevant. We, who know the right answers, know that change of place and container does not affect the identity of the liquid or its volume, and that volume is not a simple function of depth. But these are not factors which we can take for granted in a child, and it does not take a great deal of reflection to see that we cannot. Moreover, the notion of the identity of a liquid (or of any other object) is not necessarily an obvious one. After all, we allow some changes in things without thereby denying that they retain their identity. Liquids expand when heated without becoming thereby different liquids. If we were to maintain that the identity of a liquid has something to do with its mass, this is obviously by no means a simple notion, and is not one that could at all be taken for granted in a child. What *does* identity depend on for a child? I am anxious here only to raise such questions for consideration, and to bring out the complicated relationships that may exist between the concepts which we use even in situations which may seem obvious to us. *We* tend to take notions like that of identity for granted (even when we cannot give an account of them); but there is no saying that a child does. Nor should we expect insight into these relationships to emerge all at one time; for, some of them are more complicated than others. The notion of volume, for example, is a more complicated notion than that of depth – it introduces another dimension. The volume of a liquid is therefore necessarily more difficult to estimate than its depth. Hence, the apparent relationship between the identity of an object and its depth or height may well seem more obvious than that between the identity of an object and its volume. All this should be evident to one who is prepared merely to reflect about the situation, provided that he has the requisite concepts.

Furthermore, it is not surprising that at a certain stage of development a child may be pulled in different directions: it is the same object for him to the extent that nothing has apparently been done to it which could cause it to change its volume or indeed change at all; yet it is different because its apparent depth and therefore apparent volume have changed. In the development of the 'right' view of things social influences obviously play a large part – a point very much underemphasized by Piaget. Similar considerations apply to the part played by the acquisition of linguistic tools. In other words, the facility with which a child may come to see the proper relationships between such factors as volume, depth and the identity of the object will depend on the extent to which he is subject to social influences of a certain sort and on his ability to formulate the relationships in words.

I have no wish to draw any other general moral than the one which I have already mentioned, i.e. the need for reflection on such situations. I certainly do not believe that it is possible to lay down any general law of development which the child must follow in acquiring concepts and coming to see the relationships between them. I would, however, point to the fact that concepts vary in complexity and abstractness, and that this determines certain general priorities. In considering how education should proceed one has to start from a knowledge of the concepts which a child possesses and the goal to be attained, and work out the intervening steps in the light of such general considerations as I have mentioned. This, I would emphasize again, can be done only by one who knows the subject and is prepared to reflect about it. There is no short cut, but that certain things must come before others in any process of this sort is a matter of logical necessity of a kind. How exactly, how precisely the priorities could be worked out is a matter for speculation, and the steps to be followed in the teaching of any given child will obviously depend on where that child is already, on what concepts he already has and on what relationships he already appreciates. For this reason, any generalized programme for teaching children of roughly the same stage of development must inevitably be a matter for compromise; but that *some* general principles can be laid down for the development of knowledge within any given sphere is of course a presupposition of any educational programme. In some disciplines the steps to be taken by the learner are comparatively easy to establish; hence their amenability to instruction by teaching machines. In other disciplines, any programme of teaching must inevitably be a hit and miss affair. It is all a question of the complexity of the relationships which exist between the concepts in terms of which the subject matter is to be understood. An assessment of these relationships can come only from one who knows the subject. It is not a matter for one who has specialist psychological knowledge alone.

I may have given the impression that while subjects are not block entities, in the sense explained earlier, they nevertheless have a fixed order of development, and that learning consists in finding out what this is and following it up. I do not think that this would be the correct account of the situation. This is not just because it is unrealistic, not just because finding one's way may involve going down many blind alleys. Wittgenstein once described coming to understand the nature of mathematics as trying to find one's way round a strange town, and this is not a bad description of any attempt to learn a subject. Moreover, it may be that in the end one of the best ways of coming to understand the geography of a town is to get thoroughly lost and have to find one's way home despite this. The apparently blind alleys may turn out not to be blind after all. Sometimes, too, the best first step may be to acquire a habit of going in a certain direction; habits can always be adapted later, as long as they do not become ossified. All this is true, but it does not get to the root of the problem. The analogy may or may not work even at the most abstract level of a subject, although the idea of a settled geography to be discovered may be one to be retained at any rate as an ideal. But the child in a school is not so much learning the geography of an area as acquiring the tools and techniques by which he may eventually come to make a map of it. A tool is of little use until it is decided what purposes it may be used for. Maps also may be constructed for different purposes and with different projections.

The point of this analogy is that concepts too can be thought of as tools of this kind. In making a map one has to know not only the features of the terrain to be represented on it, but also what counts as a feature of a specific kind. Similarly, concepts may be thought of as instruments for the task of attaining a familiarity in thought with some range of facts and also for attaining an understanding of what counts as a fact of a given kind. And just as the map has a purpose, so too concepts may be regarded as devices for thinking of the facts in a way which may be useful for some further end. That is why I said earlier that in considering how education should proceed one should start not only from a knowledge of the concepts which a child already has but also from a knowledge of the goal to be attained. What is the goal to be attained in teaching a young child elementary arithmetic, the salient facts of an historical period or the rudiments of English grammar? Until questions of this sort are answered it is impossible to say how we should proceed or in what order concepts should be invoked. It has, in sum, to be decided what is the goal of any given inquiry. The problem is a well-known one in connection with the learning of classics. Until the goal to be attained in studying classics has been decided it is pointless to argue about how to go about studying it — whether, for example, the doing of Latin proses or the study of Ciceronian cadences has any utility. Concepts are, to change the analogy, like keys too; they open doors, but if they are to be of any use one must know what door each opens, whether the door leads anywhere and whether there is any point in opening it.

I have spoken of concepts long enough without really explaining the term. I must now say something of what it is to have and acquire a concept, and this will bring me to my second main topic, about which I have in effect said something already. It must now be made explicit. The connection is this: I said earlier, in presenting my second main point, that it turned on what was involved in understanding principles. The notions of a concept and a principle are interconnected; to have a concept of something is to know the principle in accordance with which things are said to be of the relevant kind. To have a concept of, say, man is to know the principle whereby certain things may be collected together — those things, namely, which we call men. It is thus to know what it is to be a man. This entails not only being able to give an account of what sorts of things men are, but also thereby to recognize men as such. To acquire a concept thus involves acquiring this knowledge and this ability. Of course, someone may have a *certain* understanding of a concept without being able to recognize the things which fall under it. There is a sense in which a blind man may be said to have some understanding of the concept of redness. He may be able to tell you that it is a colour, and he may be able to give a formal account of what a colour is, e.g. that it is a property of the surfaces of objects that is accessible only to vision. He may indeed be able to give some account of the structure of colours and of the relation of red to the other colours. All this is possible without sight, and therefore without the experience necessary to a full understanding of what it is for an object to be red. Such a full understanding requires both the ability to give a formal account of redness and the ability to recognize instances. A concept thus gives one a principle of organization for a subject matter. If one has a given concept one has knowledge of that principle. That is why I have already talked of the understanding of a subject as a matter of appreciating certain concepts and their inter-relationships.

It is a dogma of empiricism that one acquires a concept by reviewing a number of particular things and seeing what is common to them. This cannot be the correct view of the situation if only because in order to do this one must be in the position to regard those particular things *as instances*. It is necessary to know what things it is relevant to collect together for this purpose. Thus it might seem more pertinent to speak of applying concepts to things rather than abstracting them from things. The truth is what I have already said — that we have the concept in question only when we are both able to see a range of things as falling under the concept and also in the position to know what it is for them so to fall, what it is that makes them instances. For this reason, there is inevitably in the process of acquiring concepts a delicate balance between a kind of abstract understanding of what it is to be an X and a knowledge of what things conform to this criterion. In learning — that is to say, in the growth of knowledge and understanding of a subject matter — there must at every stage be achieved a balance of this sort if progress is to be maintained. Habits of mind, habitual ways of thinking, however useful when considered merely as stages in a transition to greater understanding, become intellectually dangerous if allowed to ossify. But there are other dangers also, those which I referred to earlier. There is the danger of becoming too concerned with particular things to the extent that it becomes just one damned fact after another. There is also at the other extreme the danger of spinning out connections between concepts without stopping to ask for their cash value.[1]

These points which I have made are, as I indicated earlier, essentially Kantian. They are to be found also in a sense in Piaget, although in his case they receive a strange biological dress. A strictly philosophical point is tricked out under the guise of a rather vague and certainly misleading psychological or biological theory. I refer here to Piaget's notions of accommodation and assimilation and the balance to be achieved between these processes. What Piaget has in mind is the idea that our knowledge of objects is partly determined by what these objects are in themselves, partly by how we regard them. This comes down to the point which I have already set out, concerning the relationship between concepts and instances. But to use the notions of accommodation and assimilation to express the point is harmful in two ways at least:

(1) The idea that perception and the acquisition of knowledge generally involve accommodation and assimilation amounts to the idea that in this context there is a mutual modification of subject and objects. (A parallel for this idea can again be found in Aristotle, in his view that perception consists in an actualization of the corresponding potentialities of sense-organ and sense-object.) But this sort of view depends on analogies which are supposed to exist between perception and other situations in which there is a reciprocal causal relationship. Such reciprocal causal relationships exist often enough in biological situations, where the attainment of a balance is the function of an organism. Thus the proper working of the body depends on the existence of physiological balances of one kind or another. The stimuli which affect certain bodily organs are themselves affected and modified by a process of feed-back when the balance is disturbed. But the relationship which comes to exist between concept and object in perception is not a causal relationship at all. A concept is not the sort of thing which can have a causal relation with an object; it makes no sense to suppose so. For, concepts are not things of this kind, as should be clear when it is remembered that as I have already said, to have a concept of X is to know what it is for something to be an X. Correspondingly, the growth of knowledge is not itself a causal matter (however much it may depend on causal factors of a physiological kind, i.e. on bodily conditions).

85

(2) If the employment of a biological model is misleading in giving us an incorrect understanding of what the acquisition of knowledge consists in, it also has misleading implications of a more directly philosophical kind. It suggests that the balance to be attained is one between something about the individual which is essentially subjective, i.e. the concept, and something about the world around us which is clearly objective, i.e. the object. Knowledge is thus a blend of the subjective and the objective. But the relationship to which I have pointed as existing between concept and instance is not one between the subjective and the objective. It is not up to an individual to organize in thought what he is confronted with in any way he pleases — or if anyone shows signs of so doing we think of him as mad. I have surely said more than once that to have a concept of X is to know what it is for something to be an X; hence, to see something as an instance of X is to see it as something to which this knowledge is appropriate. There is nothing subjective about this. In fitting something to a concept we are not imposing on it a subjective point of view; for, given what I have said, to have a concept can be as much an objective matter as anything else. The objectivity of a concept is bound up with the idea that it must be inter-subjective, inter-personal, just as knowledge is. Hence, it is impossible to look on the growth of knowledge as some kind of transaction between an individual and his environment, as if social, inter-personal, factors had no part to play. I have commented already on the serious underestimation of the social in Piaget's thought. This is borne out by his adoption of this curious biological mode, which effectively rules out the social factor, and thereby undermines the objectivity of knowledge. It is most important to note the extent to which notions like that of knowledge and concepts are social ideas, and the extent to which objectivity depends on this point. For the same reason it is impossible to think of education and learning at all except from a social point of view.

An important truth nevertheless remains in all this — that a balance must be attained between the formal understanding of the principles of a subject and an appreciation of what counts as instances to which those principles are to be applied. Unless this balance is attained one cannot be said to have a proper understanding of the concepts involved. Hence, being aware of the general principles of a subject, which itself presupposes having the concepts, the particular forms of knowledge, in which the subject matter is to be formulated, implies also attention to instances. Of course, this is of itself to take an over-simple view of the situation, since concepts do not come by themselves, and any subject will involve connections between concepts of one degree or another of abstractness. To be made to learn these connections without any prior understanding of their relevance to instances would be to be given knowledge which was formal only, and therefore empty; the lack of understanding would make the learning equivalent to rote-learning. It would be the learning by rote of empty phrases. It is perhaps arguable that in certain spheres of knowledge progress might be better made by instilling the formal knowledge and then cashing it in instances than by building up from instances in the first place. But this is merely to make the point which I have laboured all along – that at every stage in the development of knowledge a balance is required between formal knowledge of principles and appreciation of what counts as instances, and that it is of less importance which one invokes first than that a balance should be attained. Nevertheless, it is clearly futile to expect a child to move from one extreme to the other, and the concrete and particular is clearly more obvious than the abstract and general. Is it, therefore, any surprise that what Piaget calls the stage of concrete operations must in general precede that of abstract operations? As Aristotle said, while in knowledge the general is prior in itself, the particular is prior relative to us. This is what Piaget's point come down to.

What do I mean when I say that the concrete and particular is more obvious than the abstract and general? I do not present this as a mere fact of human psychology. It seems to me a consequence of the situation in which human beings find themselves, of the nature of human experience. The possibility of creatures who come to knowledge of, say, the principles of physics before knowledge of their immediate surroundings is a science-fiction conception, but it corresponds to nothing human. In so far as our concept of knowledge is really a concept of *human* knowledge, it is doubtful whether the possibility which I have mentioned is even one which is intelligible to us. The development of human knowledge may be represented as an enlargement of experience, an enlargement of the individual's intellectual environment. (The part played in this by social factors is obvious.) The things which are the individual's immediate and original concern are particular and concrete. As experience is widened and enlarged, as too it becomes more inter-personal, so it must inevitably become more general and abstract.

87

Given all this, what seems at first sight to be merely a natural transition from the concrete to the abstract in the development of human thinking emerges as some sort of necessary principle. It is necessary because this transition is just what, as we conceive it, the development of human experience must consist in. That development can of course fail to take place, but it can have no other order; otherwise it would not be *development*. But, it may be said, has not Piaget shown by empirical investigations that the concrete comes before the abstract as matter of fact? How can something which is supposed to be a necessary truth be discovered by empirical investigations? We must be careful here. Let us consider what Piaget's response might be to hypothetical counter-examples to his thesis. Presumably, if children did not develop from the concrete to the abstract at all, he would have to say that they were not normal children — and we would agree. If the development occurred in the reverse order, would he not have to say, as I have already indicated, that they were not human? The presumption in his investigations is that he is concerned with normal human children. One thing that he may be said to have discovered is that the subjects who at one stage employ concrete operations and only later abstract operations are indeed normal human children. What else should we expect to happen in such circumstances? The situation is similar to the one which I mentioned earlier in stressing the connection between abstractness and complexity on the one hand and difficulty on the other. If there is a way of establishing the abstractness and complexity of a subject, this is *eo ipso* a way of establishing that people normally find it difficult, and vice versa. Similarly, if there is a way of establishing that children are normal human children, that their experience is what is normal, then this will *eo ipso* establish that their intellectual development will be along certain general lines, and vice versa.

It seems to me that Piaget's discoveries here are like discovering that circles when presented to people in a frontal plane look round to them. To insist that they generally do would be to labour the obvious. The point is that this is the normal case, and it is by reference to it that the application of concepts like 'roundness' is established; it is the norm for what counts as round. If circles presented in a frontal plane did not normally look round our understanding of notions like that of a circle and roundness would be completely different; indeed, we should not know what to think. Hence, given that the people and the situation are normal, it could not be otherwise. It needs no empirical investigation to discover that circles seen in the frontal plane look round in normal conditions. Analogously, I do not claim that the stages found in Piaget's subjects are not there as a matter of fact; I do claim that *if his subjects are normal human children*, we could not conceive it otherwise. Hence, the priority of the concrete to the abstract is something that all normal human beings could discover by reflection on what they know about the nature of human development, of human learning; it needs no further empirical investigation. On the other hand, of course, it does need empirical investigation to discover *when* John or Mary pass from one general stage of development to another, and whether they do so at roughly the same age. But such findings of course presuppose our present educational and cultural set-up; there is no reason to suppose that the norms are unalterable. Hence, what needs even further investigation is whether what is true of John and Mary is also true of Fritz, Ali and Kwame, i.e. we need to know the effects of different cultural and perhaps genetic backgrounds on the general development of children.

Finally, let me say again that if it is thought desirable that the process of intellectual development be accelerated (something that is perhaps arguable, considering that *intellectual* development is not the only thing), then the best people to provide the answers how this is to be done are those who have reflected most deeply on what is involved conceptually in their own subject, what is best understood first, and so on. That is to say that the best person to say how the teaching of, say, mathematics should proceed is the mathematician who has reflected adequately, and perhaps philosophically, on what is involved in his own subject (especially, in the first place, in its application to experience). Of course, here again the difficulties in the way of coming up with any firm answers may be insurmountable; in which case, the only hope is to find out empirically what courses of learning children do as a matter of fact normally find most easy. For, as I have said, easiness goes with concreteness and simplicity of subject matter, and this provides a clue to what should come first and what second in learning.

My intention in what I have had to say has been above all perhaps to delimit the roles to be performed by philosophy and psychology in this field, and to emphasize the differences between empirical and conceptual inquiries here. Psychology has much to tell us about learning — about, for example, particular cases and individual differences. It can also tell us about the effect on learning of all those factors in people which we can call psychological-personality traits, intelligence, and so on. What I have been urging is, amongst other things, that there is also required proper reflection on what learning and education are, and what they involve in consequence. For, only in this way can we be rid of misleading models which may inhibit our understanding of intellectual development and education.[2]

## NOTES

1　I ignore here the possibility of *a priori* concepts, but these would be intelligible only in some sort of connection with concepts which do have the application discussed above.
2　(Note added 1981). I now think that I do not in this paper distinguish clearly enough between abstractness and generality. See my *Experience and the Growth of Understanding*, pp. 116ff. What is said about development also needs qualification; see this volume, chapter 9.

# 6

# CONDITIONING AND BEHAVIOUR

I am not sure whether my main thesis might be better put by saying that the concept of conditioning has outlived its usefulness or by saying that it never had any utility in the first place. To say that the theoretical pattern of Pavlovian conditioning is an artificial abstraction which was not really exemplified even in Pavlov's actual experimental situation would not be to say anything new. It would not be new to say even that Pavlovian conditioning never in fact occurs. These things were said by some of the classical exponents of S-R learning theory. Hull maintained the more radical thesis and Guthrie and Skinner have maintained the only slightly less radical thesis that Pavlovian conditioning, type $S$ conditioning as Skinner called it in *The Behaviour of Organisms* (1938), is an artificial abstraction, so that it does not appear in a pure form. These doubts about the notion of conditioning have not, however, prevented the notion from being used in some form or other. Indeed, we now hear of sensory conditioning and conditioned imagery, notions which are a far cry from the original conditioned reflexes of Pavlov's dogs. Moreover, the applications claimed for conditioning, e.g. within psychiatry, are manifold.

There can be no objection simply to the extension and stretching of a theoretical concept. It might indeed be argued that it is in such extensions of the application of theoretical concepts that the progress of science lies. But the fruitfulness of possible extensions of the application of a concept (and thereby of the concept itself) depends on what underlying analogies exist between the phenomena which the concept is invoked to explain. The question, therefore, is whether there are any appropriate analogies between the phenomena in connection with which psychologists have spoken of classical conditioning, operant conditioning, sensory conditioning, etc. Of course, what they all seem to have in common is that there takes place some process whereby a connection *appears* to be set up between two factors in the situation — between stimulus and response, between response and reinforcement, or between stimulus and image. I say 'appears to be set up' because strictly speaking it is merely a matter of hypothesis that there is such a connection. All that can be observed is that the response, or whatever it is, takes place and becomes more probable in the given situation. Whether this is due to an underlying connection and of what kind is another matter. That is where theory comes in.

I make this point because it may seem to some that the term 'conditioning' is not a theoretical term at all; it is merely a loose term used to cover any situation in which the probability of a response increases due to its association in some way in the experience of the organism with some other factor in the situation. Thus if someone could be got to have an image of a certain kind whenever a situation of a certain kind obtained (e.g. on being given a signal by an experimenter) this would be enough to justify the use of the term 'conditioning', and saying that the image had been conditioned. But this cannot be so, or at least to say this would be proof of the unhelpfulness of the term 'conditioning', since the label would then cover a wide range of quite different phenomena, having in common only that a certain response, image, etc., has the probability of its occurrence in situations of a certain kind increased, as a result of what has happened during a certain period. Surely it is not just *this* that is meant by 'conditioning'. If it is, then the term has certainly no explanatory value; and psychologists have certainly behaved as if it did have such value.

In fact, I think it impossible to separate the concept of conditioning from the other concepts which form its theoretical background. Any reference to conditioning must imply recourse to a certain kind of explanation of the phenomena in question, and that is where the theoretical background becomes relevant. In Pavlovian conditioning what is supposed to happen is that there is initially an understood connection between stimulus (the so-called unconditioned stimulus) and reflex reaction. By repetitive presentation of another stimulus (the so-called conditioned stimulus) in the same context, the reaction is transferred to it, so that conditioning takes place. There are certain things to note about this, things which may seem very obvious and boring but which require attention all the same. First, I have spoken of an 'understood connection' between stimulus and reflex reaction. I do not mean by this that we have to understand completely why the connection exists, although we must have *some* idea of why it does so. We do know at least the general pattern of the neurological mechanisms responsible for reflexes. But, second, this determines the sense which has to be given to the terms 'stimulus' and 'reaction' in these circumstances. For it is implied that the application of some form of energy to a group of nerve endings produces in the end, and if it is not inhibited (i.e. in normal circumstances), certain muscular contractions or other physiological effects. In the case of the patellar reflex one can speak loosely of tapping the knee and of a subsequent knee-jerk, but this is loose talk all the same. Similarly, in the original Pavlovian situation one can speak of food producing salivation in the dogs, although it is presumably the smell or taste, or rather the chemical effects on the olfactory or gustatory nerve endings, of the food which produces the reflex, and then only if the reflex is not inhibited, because, say, the animal is satiated with food. However, it may plausibly be claimed that even if one is constrained in the interests of economy to speak loosely concerning the phenomenon, one may have some idea of what is supposed to be going on and one can always in principle provide the more exact account. (Though what I have said about inhibition and normal circumstances reveals the fact that the reflex arc cannot be treated as an isolated mechanism, and that the stimulation that takes place in producing the reflex is not without its effect on the rest of the neurological system; that should go without saying. That the reflex is an abstraction has often been recognized.)

We have so far a phenomenon which is explicable in terms of a relatively isolable system. The transfer of the reaction to another stimulus must, if the account is to be more than superficially descriptive of what is seen to take place, be intelligible in similar terms. The connection with the new, conditioned stimulus must be capable of being understood in terms of the same or an analogous system, and what is colloquially referred to as the stimulus must be capable of being interpreted in terms of effects on nerve endings. The sound which Pavlov caused to occur in the case of his dogs is so capable of being interpreted in terms of its effects on the ear, and, as is well known, Pavlov put forward certain theories about the kind of neurological system which could make possible the connection which he supposed to be set up. There are no problems in his case about the end effect, the salivation, since this again can be seen in terms of the physiological workings of certain bodily organs. The mechanics presupposed in all this are, in physiological and therefore more plausible terms, what was supposed to take place in the association of ideas, according to nineteenth-century associationist psychology. It is no coincidence that the notion of conditioning was taken up with a certain alacrity by the behaviourist successors of the associationists (cf. Taylor, 1964, p. 143); but it was not only taken up, it was also extended, and that in questionable ways.

Such an extension took place in a variety of ways, but these fall into two main categories. There is first the extension of the notion of conditioning to phenomena which are not interpretable in terms of the notions of stimulus and reaction discussed above, and in which a mechanism of the kind postulated is to say the least dubious. Thus J.B. Watson (1925) spoke of conditioning where what calls out the reaction is not a stimulus in the above sense, but what he called a 'situation'. It is true that he attempted to construe situations as complex groups of stimuli, but this is not a plausible move. To say this is not to deny that when we are in a given situation our sense-organs are being stimulated in an extremely complex way. But this pattern of stimulation is not necessarily related to the situation *as it is seen by the subject*; and it is the latter to which the reaction is made. What Watson tried to explain in these terms is a subject's responding in an habitual way to a situation; but in that case it is what the subject *sees* the situation *as* that is pertinent. To put the matter in another way, while the sound in Pavlov's classical case might be said to cause the salivation when conditioning has taken place, a situation cannot be said to cause a response in the same way. But I have here spoken of a response, rather than a reaction; and it is clear that one must speak in this way; or at any rate if one speaks of a reaction, it is a reaction *on the part of* the subject, not one *caused in* the subject. It is not a contingent matter that in the classical conditioning situation the reaction is a reflex movement, a muscle movement or the workings of a bodily organ, such that the subject does not necessarily have control over it. The reaction or response that might be made to a situation, if it is to be an intelligible one, must be one made by the subject in the light of that situation. One could always construe Pavlov's dogs as having responded to the sound of the bell in the light of their perception of it (i.e. in the light of their perception of it as connected with food). This might not be a very plausible interpretation, because the response appears so automatic. But an interpretation of this kind would be the only possible one in the case of what is recognizably a subject's reaction or response to a situation. For how could a reaction of an automatic kind, similar to that of salivation to its stimulus, be at all intelligible in relation to a *situation*? Or rather, how could any intelligible claim be made that the mechanisms in this case are at all like those which might be invoked to explain Pavlovian conditioned reflexes? In other words, the extension of the notions of stimulus and reaction, if applied to this case, affects drastically our conception of what mechanisms may conceivably be involved; so that the case may be seen to be so different from the Pavlovian case that it is very unlikely to be an instance of the same phenomenon. What I am saying is that it is not a trivial matter that the notion of conditioning has been extended from conditioned reflexes to conditioned responses and that the notion of a stimulus has been extended so that more or less anything with which an organism might be concerned can be called a stimulus. In the process of this extension the cases have altered fundamentally, so that neither the application of the notion of stimulus, nor that of the notion of reaction, nor the possible mechanisms involved, are at all the same. It is difficult to see why one should suppose that one is therefore concerned with the same phenomenon, and why there is any analogy between the cases beyond a merely verbal one. Given this, it is also difficult to see what explanatory role is played by the notion of conditioning in the extended case.

Another facet of this problem is that while in the case of a conditioned reflex the eventual movements of the animal can be seen to be superimposed upon a natural causal connection between a stimulus and a physiological reaction, the natural *response* to a given stimulus (and it is worth noting that we should normally speak of a response *to* a stimulus rather than one caused by it) is not so easy to determine. If it *can* be determined it is not on causal grounds; or rather, it is not our understanding of the physiological apparatus which makes it seem natural. Our understanding of, say, the withdrawal of a limb on receipt of an electric shock is based on our idea of natural reactions to pain rather than on any idea of the physiological connection between the application of an electric current to the skin and the subsequent movement of the limb in question. Thus when a movement of a limb is 'conditioned' to, say, the sound of a buzzer via the application of an electric shock, it might seem more plausible to say that what happens is that the subject takes the buzzer as a *sign* that pain will ensue, and for that reason moves his limb away from the source of the pain; such a response might indeed become more or less automatic. To say this serves also to meet a possible objection that the movement is not phenomenologically different from that which occurs in cases of genuine conditioning; or, in other words, that the movement looks and perhaps feels like one which is caused by a buzzer in the same way in which it was previously caused by a shock. Phenomenology is certainly unreliable in such cases; there are many instances of movements which are automatic or habitual, without being in any way like a reflex reaction. And such movements may feel to the subject just like a reflex reaction, at any rate in the sense that the movement took place without previous consideration by the subject and in a certain sense involuntarily. But this does not prevent the one being a movement *caused by* the stimulus, the other a movement *made by* the subject in response to the effect of a stimulus. And once we have said *that* our understanding of the two cases must be quite different.

These considerations affect also the conception of stimulus generalization, which is often taken to be part and parcel of conditioning; for it often happens that a response or a kind of response is as a result of conditioning called out not by a given stimulus but by stimuli of the same or similar kind. In the case of a straightforward conditioned reflex, where the reflex movements or movements are *caused* by a stimulus, the possibility of a range of possible stimuli with the same general effect might be put down to indeterminacy in the cause and/or in the mechanism involved. Indeed this kind of indeterminacy might be put down as a characteristic feature of physiological mechanisms. On the molar or macrological level we tend to think of a limb movement being produced by some gross cause like a tap on the patella, although on the molecular or micrological level the actual pattern of stimulation of nerves and the actual pattern of muscle movement may vary from occasion to occasion. It is this to which I referred when I spoke of indeterminacy above. It is not that the cause is in any disturbing sense indeterminate; it is that the exact pattern of stimulation and physiological response is only indeterminately given when the phenomenon is identified as a reflex; and the same applies to a conditioned reflex. Here again the stimulus which calls out the conditioned reflex can be specified only as one of a certain kind, if one is working on the macrological level; and this is compatible with a whole range of patterns of actual stimulation. (It is to be noted once again how slippery the notion of a stimulus is in all this.)

But in the case of a response *to* something, if the response is one that takes place because the subject takes the so-called conditioned stimulus as a sign of something else and it is in virtue of this that the movement is made, the notion of generality has relevance in a quite different way. It is not now a question of indeterminacy in the identification of the pattern of stimulation. What is now to the point is that the subject takes not just, say, a particular buzzer sound as a sign of ensuing pain, but anything of a similar kind. And it is important what he does take as similar, what he classes together. This classification can be a matter of habit, not necessarily something conscious; a person or animal may have come to see certain things in a similar way without there being any conscious classification on any specific occasion. Thus the generalization, if it takes place, must be in what the subject perceives the so-called conditioned stimulus *as*. I say 'if it takes place' only to indicate that it need not take place to any significant degree. Yet to see *X* as anything at all involves inevitably *some* generality. Thus the extent to which a person may respond to different sounds, and not just to a buzzer, in ways appropriate to the belief that these sounds are signs of ensuing pain in a certain part of his body, depends on the extent to which he takes these sounds to be alike in this respect or in some relevant respect. What is actually relevant here is not easy to determine in any absolute way, since the similarities that a person takes to exist between things depend on such considerations as his past experience, his interests and his sensitivities. At all events, if this is the sort of thing which takes place in this kind of conditioning, to speak of stimulus generalization is at the least misleading, since it is not the stimulus or its effect that is generalized, but rather how the subject perceives the situation in which he finds himself. This reference to perception is vital and cannot be excluded.

It may be said at this stage that my discussion shows only that the kind of case with which I have been concerned is not one of classical Pavlovian conditioning, and that the necessity to make reference to it affords additional doubt as to whether Pavlovian conditioning really occurs. What I have been describing is a case of what Skinner has called operant conditioning or conditioning of type *R*, which functions in a quite different way from classical conditioning. This brings me to the second category of extension to which the notion of conditioning has been subjected. What is essential to this second class of conditioning is that the factor which plays the main part is not what Thorndike called the 'law of exercise' (the function of practice or repetition) but what he called the 'law of effect'. There is not a simple association between two stimuli in relation to a given response, but association between a response to a situation (or operant) and the

97

stimuli which this produces and which reinforce that response. This is instrumental conditioning, in the sense that the person's or animal's behaviour is instrumental to some given effect which is desirable for that person or animal, e.g. the production of food by the pressure of a lever by a rat in a Skinner box.

I have spoken in this of a 'desirable effect', but I do not pretend that this would generally be taken by those who refer to conditioning in this context as a desirable way of speaking. It would be *theory* that it is this which provides the reason for the continuance of the form of behaviour in question in the context; all that we can observe is that the production of a certain effect, e.g. the provision of food, does in certain circumstances itself produce further instances of the behaviour which produces the effect. What these circumstances must be and why they are contributory causes is another matter. The natural thing to say would be that the animal is hungry, that it is thus in a certain state; but the nature of that state and of the way in which it contributes to the behaviour in question has been the subject of much dispute (obvious though the answer may be to some).

Skinner's notion of an operant is meant to cover all forms of be-haviour on the part of an animal which are not reflexes simply elicited by a stimulus. Whether or not stimuli are impinging upon the animal (and it is clear that there will generally be such) the behaviour is not directly elicited by them in the way that a reflex reaction is directly caused by its stimulus. The stimuli are simply occasions for the be-haviour in question. Whether or not it is happy to speak of such behaviour as consisting of responses which are emitted by the animal rather than elicited from it is another matter. It is at all events clear that by the notion of an 'operant' Skinner means to cover all ordinary behaviour. But in that case the similarity between what is referred to as operant conditioning and the type of conditioning involved in the Pavlovian-style conditioned reflex becomes very small indeed. What is the force of calling it 'conditioning' at all? The answer can be only that despite the differences between operant conditioning and classical conditioning they are thought of as essentially two species of the same genus. They differ fundamentally only in the relations which hold between the stimuli and the response. Whereas in classical condition-ing the connection that is set up is supposed to be that between the conditioned and unconditioned stimuli, in operant conditioning the connection is between the response and the stimuli that this pro-duces in the situation in question.

This, however, is not enough to make them just two species of the same genus; one's understanding of these connections must also be similar — the connections must also have some similarity. In the case of classical conditioning, if it ever occurs, the connection must be a fundamentally mechanical one, and to the extent that it seems that a phenomenon cannot be interpreted in that way so also it becomes doubtful whether it can properly be classified as a case of classical conditioning. One's understanding of operant conditioning, on the other hand, must surely be different, since the connection, if there is one, will be set up only in certain circumstances, and under conditions of a special sort. One would expect the behaviour in question to become established only if the effect of it means something to the animal in question. This is the sort of thing that I was suggesting when I spoke earlier of the effect being desirable to the animal. But it also has to be noted that the effect that I have in mind here is, e.g. the production of food — an occurrence which is clearly a desirable one for a hungry animal. This will, of course, have in turn further effects on the animal concerned, though the exact nature of those effects will depend on other things that happen as well as on the general circumstances. Mere olfactory stimulation need not have any reinforcing effect on the tendency of the animal to press the lever that delivers the food. The animal must be in the position to eat the food — to receive a partial satisfaction of its hunger — and one must therefore expect the production of the food to set up a complex pattern of stimulation, the exact nature of which will depend on the set-up and on the exact position and state of the animal. There is nothing here corresponding to the association between stimuli or groups of stimuli that is characteristic of classical conditioning. What is set up is a complex series of interacting events, dependent on a variety of circumstances but in particular on the kind of system which constitutes the animal's nervous system and on the state which it is in.

What I have said implies that it should be possible in principle to set out the kind of mechanism which makes possible the tendency of the animal to press the lever when hungery. I am not here denying this possibility, although I believe that we have little idea at present of the exact nature of the mechanism or even of its general character. It is, on the other hand, quite clear that its complexity makes it very unlike the mechanism implied by the concept of classical conditioning — so much so that speaking of conditioning in this case can only be misleading. Furthermore, the mechanism in question must be taken merely as one which *makes possible* the tendency of the animal to press the lever. For pressing the lever is something that the animal *does*. Whenever it presses the lever certain bodily movements take place which might indeed be explained in terms of the mechanism under consideration, given the general situation in which the animal is found. Reference to the general system which all this comprises explains why these bodily movements or ones like them tend to be repeated. To the extent that the mechanism explains these movements so in a sense it explains what the animal *does*. It does so because only if the movements take place can the animal be said to press the lever (although pressing the lever is not just having these movements take place); *a fortiori* it is only if the mechanism functions in whatever way it does that the animal can be said to press the lever and to repeat its action. The 'only if' reveals therefore that the reference to the mechanism is reference to the *necessary conditions* of action, not the sufficient conditions. This is not the case in the classical conditioned reflex, where the reaction is produced by the conditioned stimulus, so that the story about the stimulus and the system which it interacts with is a story about the *sufficient conditions* of the resulting movements. If one wishes to give the sufficient conditions of the *action* of the animal in the lever-pressing situation, as opposed to the conditions of the movements of its body that take place, one must make reference also to the kind of factors which I mentioned earlier.[1] One must, that is, say such things as 'The animal continues to press the lever because the effect of doing so is a state of affairs which is desirable to it.' The conditions that thus have to be mentioned include its recognition that a certain state of affairs is desirable to it and that this state of affairs will be brought about by what it does. None of this would be possible but for the mechanism which is affected by stimuli which impinge upon it, and it is in that way — as constituting necessary conditions of action — that the mechanism furnishes an explanation of the action, but only in that way.

At all events, to say simply that the animal's action in pressing the lever is to be explained by saying that its action is reinforced by its getting food by that means is not in itself to offer any sufficient explanation; the story needs to be filled in by further details and what is important is the direction in which we must look to provide such details. As I have indicated, to look to the possible mechanism underlying the responses is to concern oneself with necessary conditions only, not sufficient conditions. The details that one needs when concerned with sufficient conditions are such facts as that the animal sees that pressing the lever produces food, that this is what it wants, and so on. If it does not see that pressing the lever produces what it wants why should it go on pressing the lever? This consideration is very relevant to other examples such as Guthrie's cat. (Guthrie & Horton, 1945), which in moving a lever in order to open a cage from which they wanted to escape, tended to do so in a stereotyped way; if they originally moved the lever, so opening the case, by backing into it rather than by moving it with a paw, they continued to open the cage in this stereotyped and uneconomical way. But is this surprising? If it is the case that the animal's action is explained by saying, amongst other things, that it sees that moving the lever causes the cage to open, we are demanding of it some kind of insight into the connection between the lever and the door. Why should one suppose that the cat must see the principle of this connection? To find the cat's stereotyped action surprising is really to suppose that intelligent action here is to be expected; and intelligent action would involve seeing the connection as it really is, with the result that moving the lever with the paw would be the rational form of action. But the real situation is quite different. We have no grounds for expecting the cat to see the principle of the connection between lever and door. Anything that happens as a result of the movement of the lever must in a sense be to the cat a form of magic, and in a magical situation of this kind the obvious behaviour to which to have recourse is that which originally produced the effect. We have no reason to expect in a cat behaviour which looks more rational. The same applies to the rat in the Skinner box; what it has to see is that pressing the lever produces the food. (It does not matter *precisely* how it happens, except that here efficiency will produce more food, while with the cat in the cage efficiency has the same effect as before.)

Without such considerations the actions of these animals remain unintelligible *as actions*. And even if one could explain the physical movements which take place in terms of physical and physiological mechanisms, it would still not be *actions*, what the animal *does*, that is so explained. What I have been trying to make clear, and the reference to the type of explanation which is relevant reinforces the point, is that with so-called instrumental or operant conditioning one is certainly concerned with what the animal does, not what happens to it, as may be the case in classical conditioning. There is all the difference in the world between the salivation of a dog in response to the smell of food, or the patellar jerk in response to a tap on the knee, and the pressing of a lever by an animal in the cage. The difference is not that between two sets of phenomena which remain nevertheless instances of the same genus of cases; it is a more fundamental difference, one between radically different phenomena, and it is this which makes any suggestion that they are all cases of conditioning so misleading. What I have said about the relevant explanations reinforces this point, since the explanation of what the animal does makes reference to what it sees to be the case, etc. – something quite foreign to the concept of conditioning in its classical form.

It is possible to make a larger claim still in this connection – that it is only in this second kind of case that it is feasible to speak of learning, and that for this reason classical conditioning is irrelevant to learning, while learning proper has nothing to do with conditioning in any intelligible sense of that term.[2] By 'learning proper' I mean the following. Not all modifications of behaviour can be taken as the result of learning, not even if they lead to a form of success in behaviour that has not previously been the case with the person or animal concerned. Analogously, not all cases of the inducement in a person or animal of such modifications of behaviour can be taken as teaching or training.[3] Certainly, not all processes which lead to the increased probability of a given response can be called 'learning processes'. What then is the proper characteristic of learning? It seems to me that what is essential is the use of experience, however that is to be analysed; a person or animal which has learned to do something does it by making use of past experience. It does not have to do so consciously; it does not have to be clear to it at any one time that it can do the thing in question because of the experience that it has had. Thus the possibility of learning while asleep or under drugs, etc., does not invalidate my claim, although there are obvious difficulties involved here. In order to make use of experience it is necessary at least that one's consciousness be modified as a result of something that happens to us which is in principle an object of experience.[4] I use the term 'in principle' so that learning while asleep is not ruled out, but in order to rule out the effects of processes which cannot be called learning processes.

Given all this, it should be clear why I say that the rat in the Skinner box can be said to be learning to press the lever in order to obtain food; it is doing so because it is making use of the experience of the effect of pressing the lever, even if its idea of the connection between cause and effect is rudimentary. On the other hand, Pavlov's dogs were not making use of experience in salivating to the sound of a bell, or at any rate were not doing so if the situation was as Pavlov supposed. If, on the other hand, the situation was really different and the animals were salivating because they took the bell as a sign of food, they were indubitably making use of their experience, even though they were not properly speaking *doing* anything. They were not then learning to salivate in response to a bell; they *had* learned that a bell means food and salivated as a result. The salivation is in some way a causal result of the belief that they had come to hold. In just what way this can be so is a further matter.

(What I have referred to as the use of experience could be described as the use of *information*. To describe the matter in this way would be in line with the approach followed by J.J. Gibson (1966) in his *The Senses Considered as Perceptual Systems*. Gibson, indeed, says explicitly (p. 272) that sign-learning at least can be subsumed under the theory of information pick-up, and he speaks of both Pavlov's dogs and Skinner's rats as detecting invariant associations in the situation. Learning that something is the case thus involves the recognition of connections of one kind or another. Implicitly if not explicitly, Gibson's approach entails a rejection of stimulus-response theory, as at any rate a significant theory of our perception of the environment and, *a fortiori*, of our behaviour in accordance with our perception of the environment. And how is the behaviour of men and animals to be explained without reference to how they see the world?)

The situation which we have reached, then, is that there are the following alternatives: (1) There is such a thing as conditioning, and its prototype is the Pavlovian or classical case. Being restricted to the production of muscle-movements, glandular reactions, etc., in the animal, it cannot serve to explain behaviour, if this is something that the animal does. The explanation of behaviour, even simple and relatively stereotyped behaviour, must involve reference to other factors, how the animal sees things, what it takes to be the case, etc. (2) There is no room for a concept of conditioning even in the Pavlovian case, since even there, for the phenomenon to appear, the animal has to take something as a sign of something else. Why an autonomic reaction should then follow may then seem a problem, but it is no more of a problem than why it follows the smelling of food in general. It might be held that even though the animal *could* be taken to be treating the sound of the bell as a sign of food, a more plausible hypothesis in view of the automatic character of the reaction is that a connection is set up between the effects on the nervous system of the conjunction of two

103

kinds of stimulation. As explained earlier, the fact that a reaction *appears* automatic may be very misleading, and this would be true even of a subject's introspective reports on his own reactions. The fact that a person is not explicitly aware of taking something as a sign of another thing is not in itself clear evidence that he is not doing this. In saying that a person does take one thing as a sign of another we are saying that he has certain beliefs about the situation, and people can certainly believe things without being aware of the fact that they are doing so. The most persuasive factors in this connection are the facts that the salivation is a *reflex* reaction, and that the transference of a reflex reaction to a belief raises some difficulties. But this in turn may simply raise doubts about the validity of the concept of a reflex in this connection. For, as suggested earlier, the reflex is itself something of an artificial abstraction, since the notion presupposes the isolation of one neurological connection from the rest of the nervous system. Moreover, that reflexes can be inhibited is a well-known fact; if this kind of modification is possible, why should not other modifications be possible without changing the apparent nature of the phenomenon? The matter must be left with a question-mark hanging over it.

Nevertheless, what remains clear about alternative (1), if this be accepted, is that conditioning is not a concept that can be applied to what animals and people *do*, as opposed to what happens to them. It thus has no proper role in the explanation of behaviour, if that notion be applied to what they do. *A fortiori*, it has no proper role in theories of learning. A final question that might now be raised is whether the notion can be applied to such phenomena as imagery. Can one speak of conditioned imagery? After all, is it not the case that images sometimes simply come into our mind, so that there is no question of our *doing* anything? They are then something that happens to us. The difficulty here is that if the image which is to be conditioned is to be something that occurs to us it must be *made* to occur to us in the first place; it must, that is, be produced causally in the way that a knee-jerk is produced by a tap on the knee. The causal connection must then be transferred to another cause. But how can the initial image be set up, except by suggestion or a process like the association of ideas, unless what the subject is being asked is to *do* something, e.g. to think of something. I mention suggestion and the association of ideas, because these might be represented as possible ways in which someone might be got to have a certain image, without being told to think of something by its means. But they are, of course, notoriously unreliable

104

ways and it could not be claimed that any means whereby someone could be got to have an image in this way has the same kind of putative intelligibility that belongs to the reflex. It may be the case that when someone generally or characteristically has a certain image in certain circumstances he may be got to have that image in response to some further occurrence like the sound of a bell, if that sound is correlated sufficiently often with the situation in question. But the ordinary explanation of this would be that the sound of the bell conjures up the image or suggests it to the man because of its association with the original situation. This is not an association between stimuli, since it was not postulated that the original situation acted in any way as a stimulus to produce the image. There is *no* way of producing an image in someone's mind in the first place which has the reliability and explicability of the reflex. We may have devices for making people think of certain things, but their intelligibility is as *devices* not as mechanisms, and we have no idea of what underlying mechanisms may be involved. Thus once again, there are important differences between this kind of case and the conditioned reflex proper.

I began this essay by expressing doubt whether it was better to say that the concept of conditioning has outlived its usefulness or that it never had any utility in the first place. That doubt has not really been resolved, since it remains unclear whether conditioning in the sense explained in Pavlov's official theory ever occurs. What *is* clear is (*a*) that if it occurs the number of cases in which it does so is very restricted and (*b*) that most of the instances which have come to be subsumed under the concept of conditioning should not be so subsumed. There are great and substantial differences between these cases, and for the most part they imply some recognition of or belief about what the situation is on the part of the animal or person concerned. They involve, that is, the animal or person taking something, e.g. as a sign of something else; they involve the idea that the animal or person must derive information from its environment and put it to use. This cannot be expressed in stimulus-response terms. But only a story of this kind will be relevant to behaviour; conditioning applies at the most to what happens to an animal, not to what it does. Hence, if nothing else is true, it is certainly true that conditioning is not a notion that can have a place in a science of behaviour. It is time, therefore, that the notion was dropped from psychology and with it all theories of behaviour that depend on it.

105

# NOTES

1 (Note added 1981) Mr Alan Watson, in his original reply to this paper pointed out that the argument here requires some qualification. The point ought to be made in terms of what is a sufficient *explanation*, not sufficient conditions.
2 Cf. Vesey, 1967. I read Vesey's paper after writing this one, but I am in general very much in agreement with his line of argument.
3 This point was clear to Aristotle, *De Anima*, p. 417b 2ff.
4 I should be more sceptical about the acquisition during sleep of skills which involve the organization of experience, e.g. playing the piano.

# REFERENCES

Gibson, J.J., *The Senses Considered as Perceptual Systems*, Boston, Houghton Mifflin, 1966.

Guthrie, E.R., and Horton, G.P., *Cats in a Puzzle Box*, New York, Rinehart, 1945.

Skinner, B.F., *The Behavior Organisms, of* New York, Appleton-Century, 1938.

Taylor, C., *The Explanation of Behaviour*, London, Routledge & Kegan Paul, 1964.

Vesey, G.N.A., 'Conditioning and Learning', in *The Concept of Education*, ed. R.S. Peters, London, Routledge & Kegan Paul, 1967.

Watson, J.B., *Behaviourism*, New York, Mouton, 1925.

# 7

# EPISTEMOLOGY AND CONCEPTUAL DEVELOPMENT

## I THE STATUS OF GENETIC EPISTEMOLOGY

Piaget has invoked the term 'genetic epistemology' to describe his theory of intellectual development in the individual.[1] The term is in some ways a curious one; it does not entirely reveal its meaning, and it may well be that many philosophers in the Anglo-Saxon tradition would consider it to be incoherent. It savours somewhat of what Locke called the 'historical, plain method', which he used to 'inquire into the original, certainty, and extent of human knowledge'. Many, if not most, modern philosophers would reject such a method of clarifying what is involved in the concept of knowledge. Questions about the genesis of our ideas, if by this is meant the genesis of ideas in the individual, are questions for psychology, not epistemology. But of course whatever term Piaget uses for his theory, he would also hold, and it would usually be held by others, that his investigations are a branch of developmental psychology. Hence the kind of objections to genetic epistemology that I have hinted at might be thought to be terminological only, and for that reason not worth serious consideration for more than a moment.

Still, Piaget does think that his theory has philosophical implications, and there are indications that he would not draw such a hard-and-fast line between psychology and philosophy as I have been presupposing. He opposes his theory, for example, both to empiricism and rationalism (or 'apriorism', as he calls it) (Piaget, 1969, chapter 8), and associates these philosophical theories with certain well-known approaches to psychology — associationism and Gestalt theory, respectively. Indeed, he says of these theories that the first is 'geneticism without structure', while the second is 'structuralism without genesis'. These are not bad slogans to sum up the views in question, and I think that he is quite right to see in them essentially philosophical points of view (see Hamlyn, 1957). His own position seems to be meant, from this viewpoint, to be a kind of Kantian reconciliation of the opposing theories, though a reconciliation that can be achieved only by the recognition of new elements, in particular the recognition of the importance of the active role played by the individual. (Apart from the Kantian influences, there are here, perhaps, shades of the reaction of M. de Biran to the empiricism of his day. Indeed, Piaget sometimes contrasts his own view with that of de Biran; see, for example, the last chapter of *The Child's Construction of Reality*, 1955.) A reconciliation between opposing philosophical views can itself be nothing less than a philosophical point of view, and I do not think that Piaget would deny this. Hence my point about his not drawing a hard-and-fast line between philosophy and psychology. Some of the questions that he raises about the origins of our ideas are meant to be questions in the same tradition as that asked, for example, by Hume when the latter asked about the source or origin of our idea of cause. Causality, Piaget says, is 'seen to originate in action' (Piaget, 1969), and in saying this he seems to be putting forward a perennial answer to this question. Yet, in his case, the answer is supposed to rest on empirical evidence. Is this or is this not confusing? Many philosophers would say, I think, that it must be, and I am of their number. The ways in which an individual may come to an understanding of a certain notion are various, depending on his prior understandings, experience, and so on. We may be able to say something general about the conditions which are normally necessary for a given form of understanding; but a story of this kind will be about the criteria for being properly said to have the concept in question, not about the origins of the concept, about the ways in which it is acquired by individuals. This in turn makes it necessary to ask questions about the status of Piaget's account of the ways in which conceptual development in general takes place. This is a point to which I shall return – not necessarily to dispute the facts, but to ask what is to be made of the facts so described.

What I have been suggesting so far is that Piaget's approach has philosophical implications and presuppositions, and that it may be necessary to sort out what is acceptable and what is not. This will involve asking which questions are genuinely philosophical and which

108

are not, for the most important part of trying to assess any theory is determining which questions are being asked. Only then can one go on to determine whether the questions have been properly answered. I have already hinted, for example (and I cannot claim to have done more than this), that questions about the conditions which are normally necessary if one is to be said to have a certain form of understanding are different from questions about the origins of that form of understanding. I have also suggested that the former kind of question is a genuinely philosophical one. As far as concerns the second kind of question – that about origins – I have allowed that questions about the development of a given form of understanding in an individual may be genuine psychological questions, but I have suggested that questions about the development of forms of understanding in people in general should be considered for the time being as of undetermined status. It will be part of our task to settle the question of their status. If it were the case, for example, that people always came to a certain form of understanding in certain distinct and determined environmental conditions, this would be a very interesting psychological discovery, although it might raise many other questions in its train (questions so different as that about the criteria for being said to have this understanding and that about what there is in these environmental conditions that explains the acquisition of the understanding under consideration). But Piaget's discoveries are not obviously of *this* kind, and it is this among other things that raises the question of their status. It is also not obviously clear that questions about intellectual development are analogous to questions about physical development or even to questions about the development of such psychological factors as personality.

Thus, if it turns out that genetic epistemology is relevant to epistemology as it is usually taken by philosophers, this may be because genetic epistemology is, if not a branch of philosophy proper, at least intimately and closely involved with it, whether in an acceptable way or not. This would have obvious consequences for the status of at least this branch of genetic or developmental psychology. It might, however, be held that my premises are incorrect, and that I am wrong in thinking that philosophical questions about the nature of a certain form of understanding and about its conditions and criteria are utterly divorced and distinct from psychological questions about the conditions in which such understanding develops in individuals. It may be that if a philosopher thinks that the question of what it is to have a concept can be illuminatingly discussed independently from questions about the acquisition of that and other concepts, he is wrong. If so, co-operative inquiries on the part of philosophers and developmental psychologists are not only desirable, they are necessary. It is to this question that I must now turn. (If it is implied in what I say that I think that the questions which I have mentioned can be illuminatingly discussed independently from each other, this should not be taken as also implying that I am quite against co-operation between philosophers and psychologists. One form of co-operation, for example, may consist in a joint sorting out of the questions that they are asking.)

## II  CONCEPTUAL DEVELOPMENT AND CONCEPTUAL UNDERSTANDING

A suggestion that the supposition on which I am working is wrong was made, in effect, by Toulmin (1969) in his contribution to the first colloquium of this kind. He suggested that 'the analysis of concepts cannot be divorced from a study of their genesis in quite as sharp a way as philosophers frequently suppose' (Mischel, 1969, p. 36). Toulmin (1969, p. 83) claimed that: 'We may accordingly conceive a possible collaboration between philosophers and psychologists, designed (*a*) to analyze our concepts, and at the same time (*b*) to show how they are acquired.' And in his conclusion (Toulmin, 1969, p. 102), he raised the question, 'Can philosophers, after all, hope to "analyze" concepts without considering their ontogenies as well as their finished structures?' And he makes use of the notion of a 'standard ontogeny' in this connection. At the risk of appearing ungracious both to him and to the psychologists whose co-operation he invites, I would like to examine and challenge these claims.

It is best to start from the question which Toulmin himself started from, 'What is a concept?' or better in this context, 'What is it to have a concept?' To have a concept is to have a certain form of understanding; to have a concept of X is to understand or know what it is for something to be an X. (To this extent understanding is a form of knowledge, and a thesis about concepts and understanding can properly be part of a theory of knowledge.) The knowledge of what it is for something to be an X can be manifested in a great variety of ways, although the range of ways in question will to some extent be delimited by the kind of concept that X is. Toulmin is therefore quite

110

correct to be critical of Geach's view (Geach, 1957) that the knowledge in question is the knowledge of how to use relevant words (though it has to be admitted that this is Geach's initial suggestion only and that the final view presented by him presupposes a complex theory of judgment which is only analogically based on the making of statements). Many concepts of course could be had only by language users, since in order to have the understanding in question we need the means provided in language for symbolizing the complex relationships involved. It would be quite wrong, on the other hand, to rule out understanding completely where there is no linguistic ability. If knowledge of what it is for something to be an X is clearly manifested in behaviour, there can be no reason to refuse the attribution of the relevant concept. To this extent there can be no objection to the attribution of concepts to animals. I am not, of course, saying that it is always clear whether the knowledge involved in the concept *is* manifested in the behaviour, and I am not, for that reason, suggesting which concepts *can* be attributed to animals. I am saying only that there can be no objection in principle in attributing concepts to animals, as long as we are willing to attribute to them other things which presuppose that knowledge, for example, perception of the world in certain ways, since perception of something in a certain way presupposes understanding of what it is for something to be like that.

Toulmin's first thesis is, therefore, that to know what it is to have a concept, we need to know what is involved in having the understanding or knowledge which the concept embraces. The understanding may manifest itself not only in language use but in a variety of forms of life, to use Wittgenstein's expression. (Whether or not Wittgenstein meant that expression to be taken in the relative and culture-dependent sense that Toulmin gives it is another matter to which I shall return.) It is, however, the second thesis that is the important one for present purposes. This is that to have a full knowledge of what it is to have a given concept we need to know how it is acquired. Toulmin takes Wittgenstein to have held that one can gain a better understanding of what it is to have a given concept by considering how we acquire it, how we learn the connected 'language game'. Whether this is a correct interpretation of Wittgenstein I do not know, and for present purposes it probably does not matter. It is clear enough that light *can* be cast on a concept by asking how it is typically acquired; the question is whether an understanding of what it is to have that concept *requires* us to ask how it is typically acquired. For that is what is implied by

111

Toulmin's thesis about full understanding in this context. It surely cannot be the case that there is any *one* way in which a concept must be acquired. People acquire concepts in a variety of ways, and although we may be able to say what must be true of them if they are properly to be said to have acquired any given concept, we cannot insist that they do not have the concept unless they have acquired it in some particular way, or even the way that people typically use. To suppose otherwise is to confuse the routes to understanding of a given matter with the conditions under which alone that understanding can exist.

The justification that Toulmin (1969, p. 80) offers for his thesis (and as far as I can see the only justification) is contained in an inset passage of his paper. The first sentence reads: 'All scientific experience indicates that one cannot analyze the criteria for recognizing when a process is *completed*, in a final and definitive form, until the actual *course* of the process has been studied.' It is difficult to know what to make of this claim, and in any case where scientific experience is concerned I am in the position of one who rushes in where angels fear to tread. Yet I would suggest that the claim begs the question when applied to the putatively parallel question about the understanding of concepts. It assumes first that we have the right to speak of a process in this connection, or rather it assumes that there is a single process such that grasping a concept or set of concepts is its completion. It seems to me that there might well be many processes of acquiring a given concept or even none at all. People can acquire understanding in different ways, and there need not be one or any process which leads to the understanding. If that is so, how can an understanding of what it is to have grasped a concept presuppose as a matter of necessity an understanding of the process of acquiring it? I am in any case inclined to dispute the claim as a general truth about processes. Does a knowledge of the criteria for recognizing when a journey is completed entail studying the course of the journey? Surely I may know what it is to have arrived somewhere without any knowledge of the actual journey.

It is another matter the other way round. I cannot know the details of a journey unless I know what its end is and thus what it is to have arrived. This is a conceptual truth turning on what it is for something to have the relation of means to end. I cannot for this reason know what is involved in the acquisition of a concept of a certain kind unless I know what it is to have that concept. It is the same truth that underlies the Aristotelian claim that things have to be understood in terms

112

of their *telos* or end. If something is construable only as a means to an end, then it is unintelligible except in relation to that end. Any deviation from the process to that end is therefore readily construable as a blind alley. The end in the case of concept acquisition is a common human understanding; it is only given such a common understanding that we can speak of *the* concept of X. Objectivity in understanding does not entail that people should necessarily and always be agreed in that understanding; if it did have that entailment, the growth of new understanding against the current of tradition would be impossible. But objectivity in understanding presupposes both the *possibility* of common human agreement and the fact that it is the norm that what is commonly agreed is objective. This is implicit in Wittgenstein's well-known remark that 'if language is to be a means of communication there must be agreement not only in definitions but also . . . in judgements' (Wittgenstein, 1953; see also Hamlyn, 1971). This in turn brings out the importance of the social in any consideration of concepts and the understanding. As I have commented on a previous occasion (Hamlyn, 1967), there is a considerable underestimation of the social in Piaget's thinking. He tends to think of the growth of knowledge and understanding as a matter between the individual and his world, as a product of interaction between subject and object. (This is implicit in Piaget's heavy reliance upon the notions of assimilation and accommodation, but see also Piaget, 1969, chapter 8.)

Given this common understanding, we can view the learning process as a set of necessary steps towards it, and we are liable to see earlier stages in its light. That is why the philosophical operation of sorting out what is involved in the understanding of a given concept is relevant to an assessment of a theory of concept acquisition and development. It is easy for example, and perhaps in some ways right, to think of children as incomplete adults (just as it is possible to think of animals as incomplete human beings). In this light a childlike way of thinking may appear defective, even misconceived, but very much in the way that a mistaken belief on the part of an adult may be thought misconceived. Piaget gives the impression of thinking in this way in connection with what he calls the horizontal displacement of structures. The same kind of operations, involving structuring of the world, may be involved in the understanding of such things as conservation of substance and volume; yet they may appear in children at quite different ages, appreciation of conservation of substance occurring at about six, that of volume at about ten. What then of a child who thinks that when water is poured from a shallow, broad glass into a deep, narrow one it changes in amount? It is easy to say that this is a misconception on the part of the child, because within *our* system of concepts we know how the situation should be viewed. Yet it is not in any ordinary sense a false belief, since where a certain kind of understanding has not developed it is inappropriate to speak of belief at all (compare Toulmin, 1969, p. 84, and Hamlyn, 1967, pp. 33-4). At the same time, this should not be construed simply in terms of the idea that the child has not at this stage acquired a certain concept, as if there is just something missing at one time that will be present at another − as the idea of the horizontal displacement of structures may suggest. For it is not the case that the child knows well enough what water is, but simply fails to appreciate that it retains its volume when poured from one kind of vessel into another. The child is seeing the world in terms, rather, of a quite different set of concepts; the concept which goes for him with the word 'water' is not our concept at all, and we have no right to suppose otherwise.

Likewise, we have no right to suppose that during the development of the scheme of concepts in question the connection between the concepts of water and, say, volume, is anything like that between the concepts of water and, say, mass. That is to say that we have no right to suppose that there are bits of understanding − the understanding of what water is, the understanding of what volume is, and the understanding of what mass is − so that we can compare and contrast the relations that hold between them in a linear way. The child's understanding of what water is will be quite different on the occasions when he does not know or appreciate that water poured from one vessel into another of a different kind remains the same water, when he appreciates this but does not appreciate the constancy of volume, and when he appreciates all of these things. Hence there is danger in speaking of a concept of water as if a child might have this by itself without other connected concepts of the kind which I have been considering. To have a concept is not an all-or-none affair; there are degrees of understanding and degrees in the complexity of what is understood. Conceptual development is as much as anything an initiation into a web of understanding which may be more or less involuted at any given time. Piaget's use of the term 'structure' in order to speak of conceptual relationships implies a kind of ordering of elements, such that the relationships can be repeated at different levels or between different concepts. This does not seem to me an adequate picture

114

of the understanding or of what having a concept is, and may be a carry-over from the atomism inherent in the associationism against which he is reacting. It is perhaps part of what is involved in the attempt to strike a compromise between that 'geneticism without structure' and 'structuralism without genesis' to which I have already made reference. But if having a concept of X is knowing what it is for something to be X, it should be apparent that such knowledge is not and cannot be an all-or-none affair, and that it is not formed out of fixed and constant units of understanding, so that we can without qualification speak of identical or similar structures, as Piaget does.

Hence the implications of the idea of horizontal displacement of structures (to say nothing of what may be even more misconceived — the idea of vertical displacement of structures, according to which there may be structural similarities or identities between different levels of the mental life) are likely to be very misleading. Conceptual development is unlikely to be a matter of progressive steps towards a goal that we can take for granted because it is the accepted goal. The child has to learn that some theories and ways of taking the world have to be rejected, because they do not work. What 'working' and 'not working' consist of in this context is of course an extraordinarily difficult matter to make clear; to give an adequate account of it would be to give a complete theory of education which I for one do not feel competent to give. At all events, the child does not have to systematize phenomena for himself; there are social pressures and influences, generally accepted standards and norms of what is right and correct. It would equally be wrong to ignore the role of feeling and emotion in the process. I mention these points because they are both factors which Piaget seems to me to underestimate. Thus, at a given time a child may, just like an animal in its own way, see aspects of the world in ways which are not simply like ours but defective; the child may see those aspects of the world in ways which are radically different from what is adult and accepted, and in ways which are suited to its needs, its emotional attitudes, and its interests. It is only our final conception of how the world is, the one which constitutes the norm of how the world really is, the one that is agreed, that makes the child's thinking appear just a stage in the development to that goal. It may, however, be both less and more than this. It may be less in that it does not constitute a stage in a process towards that goal; it may be more in that given the child's needs and interests it serves his immediate purposes admirably, and is in that respect not defective at all.

Why, then, if I stress the dangers of thinking of the child's concepts and of his way of thinking as merely incomplete versions of ours, do I also say that we can view the learning process as a set of necessary steps to its final goal? The truth is that we can view it in this way, and indeed must do so, insofar as we think of it as a *process* at all. Here I am taking what Toulmin said about processes in the passage which I quoted earlier, and accepting as necessary one half of it. It is a necessary truth that the stages of a process must be seen in terms of its goal if they are properly to be seen as *stages*. It is a further question whether we are entitled to speak of a process at all. Why should we think of the development of thought as a process of this kind? Surely children's thinking, like the development of human thought in general, involves not a steady progression towards a goal, but, among other things, the occasional pursuit of what from the point of view of the goal may turn out to be blind alleys, but which from a more local and different point of view may sometimes look like illuminating and satisfying discoveries.

## III THE NATURE OF PIAGET'S THEORY

In the light of what I have said so far, how is one to regard Piaget's general theory, his genetic epistemology? There are two sides to this. On the one hand, there is the wealth of observation and experimentation — something which is nothing less than remarkable. A great mass of well-attested empirical findings has resulted from the observations and inquiries of Piaget and his colleagues. If such things as the age norms are sometimes disputed, I do not think that the immediate findings enshrined in what might be called the case histories are a matter for dispute. On the other hand, there is Piaget's theory and the fact that so many of his books bear titles (in English) like *The Child's Conception of Physical Causality* (1930), *The Child's Conception of the World* (1929), *The Child's Conception of Geometry* (1960), and *The Child's Construction of Reality* (1955). If what I have said is right, these titles suggest that questions are being begged — how seriously it is impossible to say, except as the result of a detailed investigation which I cannot undertake here. (The title, *The Child's Construction of Reality* is particularly interesting. Does the child *construct* reality? All by himself?) It is of course vitally important to be told that children do not think just like adults, and in this respect Piaget's work is enor-

116

mously important; I have no wish at all to deny this. But since my concern is with the relevance of Piaget's theory to epistemology, it is important for my purposes that the *status* of that theory should be made clear. If different stages in the development of thinking in the child can be distinguished, and if these are stages of a process leading to an adult and objective way of thinking, it is society and the educational system that ensure that this process is gone through. These, as I have emphasized enough already, are not factors that loom large in Piaget's thought. Rather, his genetic epistemology might be construed as an account (perhaps in part a phenomenological one) of the progressive freeing of the individual from the chains of perception as a result of activity (operations) on his part. This emerges strongly from Piaget's *The Mechanisms of Perception* (1969), which is for this and other reasons an extremely important book for our present purposes. It is a book which, while not being in the direct line of other studies in genetic epistemology, provides a theoretical framework for those studies, both psychological and philosophical. It is a central thesis of the book that perception is not the clue to the nature of the world that it is sometimes thought to be. Perception is likely to be responsible for deformation in our view of the world. Objectivity comes through intelligence, which is active. Objectivity, he claims (Piaget, 1969, p. 364), 'is constructed on the basis of, and in proportion to, the activities of the subject.'

These suggestions raise many questions. What, for example, *is* perception on this point of view? How do the activities of the subject give rise to objectivity, and why does objectivity depend on these? Piaget's answers to these questions are, I think, essentially Kantian. The acquisition of knowledge presupposes an interaction between subject and object; an interaction which is also implicit in Piaget's use of the concepts of assimilation and accommodation, as I have suggested elsewhere (Hamlyn, 1967, p. 38). What is fundamentally wrong with the rival theories of empiricism and apriorism is that they do not allow for such an interaction; they lay all the weight on the object and subject, respectively. But Piaget thinks that the falsity of these rival philosophical positions can be shown not only by philosophical argument but also by an appeal to the facts. This is the reason for the extensive use of experimental evidence in *The Mechanisms of Perception* (Piaget, 1969). Yet, as must be the case if the facts are even to appear to support a philosophical theory, the facts have to be incorporated in an elaborate framework of theory. There is the same

117

mixture of philosophy and empirical fact as there is to be found in Gestalt theory. It embraces above all a certain philosophical position on the nature of perception.

Piaget begins his exposition and argument by considering what he calls primary perceptual illusions. Although this is not Piaget's way of putting it, these are illusions like the Müller-Lyer illusion which seem to depend entirely on features of the perceptual object, and not upon the subject who experiences them. This is not to say that the subject cannot come to be less affected by them than he was originally. Indeed it is crucial to Piaget's point of view that these illusions are liable to development so that they can be treated genetically. His main thesis is that the overestimation of some feature of an object like its length is due primarily to centration or fixation of the object, and that the reverse effect which takes place when an illusion decreases with age or practice is due to co-ordination of centrations. This works in a complex way, especially when, as in the Müller-Lyer illusion, there is over-estimation of the length of one line relative to another. The whole thing is explained on a model which presupposes 'encounters' between elements of the perceived figures and elements of the sensory receptors together with 'couplings' or correspondences between such encounters. The details of this theory are not easy to follow, but fortunately they need not be our concern at present. It is the general character of the account which is important, for the explanation of illusions of this kind is entirely in terms of what happens physiologically at the level of the retina. Or if it goes beyond this (and Piaget is not anxious to commit himself as to the actual embodiment of his model), it never-theless remains true that the explanation is entirely causal, without any reference to beliefs or anything of that kind on the part of the per-ceiver. I do not say this in any spirit of criticism, since what is clear about these illusions is that they are *not* a function of any beliefs on the part of the perceiver.

What is important for present purposes is that Piaget in effect restricts perception to the functioning of such purely sensory systems. The diminution of an illusion in time, which Piaget puts down to what he calls 'decentration' may on that account be due to, among other things, the fact that our movements put the objects in question out of fixation. Thus, what we see and how we see it is very much deter-mined by what Piaget calls sensory motor activity, and even more by further activities on our part that arise from this. Thus, while perception is initially a function of sensory stimulation and subsequent

118

mechanisms, it becomes in turn influenced by activity on our part. Moreover, it is this activity on our part which serves as a correcting influence upon the tendencies to distortion inherent in the purely sensory, as is evident in the primary illusions. It is for this reason that he says that 'objectivity is constructed on the basis of, and in proportion to, the activities of the subject.' Activities on our part, including exploration, lead to the correction of the sensory mechanisms. Yet, how this takes place remains fundamentally unclear. It is clear enough how the movements that we make may lead to the breakdown of the distortion due to constant centration of something, given the point that centration is itself a distorting factor. Decentration is in that sense a frustration or blocking of the naturally distorting mechanisms which the sense organs by themselves involve. But much perception is dependent on our concepts and beliefs. Visual perception of this latter kind is what Dretske (1969) has called 'epistemic seeing', and his book, *Seeing and Knowing*, is in large part a persuasive advocacy of the thesis that the range of epistemic seeing is very wide indeed. How do these concepts and beliefs latch on to the purely sensory?

Piaget is opposed to the empiricist thesis that our concepts are derived from the senses. Apart from the fact that the 'structures of perception' differ fundamentally from 'structures of intellect' despite some similarities (perception, for example, is always perspectival, while intellectual understanding is not), the most that perception can do is to provide the conditions for the application of the concepts formed through operations of intelligence. 'Perception is of the *here and now* and serves the function of fitting each object or particular event into its available assimilative frameworks' (Piaget, 1969, p. 359). Thus the structures of perception may prefigure those of the intellect, so as to provide a ground for the application of intellectual structures, but they do not provide a source for those intellectual structures; the latter are derived from our own activity in the operations that we perform. The prefiguring of the intellect by perception is due to the fact that 'they share sensory-motor roots' (Piaget, 1969, p. 362). This then is an aspect of what Piaget elsewhere calls 'vertical displacement of structures.' In our activity towards the world of perceptual objects we operate according to the same or similar rules, so to speak, as in our activity in formal operations. As experience develops and grows there is an interaction between subject and object which is 'due to an endless construction of new schemes by the subject during his development, schemes to which he assimilates the perceived objects and in which there are no definable boundaries between the properties of the assimilated object and the structures of the assimilating subject' (Piaget, 1969, p. 364).

I cannot pretend that my summary of Piaget's thought is clear; it is difficult to clarify something that is far from clear in itself. Yet it appears that Piaget's central concern in all this is to give a philosophical account of the growth of experience in the individual. I would like to refer once again to the positions to which Piaget is on his own account opposed, and then try to see what his theory amounts to. First there is empiricism, which is the thesis that we are 'given' items of information in experience, in sense data, and that we abstract concepts from what is given in this way. (Nowadays it seems difficult to state the thesis without its appearing incoherent, since how can what is 'given' constitute information if it does not already presuppose concepts?) Piaget calls this 'geneticism without structure', since although empiricism can provide a theory of the development of experience, through the summations and associations of what is initially given, such development must on its account be independent of any necessary order. Experience develops simply as it happens to arise; any relationship between the elements of experience must be merely contingent. The opposing theory, rationalism, apriorism, call it what you will, presupposes that experience must from the very beginning conform to the structure that thought determines. There is nothing given in experience; the problem is rather how experience is to be fitted into what is given in thought. Piaget associates this point of view with Gestalt theory, since he holds that on that theory sense perception and thought conform to and are explicable in terms of the same structural laws. There is no real development allowed for in that theory; hence it is 'structuralism without genesis'. Gestaltism favours 'nativism' as opposed to empiricism. Piaget's task is to afford a reconciliation between the two opposing views, just as it was Kant's task to afford a reconciliation between rationalism and empiricism on a more straightforward epistemological plane. That is why it is right to see Piaget as an essentially Kantian thinker. Just as Kant's reconciliation between empiricism and rationalism came through the idea that experience is determined by categories which are a function of the human mind, so Piaget's reconciliation between empiricism and nativism comes through the idea that experience develops according to structures which are, likewise, a function of the human mind in its relationship to the world. In his introduc-

120

tion to *The Mechanisms of Perception* (1969), Piaget puts the idea in terms of what he calls 'the relational method'. What he seems to have in mind is the idea that at any stage, experience is determined by what and how the mind relates. (There are Hegelian undertones in this; one might compare some of the argument in the opening chapters of Hegel's *Phenomenology of Mind*, 1910.)

One might even compare this with the line of thought to be found in Wittgenstein. He too is very much of an anti-empiricist thinker, and is opposed to the idea that there is anything 'given' in sensation – something which I take to be implicit if not explicit in his argument in *Philosophical Investigations* (Wittgenstein, 1953, Part I, 242) about the impossibility of intrinsically private languages and of the idea that words for sensations could be given a meaning in terms of those sensations alone without reference to a common language of which they must inevitably form a part. He is equally opposed to the idea that there is a rigid form to thought that can be abstracted from the language that we use. It is this, as I take it, that is a large point of his reference to alternative language games, which imply alternative ways of construing the world. Yet this does not mean that there is an absolutely free house, that there are not limits to the organization of experience other than the relative ones which a given society imposes – important as these particular limitations are. For our thought and experience are determined by 'forms of life'. Indeed, in one place in the *Philosophical Investigations* (p. 226) Wittgenstein speaks of these forms of life as the 'given'. They are the one thing that we cannot get round the back of, so that they cannot be construed as merely conventional or in some sense relative. How we see colours, for example, and what relations we take as holding necessarily between them is a function of what Kant called our form of sensibility; it is a function of what discriminations our sense organs enable us to make in relation to the world as it affects those sense organs (see again Hamlyn, 1971, and compare Aune, 1967). There are analogous limits on the possibility of experience imposed by the nature of thought in general (though I feel far less certain about the direction of Wittgenstein's thought on this issue). These are limits in forms of life, in the sense that we cannot think of perception, thought, or any of the other faculties which human beings (and to some extent animals) are capable of except as functions of the life that they lead in the world in which they find themselves. The important point that Wittgenstein is trying to make is that our experience and what we can be said to know must be seen in this light and against this background. The limits which circumscribe what we *can* know and experience are neither conventional nor simply contingent in the sense that we can conceive what it would be like for things to be otherwise. If other forms of life are possible, we can have no real conception of what it would be like to experience them.

One clear implication of all this is that although what we *can* experience has its limits, all experience which, as perception does, gives rise to knowledge must be concept-dependent, conceptually mediated. To perceive the world at all one must have some understanding, if only of a rudimentary kind, of what one is perceiving. William James said that the first object of acquaintance in the individual is the universe; and there is something in this, in that we must, if we are to attribute perception to a child at all, attribute to it the awareness of an object as opposed to merely passive sensations. At first there can be no distinction of one object from another; hence the first object of awareness is indeed everything. The distinguishing of one object from another and the general elaboration of awareness of the world is thereafter a product of the individual's interaction with his environment, including his social environment, and is therefore conditioned in part by what he is, by his form of life, and in part by what there is to interact with. But understanding and experience must develop hand in hand. To have a concept of X we must have not only a formal understanding of what X is, something that could be given in formal definitions, but also a knowledge of what X is to be applied to, of what sort of things count as being X; and the latter demands experience. This point is the other side of that quoation from Wittgenstein that I have referred to before — that 'if language is to be a means of communication there must be agreement . . . in judgments.' The agreement in judgments referred to is agreement about what counts as falling under the description that language makes possible. It is not, then, that we have experiences from which we abstract our concepts, nor the reverse, that by some mysterious means we develop concepts which we apply to experiences. Both of these views take too limited a view of the concept of 'experience'. We have sensations of course, but these provide merely the conditions for the application of concepts in experience. In the sense of 'experience' in question, sensations provide none in themselves. Experience involves knowledge, and for this concepts and understanding are necessary.

In this light let us now go back to Piaget, for in many ways, but not all, Piaget's line of thought fits in with what I have said. In the first place, although he restricts perception, at least some of the time, to the purely sensory, he seems to think of it merely as providing the conditions for the application of concepts in experience. That is the implication of the remark that I quoted earlier — 'Perception is of the *here and now* and serves the function of fitting each object or particular event into its available assimilative frameworks' (Piaget, 1969, p. 359). It also provides one way of taking his view that the intellect is prefigured by perception. I am not sure, however, that this it all there is to it. For he sometimes includes under the heading of 'perception' the sensory motor system, and in that case it would be the movements that we make at that level that would prefigure the operations performed at a higher and more cognitive level. This view is reinforced by the fact that he tries to subsume the corrective process that takes place as we build up experience of the world under the single concept of 'decentration'. The use of this concept implies, at the sensory motor level, that the movements that we make bring about causally a multiplicity of fixations which serve to counteract the distorting effect of any one centration. Correction is in this case a purely mechanical process which is a statistical effect of the plurality of points of view produced by, for example, movement. But the corrections that we make in our view of the world as a result of fresh experience and new understandings are not of this kind at all. That is why I said earlier that it remains fundamentally unclear how correction of sensory mechanisms takes place once concepts are involved; such correction can take place only with regard to what is already conceptually mediated. I think, therefore, that Piaget uses the notion of 'decentration' quite equivocally.

It may be that Piaget would not be upset by this criticism. He speaks frequently of the 'filiation' between perception and intelligence. He also maintains, in the introduction to *The Mechanisms of Perception* (Piaget, 1969, p. xxiii), that while 'neurophysiology is exclusively *causal*' and 'psychology is based on implication' (a remark to which, perhaps, some contemporary philosophers in the Anglo-Saxon tradition might be sympathetic),

> there need be no conflict between physicochemical causality and psychological implication any more than between physical or material experience and the logico-mathematical deductions used to explain it; there is an isomorphism between causality and implica-

123

tion (which is the source of psycho-physiological parallelism), and the future harmony between causal physiology and analyses based on implication should be sought on the basis of the relations now existing between experimental or causal, and mathematical or implicative physics.

There is much in that remark which requires examination, though I have no space to do so here. It is, however, clear that it will not do to explain the relationship between neurophysiological mechanisms and 'psychological' operations of a corrective sort on the analogy of the relationship between experimental and theoretical physics. It seems to me that if it is in this sense that perception prefigures intelligence, the prefiguration rests on an analogy only — an analogy between the sense in which a mechanism of the kind envisaged by Piaget for perceptual decentration can be corrective, and that in which the process by which we develop our experience and knowledge of the world is corrective. It is, I suggest, no more than an analogy, and we should not think of decentration in the strict sense as corrective at all if it were not for the fact that we have a prior conception of how a thing should look, and that decentration is supposed to be a counteracting influence against a tendency which is by the same standard deforming. In fact the story about centration and decentration is about the mechanisms (much more complicated than is ordinarily supposed, if Piaget is right) which make perception possible. They are, strictly speaking, neither corrective nor noncorrective; they merely make correction possible. Why there should be mechanisms of such complexity and cumbrousness that fixation leads naturally to distortion, so that counteracting mechanisms are necessary, is another matter.

If we waive all these (perhaps rather crucial) objections, there is still one further question to ask. If Piaget is right in thinking of perception as supplying the conditions for the development of concepts in experience, what are the grounds for thinking that development must have a determined order and structure? In attempting to answer this question we are confronted with the further question of the relationship of empirical findings to philosophical theory. For there is, on the one hand, the wealth of empirical observations which I have already acknowledged; and on the other hand, there is the claim for some sort of necessity in the order of development, a necessity which could not be inferred from empirical observations alone. I suspect, as I have suggested earlier, that Piaget thinks that the necessary order and structure of development has a status something like that of Kant's categories; it is a necessary feature of the human mind in its relation to the world, it is part of our form of life. It is a necessary condition of what we call experience. It is *prima facie* difficult to see why this should be so in all its details. There might nevertheless be something to be said for the position that there are necessary priorities and posteriorities in the ordering of experience, and it is to this question that we must now turn.

First, however, let me sum up in a general way what I have been saying about Piaget's position. In effect I have put Piaget in that tradition of psychology, of which the Gestalt psychologists are the most obvious example, which comprises to one extent or another a reaction against the sensationalist/associationist position. That position involved a mixture of philosophical and psychological issues, and the same must be true, in consequence, of the reactions. The only real basis for the atomism of associationism was the doctrine of atomic sensations and ideas which it inherited from the British empiricist philosophers such as Hume. The Gestaltists put in its place another theory of the 'given' derived from Husserl and ultimately Brentano. Piaget's own reaction is more in the Kantian or idealist tradition, but his theory is as much dependent on a philosophical position as were those of the others that I have mentioned. My own opinion is that the mixture of philosophical and empirical issues involves in each case a muddle, that the philosophical and psychological questions which are at stake are different from each other, and that there are no grounds for the belief that philosophical questions can be answered by appeal to empirical evidence or vice versa. On this I can at present only be dogmatic, although I can refer for the argument in the case of Gestalt theory to my *Psychology of Perception* (Hamlyn, 1957). If I am right, however, my answer to the question, 'What relevance has genetic epistemology in the more orthodox sense?,' must be that in a certain sense genetic epistemology *presupposes* a traditional epistemological position. If it has implications for epistemology, it is in that sense and for that reason, and not because of its status as a psychological theory.

## IV EPISTEMOLOGICAL PRIORITIES IN THE GROWTH OF UNDERSTANDING

I have argued elsewhere (Hamlyn, 1967, p. 32) that there are such things as epistemological priorities in the learning of a subject, and

Toulmin (1969, p. 81) has argued similarly in terms of the notion of conceptual stratification. It is to these priorities that one must look in deciding how a subject is best presented to those who have to learn it; or at least they will provide one of the considerations, for it must not be forgotten that there are many other factors including motivational and emotional ones that will determine how a subject is best learnt. Now if it is the case, as it might well be, that a person cannot understand X unless he understands Y, it is still not open to a philosopher or anyone else to say on those grounds alone that people must be taught to understand Y first and then X afterwards. In other words, priority for understanding does not imply temporal priority. All that a philosopher can say on the basis of his analysis of epistemological priorities is: 'You cannot really understand X, because you clearly do not understand Y.' In effect, epistemological priorities are logical priorities of a kind. It might be argued, for example, against the current of the empiricist tradition, that one cannot really understand *red* unless one already understands *colour*, since 'red' means 'red colour', and that an understanding of *red* is not complete unless one also understands the way in which red differs from other colours in general and how it is related in particular ways to certain particular colours (for example, how red is in some sense 'close to' purple or orange as it is not to, say, green). Thus *red* entails *coloured* and has also certain relations with other colours. But it would scarcely make sense to suggest that one should teach someone what colour is and only then what red is. It would equally make no sense to suggest that one should teach someone what red is and thereby what colour is, independently of other colours. A full understanding of what red is brings along with it a nexus of understanding of other things, and one cannot be said fully to understand it until one understands that whole nexus. How far the nexus extends is something that can be decided only in particular cases; there cannot be a general rule which determines the answer for all cases. It should be noted, however, that I have spoken of a full understanding. The understanding of a concept need not come all at once; there can be degrees of understanding of it, and degrees of understanding of the surrounding nexus. That is why all that can justifiably be said in accusing someone of a failure to understand is, as I have expressed it above, 'You cannot really under X, because you do not understand Y.'

There is, moreover, the point that I have laboured already — that a condition of fully understanding a concept is that one should be able to apply it in relevant and suitable instances. The nexus of surrounding concepts is not an abstract network only; it must touch reality at some point or points. But one cannot say in general when and to what extent the application of the concept or of one of its surrounding concepts should come under consideration. Learning and teaching must always involve a delicate balance between abstract concepts or principles and the application of these in instances. Hence, once again there can be no rules for the promotion of understanding. Yet when these caveats have been made it is obvious that there is such a thing as conceptual stratification, as Toulmin puts it, and that to suppose that one could have certain concepts without some understanding of others would be foolish. Yet what could be inferred from this about any *temporal* ordering of the understanding, about any principles for conceptual *development*, is very uncertain. Is there anything that could be safely said on this matter, even at the most general level? For the firm points in Piaget's theory *are* very general in character — the general nature of the three stages of development and perhaps some subdivisions of them. Perhaps the main point is the general precedence of the concrete over the abstract, as exemplified in the fact that according to Piaget the period of concrete operations always precedes that of abstract operations.

The suggestion that in the growth of the understanding we are initially tied to the concrete and particular, and only gradually extend our thought into the abstract and general is a very natural one. It is a suggestion to be found in Aristotle's observation that the particular is prior relative to us even if the general is prior for knowledge in itself. Our normal picture of human beings is that they gradually extend their understanding so that what is initially understood in particular and concrete instances comes eventually to be understood in a more general and abstract form. How indeed could it be otherwise? One answer to this question is that it could not be otherwise, because the development of understanding comes through learning. Learning involves the acquisition of knowledge and understanding; indeed, it involves the use of experience. Experience itself involves confrontation with particulars, even if, as Aristotle would say, the knowledge that this confrontation entails is knowledge of the particular as a such and such. It is thus inevitable and necessary that the development of understanding involves a progression from the more particular and concrete to the more general and abstract. No acquisition of understanding based on learning could be otherwise. I do not think that

127

this is Piaget's answer, since my impression is that he thinks of the progression as a natural order of development, not based so much on what learning is as on the natural constitution of the human mind in its relation to the world.

We could *in a sense* conceive of this progression not taking place in this order. Indeed, an extreme rationalist theory of knowledge provides such a conception. We could think of the individual as being born with a set of innate ideas which only need experience to be made explicit. Or we could imagine a science fiction story about people who are provided in some nonexperiential way with a system of understanding which then requires exemplification in experiential terms. (I do not know whether this would make an interesting science fiction story if worked out, but it conforms at least to the principle to which I adhere — that the best science fiction stories turn on philosophical points!) In such cases the growth of knowledge would not depend on learning as we understand it, but that does not matter. Or at least it matters only in the sense that this fact reveals that the story in question does not fit our form of life. It is indeed important, if it is to be used as suggested, that the details of the story that I have referred to should *not* be filled in; for any attempt to fill them in would be intelligible only to the extent that it presupposes our form of life. Hence when I say that the story does not fit our form of life, I am saying that at certain points the story remains mysterious and unintelligible. Our form of life, as I said earlier, imposes limits on our understanding, and while it is in one sense possible that there might be alternative forms of life to ours, we deceive ourselves if we think that we can make any *real* sense of that idea. Our understanding is built up from and dependent upon the common experience that we have. While we should make continual attempts to enlarge that understanding, we cannot transcend the limits that make it *human* understanding. I therefore conclude that while we can give a partial sense to the supposition of a growth of understanding which is unlike ours, it is partial only, in the sense of being merely formal; any attempt to fill in that understanding would reveal how little of an understanding it really is.

There are thus very good grounds for thinking that the direction of the growth of the understanding must be in general terms as Piaget says it is. But this is not a merely contingent fact as the reliance upon empirical observations, so necessary to developmental psychology, would suggest. Nor is it *just* a consequence of a very general fact about the nature of the human mind in its relation to the world, as the philosophical position inherent in genetic epistemology would suggest. It is that given our understanding of normal human experience, learning, and knowledge, we cannot conceive of how it might be otherwise. For this is an understanding of the *norms* which provide the criteria of application for the concepts of experience, learning, and knowledge.[2] There are thus conceptual relationships between these concepts and our understanding of normal human development. Given, then, that we are operating with these concepts, we must take the development of understanding from the particular to the general as the norm. Abnormal cases need special explanation, and this may sometimes be provided. But we can have no real conception of what it would be like for the abnormal to be the norm (see Hamlyn, 1967, pp. 41-2).

What then of the details of Piaget's account of cognitive development? It seems to me that these can only be contingent, and for that reason alterable in principle. This applies to the age norms as much as to anything else. There are a multitude of factors that become relevant here — social influences, cultural influences, motivational factors, the role of emotion, and so on. A human being is not after all a merely cognitive being who develops and grows in isolation. Piaget's discoveries of the details of cognitive development are interesting and important, but they should be taken in that spirit. I would stress what I have said about the details being alterable in principle. Perhaps I may be forgiven if I say a few words about the moral of this. It seems to me that in practical terms the rather wholesale way that Piaget's theory has been taken up by many educationalists has its dangers. Piaget's psychology is a cognitive one and it is excusable that it leaves emotional development largely out of consideration, but this side of things must be remembered. I have spoken already about Piaget's underestimation of social and cultural factors. There is also, perhaps, the overestimation of the efficacy of *operations*, that is, activity as such on the part of the child. But it seems to me that the worst danger in the application of Piaget's theory of education is that the details may be accepted as overly rigid, and teachers may argue that there is no point in trying to teach children certain things before certain ages. Such an attitude could be educationally disastrous. John Wisdom used to speak of the necessity within philosophy of trying to say what cannot be said. There is an equal necessity within education of trying to teach people what they cannot understand. This may be a paradoxical way of stating a truth, but it is a truth nevertheless.

## V CONCLUSION

It seems to me that Piaget's theory is a blend not only of the empirical and the conceptual (which would be both acceptable and inevitable), but of the empirical and the philosophical. While empirical investigations may throw up suggestions for the philosopher and vice versa, and while these suggestions may well be valuable, I am still inclined to think that a theory that rests directly upon both empirical and philosophical considerations must have a degree of incoherence. This I take to be the case with Piaget's theory. If Piaget's genetic epistemology has relevance for epistemology in the more traditional sense, this is because genetic epistemology involves as at least one component a traditional philosophical position of its own. I do not think that Piaget would deny that his theory involves a philosophical position, but he might deny that there is the kind of gap between the empirical and the philosophical that I have presupposed. Nevertheless, despite argument to the contrary, I still think that the gap exists and must be reckoned with.

## NOTES

1 B. Kaplan points out that Piaget, in his *Introduction à l'épistémologie génétique* (1950a), defines genetic epistemology as the study of successive states of a science as regards its development, and thus distinguishes between genetic epistemology and the psychology of intelligence. This raises many questions about Piaget's attitude towards the thesis that there is a parallelism between ontogeny and phylogeny, but I cannot think that Piaget in general excludes the study of intellectual development in the individual from genetic epistemology.

2 Since objectivity involves (though it is not entailed by) community of understanding (the interpersonal agreement to which I have referred), these norms must, in a sense, be social. Hence the development of understanding cannot be a matter merely of the relations between the individual and his world. Piaget does, to some extent, associate objectivity with the social, but on his terms it remains something of a mystery why the association should exist.

# REFERENCES

Aristotle, *Posterior Analytics*, translated by G.R.G. Mure, London and New York, Oxford University Press, 1928.

Aune, B., *Knowledge, Mind, and Nature*, New York, Random House, 1967.

Dretske, F., *Seeing and Knowing*, London, Routledge & Kegan Paul, 1969.

Geach, P., *Mental Acts*, London, Routledge & Kegan Paul, 1957.

Hamlyn, D.W., *The Psychology of Perception*, London, Routledge & Kegan Paul, 1957.

Hamlyn, D.W., 'The logical and psychological aspects of learning', in R.S. Peters (ed.), *The Concept of Education*, London, Routledge & Kegan Paul, 1967 (this volume pp. 71-90).

Hamlyn, D.W., 'Objectivity', in R. Dearden, P. Hirst, and R.S. Peters (eds), *Education and Rationality*, London, Routledge & Kegan Paul, 1971.

Hegel, G.F., *Phenomenology of Mind*, J.B. Baillie (ed.), London, Allen & Unwin, 1910.

Hume, D., *Enquiry concerning the Human Understanding*, L.A. Selby-Bigge (ed.), Oxford University Press, (Clarendon), 1894.

James, W., *Principles of Psychology*, New York, Holt, 1890, 2 vols.

Kant, I., *Critique of Pure Reason*, translated by N. Kemp Smith, London, Macmillan, 1929.

Locke, J., *Essay concerning Human Understanding*, A.C. Fraser (ed.), Oxford University Press (Clarendon), 1894.

Mischel, T., 'Scientific and philosophical psychology: A historical introduction', in T. Mischel (ed.), *Human Action: Conceptual and Empirical Issues*, New York, Academic Press, 1969.

Piaget, J., *The Child's Conception of the World*, London, Routledge & Kegan Paul, 1929.

Piaget, J., *The Child's Conception of Physical Causality*, London, Routledge & Kegan Paul, 1930.

Piaget, J., *Introduction à l'épistémologie génétique*, Paris, Presses Univ. de France, 1950, 3 vols. (a)

Piaget, J., *The Psychology of Intelligence*, London, Routledge & Kegan Paul, 1950. (b)

Piaget, J., *The Child's Construction of Reality*, London, Routledge & Kegan Paul, 1955.

Piaget, J., *The Mechanisms of Perception*, London, Routledge & Kegan Paul, 1969.

Piaget, J., Inhelder, B., & Szeminska, A., *The Child's Conception of Geometry*, London, Routledge & Kegan Paul, 1960.

Toulmin, S.E., 'Concepts and the Explanation of Human Behaviour', in T. Mischel (ed.), *Human Action: Conceptual and Empirical Issues*, New York, Academic Press, 1969.

Wittgenstein, L., *Philosophical Investigations*, Oxford, Blackwell, 1953.

# 8

# HUMAN LEARNING

The two great classical theories of knowledge — rationalism and empiricism — bring with them not only different conceptions of knowledge, but also different understandings of the acquisition of knowledge. They also involve different philosophies of mind, at any rate to the extent that for empiricism the mind is, as Locke put it, like a great mirror which passively receives reflections from without, while for rationalism the mind is more active, involved in its own operations. Like any characterization in terms of 'isms', what I have said is a caricature of any actual philosopher, but the tendencies are undoubtedly there. If that is so, one would expect similar tendencies in accounts of learning and the acquisition of knowledge based on these theories of knowledge and mind. With the development of psychology as an empirically orientated science, accounts of learning inspired by empiricist ways of thinking have become the accepted thing, as was only to be expected. Charles Taylor has noted[1] that S-R theory can be construed as 'a mechanistic transposition of the traditional empiricist views on epistemology', and he has sought more recently (e.g. in lectures given at the University of London) to show how theories of human behaviour based on the ideas of computer simulation and machine analogies tend to reflect the atomism which is to be found in traditional empiricism with its apparatus of, for example, impressions and ideas. That atomism is there because a theory of behaviour must have as an essential part a theory of the acquisition of knowledge about the environment, in the light of which knowledge behaviour ensues. The theory of the acquisition of knowledge in question reflects traditional empiricist epistemology which is based on the idea that all knowledge is built up from certain atomic elements derived directly from experience. I am not here concerned with the explanation of behaviour in general, but with the acquisition of knowledge, and theories of this might be expected to have a direct relationship to theories of knowledge themselves.

Some empirically minded psychologists might maintain that I have begged the question in speaking so easily of the acquisition of knowledge and in assuming that this is what learning is. Indeed there has been some tendency on the part of recent psychologists to take it that learning embraces any modification of behaviour in an organism as the result of experience, or even as the result of stimulation from the environment.[2] Some of the reasons for such a point of view lie in a preoccupation with animal, as opposed to human, learning; for it is thought that animal learning is hardly to be characterized in terms of the acquisition of knowledge, understanding, etc. Whatever may be said on that issue, human learning is of course much more complicated in many cases than animal learning, and it is true that many of the abilities acquired by animals through learning involve little or no understanding of what is involved. Nevertheless, I do not think that the account of the matter under consideration will do; the definition of learning implied by it is far too wide. It will not exclude, for example, sudden and apparently irreversible changes of behaviour brought about by certain experiences; it will not exclude, to take two quite different examples, the phenomena of imprinting described by ethologists — the tendency in certain animals for crucial experiences to produce far-reaching and more or less permanent effects when they occur at certain stages in the animal's development — or the onset of sudden madness as the result of very disturbing experiences. It is not even true that someone who has acquired a certain habit has thereby necessarily learned anything; *a fortiori* being conditioned is not a form of learning. I have maintained elsewhere, in discussing the irrelevance of conditioning to learning,[3] that learning must involve at least the *use* of experience, a notion which suggests a more active role on the part of the learner. But I am not now sure that this will quite do, unless 'use' is given an exceptionally wide sense. A person who has simply been given a piece of information may certainly be said to have learned something; yet it would be hard to say that he has in this case *used* his experience, even if the idea of a person receiving all his knowledge in this way, without his performing any role himself, is scarcely if at all intelligible. Not all learning is like problem-solving. Still, this is not an objection to the thesis that learning must at least involve the acquisition of knowledge through experience and that changes of behaviour due to learning must be the result of the new knowledge. In many cases, but not all, the acquisition of the new knowledge will entail the learner's using his experience. At all events, on our ordinary conception of learning it would, I suggest, be impossible to suppose that someone could have learned something if he had not in some sense acquired new knowledge, whatever form that knowledge may take (and it may of course include skills as well as factual knowledge).

An objection of a different kind to my association of learning with knowledge[4] would be that there are forms of learning in which the end of the learning is not in fact knowledge. We can, after all, learn to see things in new ways, to accept things, to appreciate things and so on. Does this learning involve new *knowledge*? Suppose that a man comes to see something in a certain way, even to appreciate it as it is and to have an affection for it; we may sometimes say that he has learned to do these things and in saying this we imply something about the relevance of the experience that he has acquired to his seeing it in this way, and so on. We rule out thereby any suggestion that his attitudes may have been brought about causally in ways that have nothing to do with experience. Similar considerations apply to such cases as having learned to treat someone circumspectly or to be tactful in certain circumstances. There is a whole range of somewhat disparate cases which may fall under the general heading of 'having learned to . . . .' These may not involve the acquisition of knowledge *simpliciter*. Yet I am still inclined to think that knowledge enters into the picture in other, more indirect, ways. If I have learned to love someone, rather than merely come to love them, my love follows upon and exists in virtue of what I have come to know. How this happens is another matter, and any account of this would be a complex one which I cannot enter upon here. Suffice it to say that the kinds of case that I have in mind here are in my view parasitical upon those cases of learning which do involve the acquisition of knowledge *simpliciter*; and while I recognize their experience I shall concentrate in the following on those cases of learning which do straightforwardly involve the acquisition of knowledge. It should be noted, however, that that knowledge can take a great many different forms.

Theories of learning inspired by rationalist theories of knowledge have not had much of a press until lately. When Piaget, in various places in his writings, tries to place his own approach in the spectrum of theories of human development, he characterizes Gestalt theory as rationalist in effect. While empiricism involves, he says, development or geneticism without structure, Gestalt theory involves structure without development. I suppose that this is one way of looking at Gestaltism, although I do not think that the immediate origins of Gestalt theory were in fact specifically rationalist. Piaget himself, as I have argued elsewhere,[5] seems Kantian in inspiration; like Kant he attempts a putative reconciliation between rationalism and empiricism. A more straightforward claim for a rationalist account of learning (or at any rate human learning) has been made by Chomsky, with his now notorious defence of the doctrine of innate ideas. Chomsky's claim that we need to espouse the notion of innate ideas was initially made in the context of language learning, but there are signs in recent writings that he thinks that the view has a wider application. Thus in *Language and Mind* (p. 64) he asks whether there are other 'areas of human competence where one might hope to develop a fruitful theory, analogous to generative grammar'. He suggests that 'One might, for example, consider the problem of how a person comes to acquire a certain concept of three-dimensional space, or an implicit "theory of human action", in similar terms.' It is noteworthy that the examples mentioned involve concepts where there is more than a *prima facie* implausibility about empiricism. Just as there is an immense difficulty, if Chomsky is right, in seeing how the notion of language, of how to talk, could be abstracted from experienced data, if the person concerned did not already know that these data were language-data, so there is the same difficulty, as Kant saw, in seeing how the notion of space could be abstracted from experience; and the same difficulty applies to the idea of abstracting the notion of action from observed bodily movements. There are, of course more general difficulties about the notion of abstraction as a source of concepts, but the difficulties emerge in a specially crucial form in examples of this kind. As far as language is concerned, Chomsky's point seems to be that a child could not abstract the notion of language from the data available to him.[6]

There are serious objections to this way of putting it. In the first place, the fact that a concept cannot be abstracted from experienced data does not mean that it must be innate. In Kantian terms, a concept might be *a priori* without being innate (although I do not think that it is really helpful so to speak, since the notion of an *a priori* concept implies by its contrast with *a posteriori* concepts the very abstractionist thesis that is at fault). At all events the knowledge involved in having a concept might begin with experience without arising out of experience. It is somewhat surprising that Chomsky seems to suppose that the only alternative to empiricism is rationalism. Even while operating within the terms of reference supplied by traditional epistemology, there is the Kantian point of view. Piaget, who does adopt a Kantian point of view, does not suppose that the structures of the mind which he thinks it important to recognize are innate; indeed it is a crucial point for him that they *develop*. For him, as I have already said, rationalism involves structure without genesis, without development. I do not point this out because I think that Piaget's approach is the right one, rather to indicate that there are, within the terms of reference that Chomsky accepts, other possibilities than those which he recognizes. Chomsky's brief comments on Piaget in *Language and Mind*, apart from adducing putative evidence that may cast doubt on the validity of Piaget's actual findings – a strictly empirical issue on which it is scarcely open to a philosopher as such to comment, are to the effect that Piaget does not adequately explain 'the basis for the transition from one of the stages that he discusses to the next, higher stage'. This is an *ignoratio elenchi*, since for Piaget there is no basis in the sense that Chomsky seems to demand. It is on his view merely a fact about human beings in the sort of environment in which they find themselves that there are the stages that he distinguishes in their development. It is true that Piaget seems to make this more than a merely contingent fact; the reasons for this are complicated and I cannot go into them properly here, although I have discussed them to some extent elsewhere.[7] Suffice it to say that for Piaget it is a kind of essential truth about the nature of the understanding, a kind of metaphysical truth about man in his place in the world. Or so I think. Yet whatever the status of Piaget's theory about the development of understanding in the individual, it provides a further possible view in addition to those recognized by Chomsky, and it is an *ignoratio elenchi* to force it into the mould of one or other of the initial alternatives.

But, as I have implied before, I do not think that any of these alternatives are really viable, and there are objections to Chomsky which are more fundamental than those which I have mentioned. Chomsky speaks of the child having to discover the grammar of a language from the data presented to him,[8] and thus seems to think that it makes sense to speak of there being data which the child has to survey. The term 'data' could be taken either as referring to sense-data or in a more ordinary sense where data are correlative with evidence.

The two uses of the term are no doubt connected in that sense-data may be construed as incontrovertible pieces of evidence provided by the senses, while data in the more ordinary, scientific sense provide evidence in a straightforward way, though scarcely incontrovertible evidence in any absolute sense. But in the ordinary, scientific sense of the word something can be taken as a datum only if it is already understood as such. In other words, if it is true that the child has to discover the grammar of a language from the data presented to it, the child must not only have a prior idea of what a language is, but have also a prior idea of what among its sense-experiences is relevant to the supposal that it is hearing a language being used. Data are data only relative to a prior question and thus to a prior understanding. Since this applies wherever reference is made to data, the inference to be drawn is that *any* discovery about the world, no matter what, presupposes a prior understanding of it. By this token we should need prior (innate) ideas not just of language, but of any feature of the world in which we find ourselves. The only way to short-circuit this argument would be to suppose that there are data which are absolute, which provide their own understanding without dependence on concepts. Such a conception is part of the traditional notion of sense-data, which thereby constitute pieces of information provided by the senses in a way that is independent of concepts. I shall not rehearse the objections to this whole way of thinking; they have been made by a whole host of philosophers in many places. It is not clear, in any case, that Chomsky means to have recourse to such a notion. Without it, however, once the problem is posed in the way that Chomsky poses it, one is committed to the view that there must be concepts prior to any experience of data; and once one is on this road to innate ideas there is no obvious way off it again. This is the inescapable conclusion for a rationalist — that all ideas are innate — and Chomsky does not appear to see that it is so.

A point associated with the last, and one which is bound up with an issue in the philosophy of mind which is common to both empiricist and rationalist epistemologies, is that the child, and indeed any individual, is construed as set over against a world which he has to construct on the basis of what is presented to his senses. This point of view is a legacy of Cartesianism, which involves the identification of a person with his mind, which is thus separated from the physical world; that physical world is therefore 'external'. Given all this, unless the child has a world already made for him, it must be supposed that he has to construct it from what is given to him, from the data, as if he were a scientist working on a problem, but a scientist who in the nature of the case must work on his own. The child has thus to find his own way about the world, and there is no one to help him, since other people are part of that 'external world'. If this were so, it would be impossible to see how the child could ever come to a conception of the world at all, let alone the same world as we know. I shall not dwell on these absurdities; what I have said should be sufficient to indicate that any view which in effect construes the child as a solitary inquirer attempting to discover the truth about the world must be rejected. (What after all could be meant by 'truth' in these circumstances?) But it is a view of this kind that is implicit in Chomsky's way of looking at what is presupposed in language learning, or at any rate in some of the things that he says about this, such as his remark about the child having to discover the grammar of a language from the data presented to him. It is equally implicit in his views about learning of other kinds.

There is perhaps a tendency at this point to say to oneself: 'But surely the child has to acquire knowledge of the world somehow; if it is not something like this, how does he do it at all?' To think like this is to think of the child as on a par with an adult, as indeed a little adult with adult kinds of knowledge and understanding. It makes perfect sense to ask of an adult with a certain amount of knowledge and understanding how he can go about acquiring further knowledge and understanding; but it is that prior knowledge and understanding that makes possible the acquisition of more of the same kind. If therefore one persists in thinking of the child as a little adult, then, if knowledge is to develop at all, it will be necessary to attribute to him prior, and therefore presumably innate, knowledge. But the knowledge in question must be knowledge of the world as *we* know it; the knowledge and understanding in question must be objective, not any kind of understanding will do. But surely knowledge and understanding of this kind could only be acquired. This is not to say that we are not born with equipment, physiological or otherwise, necessary for the acquisition of such knowledge and understanding. It *is* to say that the suggestion that we are born in possession of understanding, that this understanding is objective, and that this is not a mere happy accident, makes no sense. Some animals are, of course, born with ready-made dispositions to react in appropriate ways in certain circumstances, dispositions that we call 'instinctive'. But such facts are to be explained in evolutionary terms, and in terms of whatever mechanics in the individual animal are appropriate to the preservation of the species; this

138

very fact, among others, makes it inappropriate to say that they have innate knowledge or understanding. In sum, I do not think that it is intelligible to speak of innate knowledge and understanding, and there-fore of innate ideas, at least in any sense that makes the notion of any use for the explanation of the acquisition of the rest of our knowledge of a common and objective world.

How, then, is knowledge acquired? The only reasonable response to this question is to ask in return: 'What knowledge, and by whom?' A similar response is required for the question: 'How does learning take place?' It depends entirely on what it is that is being learned and who it is that is doing the learning. Knowledge may take various forms, and the ways to the various goals which knowledge may constitute are likely to vary with the nature of the goal in question. Even within the sphere of, say, skills, learning how to play the piano will be a quite different matter from learning how to type, although both involve the use of the fingers. I do not mean to suggest by this that there are no similarities between skills and methods of acquiring them; but it is equally important to stress the differences, and when one brings in other forms of learning and other things to be learned the differences become even more apparent. Psychologists, at any rate all those who are not chained to one form or another of dogma, are well aware of this, and references to forms of learning of differing kinds are now relatively commonplace in books on these matters. But the application of knowledge of these differing learning-processes to actual educational problems involves knowing about the learners too. People obviously have different facilities for learning, but even within groups of people with roughly the same facility starting-points may also differ.

I mean by starting-points the previous knowledge and understanding of the persons concerned. Even if one can be fairly sure that a child of a certain age could not, given the general framework of educational processes within our culture, have certain forms of understanding and knowledge (a fact that no doubt underlies Piaget's notorious, and probably over-rigid, conception of the stages of intellectual develop-ment, whether or not he would put it in this way), there is still room for great variety in the knowledge and understanding possessed by such children. Hence educational processes must always be a compromise and, I suspect, a question of hit and miss. (And one might add, for pro-fessional educators, that the educational processes that they often have in mind, what goes on in the school class, constitute a comparatively small part of the learning that goes on in everyday life.) Apart from all

139

this, there is a large array of motivational and emotional factors which will clearly influence the way in which learning goes on, if they do not actually prevent it. I do not see how it is possible to say anything both significant and general about human learning processes, although there is nothing against the possibility of a kind of natural history of such processes, a rough classification of their species and of the forms that thay may take. Moreover, a consideration of the goal to be attained in any process of learning may lead to a delimitation of the possible range of processes that are relevant to that goal. At the same time, it has to be said that people sometimes acquire understanding and knowledge, even knacks and skills, in surprising ways which could not be ruled out in advance; it would be foolish and unprofitable to attempt to undermine such possibilities *a priori*.

All this may suggest that we are thrown back upon an empiricist epistemology, according to which there are no prior limitations on what can be acquired through experience. It was not my intention to lead up to such a conclusion; nor do I think it the right one. For it is still necessary to meet the point that Chomsky, for example, makes against empiricist theories of language learning — how the business could even get off the ground if those theories were correct. For the possibility of learning X presupposes the existence of prior knowledge in terms of which X will make sense to the learner. In learning which involves a positive attempt to arrive at an answer to a question there must be prior knowledge of what sort of thing will count as an answer. (This is a point which Plato seems to me to be groping after in the *Meno* when he attempts to meet Meno's paradox, that we cannot carry on an inquiry since either we already know what we seek or we shall not recognize it when we reach it, by his doctrine of recollection. Plato's solution is clearly wrong, but he may have a correct sense of the problem.) But where the learning is more passive or is not a function of a positive search on the part of the learner, the prior knowledge may be more indirectly connected with what is learned. Yet, at all events, without a background of knowledge of some sort what is to be learned will not be made sense of and is in that case not a possible object of learning.

Does this lead back towards a rationalist epistemology? The answer is, I believe, 'No more than it leads to a Platonic doctrine of recollection.' The problem is real enough but not the solutions so far considered. It is not really a question of 'either an initial *tabula rasa* or an initial body of innate knowledge'. The *tabula rasa* conception implies too mechanical a view of the acquisition of knowledge apart from the other failings already noted; for it implies that the effects of external stimulation are simply imprinted on the soul, the mind, the organism, or whatever it is. The opposite conception implies too intellectual and perhaps too conscious an operation on our part; in all cases we have somehow to apply prior knowledge to what we now experience, like the application of a hypothesis to the data being acquired. But there is in any case no need for the prior knowledge which I have mentioned as necessary for learning to be *temporally* prior. This is a point that requires emphasis. The point that I was making was meant to be a conceptual point − it is simply that someone could not come to knowledge of X, if this is to be learning, without other knowledge. But this other knowledge does not need to have been acquired previously in time. The priority that is necessary is a logical priority only. Someone who has come to see that $q$ is implied by $p$ may be said to have learned that $q$, but it is not necessary for this that he should have come to see the truth of $p$ before coming to see that of $q$; he may come to see both together. A slogan which would make my point would be that all learning is, in one way or another, connecting things, and it is in this way that experience develops. But the connecting may take many different patterns. Why, then, should learning be simply like either of the two processes implied by rationalist and empiricist epistemologies? Why should we be confined to the two alternatives − either mechanism or intellectual operations? Piaget maintains that intellectual operations, when on his view they eventually occur, have already been 'prefigured' in sensory-motor movement. Whether or not this particular suggestion is helpful, could we find in a suggestion of this kind a clue to an adequate solution to the problem how learning can get started?

What I mean by this is the following. Both the approaches so far discussed (as well as any approach that can be construed as anything like a straightforward compromise between them) seem to assume that we can consider the acquisition of knowledge by a person in isolation from the other factors that go to make up that person's life. It is true that there have been philosophers like Maine de Biran who have insisted that any adequate epistemology must bring in the will as well as sense-perception and the understanding. But the force of such suggestions has typically been that resistance to the will can simply provide extra pieces of information about the environment, information that could not be provided in any other way and certainly not in the merely passive reception of information that traditional empiricism presupposes. Similar things might be said of suggestions that *action* is necessary for the acquisition of knowledge and that a purely passive and sensory consciousness is an absurdity.[9] So it may be, and the necessity of activity has equally been stressed by Piaget (among others of whom one might perhaps mention J.J. Gibson in his book *The Senses Considered as Perceptual Systems*, Boston: Houghton Mifflin, 1967; London: Allen and Unwin, 1968). I have no wish to underestimate the importance for the acquisition of some knowledge of exploration on the part of the learner, of trial and error, and of active experimentation. But, once again, without prior questions to be put to nature such exploration and experimentation cannot get a purchase, for the reasons already rehearsed. Hence it is not just this sort of thing that I have in mind when I say that the theories so far discussed do not pay attention sufficiently to the other factors that go to make up a person's life.

One thing that I have in mind is the point that an individual is not a solitary centre of consciousness for which the questions of which I have spoken have somehow to arise — and if so how? A person is a social being from childhood, and the knowledge that he has to acquire is equally socially determined in an important sense. For knowledge presupposes criteria of truth, and these presuppose the agreement in judgements of which Wittgenstein spoke.[10] Hence learning on the part of an individual is as much as anything his initiation into a framework over which there is wide agreement, even if there is also plenty of room for individual deviations from the norm. For this to be possible there has to be, and is, a background of common interests, attitudes, feeling, and, if I may put it in these terms, cognitive apparatus. There must be, to use Wittgenstein's phrase, agreement in forms of life. By 'cognitive apparatus' I mean everything that makes possible a common and shared sensibility and ways of thinking —physiological make-up, sense-organs, etc. In animals, of course, much more than is the case for humans depends on this sort of thing, upon common and inborn ways of reacting to the world, ways of reacting that we call instinctive, the explanation of the persistence of which is, as I said earlier, to be found not in its value for the individual but for the species. But even in humans there has to be something of this sort of thing, and it was to this in part that I was referring in speaking of common interests, etc. — the need for food, comfort, etc. But the child has to be put in the way of things that will satisfy those interests; he cannot find them for

142

himself, since he can have no conception of what will satisfy them or even of what it is for something to do so. The same is true of animals in a way; but there is in their case a natural disposition for the satisfaction of needs, due to a pattern of behaviour appropriate to the species; without which the species would not survive (cf. the patterns of behaviour investigated by ethologists such as Tinbergen — for example, the tendency of a chick to peck at a spot on the mother's bill, so getting food from her). In humans there have to be some instinctive patterns of behaviour, e.g. sucking, but so much more depends on what the mother puts the child in the way of. Equally much depends on such things as expressions of love and affection and on the rapport that is normally set up between parent and child.

Thus the child is not a solitary but immature consciousness trying to make sense of a mass of data which come before it in the light of certain mysterious principles with which it is born. Awareness of objects, in the formal but not material sense of 'object', is something that we must presuppose in the child. What he is put in the way of will determine the ways in which the formal notion of an object is cashed for him, what objects, in other words, he takes to exist; in the end too this will determine that the ways in which that notion is so cashed are roughly our ways. Psychologists have sometimes said that for the infant there is initially no distinction between self and not-self. If this is meant to be an empirical point it is difficult to know on what basis the truth of the claim is to be assessed. But one might contrast it with Kant's assertion in his 'transcendental deduction' that awareness of objects with an identity in space and time is correlative with awareness of oneself as such. If the psychologists' claim is correct the child has to get from a stage at which there is no distinction between self and not-self to a stage at which there is a correlative awareness of oneself and of other spatio-temporal objects as objects with an identity. Whether or not the matter is happily so put, there is no intrinsic difficulty about a child's having to learn of his own identity as a person with a body as distinct from other bodies with other identities. He could not do this purely on the basis of experiences which are in a genuine sense private; but the child is in the world and a part of the world from the beginning and is put in the way of making these distinctions by adults. His attention is drawn to them by the circumstances of his upbringing, and in particular by the treatment that he receives from and the relations that he has with his mother. Differences between objects of awareness are thus forced upon him. Of vital importance in all this is the role of correction by adults. Only through this, I suggest, can something like the concept of truth emerge and in it the concept of judgment. I am tempted to maintain that it is an *a priori* truth that a baby left on a desert island would not survive; nothing would put it in the way of making the distinctions, etc., necessary to survival. Even 'wolf-boys' receive some initiation into a 'world'.

I have in the foregoing spoken often of the child being put in the way of things; I have not said merely that the child is taught things. The vital role that I have given to other people, and to the mother in particular, in the child's learning about the world is not merely that of a teacher; although in performing the correcting function to which I have already referred, parents and other adults *are* in effect teaching or at least performing a necessary prolegomenon to teaching. For what they are doing is ensuring that the child takes things as we do. Yet the relation that exists between mother and child is, if not from the very beginning yet nevertheless soon, fundamentally a personal relation. It is a vital factor in the child's upbringing that parents and other people treat the child as a person and not just as a thing; there is a constant respect for feelings, care, love and so on, which elicit responses from the child which are, if not the same, at any rate appropriate to the situation. Thus it is part of my thesis that early learning is very much a function of personal relationships that exist between the child and other human beings; without this or something like it, it is difficult to see how learning could go on at all, let alone make much progress. How much of this is also applicable to adult learning?

Psychologists such as D.O. Hebb[11] have made a distinction between early and late learning, the former being general in character and slow in development, compared with the often dramatic jumps that sometimes occur in late learning. The distinction was made, I believe, for, among other reasons, its relevance to the continuity/discontinuity dispute that occurred in the hey-day of the argument between strict S-R theorists such as Hull and others such as Tolman who thought of learning as occurring on occasion at least by other means than the slow piling up of associations or S-R connections. Whether or not the distinction has that particular relevance, it is real and important enough. One would expect early learning to consist of a slow sorting out of categories and distinctions[12] and the gradual acquisition of general principles. The application of these distinctions and principles to cases, even to new and previously unforeseen cases, might well be sudden and quick. If late learning is dependent on personal relations at all, it clearly must be so in a quite different way from that in which the earliest learning is so dependent. In the case of late learning, factors concerned with personal relationships may enter the scene as providing motivation or the reverse, insight or the reverse, but they are not a condition of learning taking place at all. Initially in the life of the child I think that they do constitute such a condition.

How does this apply to the problem with which Chomsky is concerned — the acquisition and learning of language? Chomsky postulates an innate language faculty because it is for him inconceivable that the child should acquire familiarity with the idea of language merely from the noises that he hears from other people when they use language; once given the idea of language itself it is more intelligible how the child should pick up the details of the language spoken by those in his environment. But this account of the matter not only presupposes the view of the child as a little adult having to deal with a problem, it also assumes that the child does it alone and *ex nihilo*, except what it is born with. But surely the idea of language is merely one idea that the child has to pick up in its early years and it is not an idea that lacks connection with other things. The point might be put in the following way. Chomsky's problem is that of how the basic categories and phrases of deep structure could be abstracted from the data available. The answer is that they could not be; but it is not entailed by this that they are in consequence innate in the child, since much has gone on before the ability to use and understand language emerges. In particular much has gone on in the way of communication, and communication itself has its foundation in the mutual emotional responses that take place between child and parent. Admittedly communication by language is something in many respects new when it emerges, and it would be very surprising if every aspect of the grammar of language at the level of deep structure had its counterpart in some aspect of pre-linguistic behaviour. On the other hand, from the earliest days when interchange of smiles, for example, are possible, communication is built into the web of behaviour that takes place in the context of personal relations between child and mother, and then child and other people. It is not language alone that the child has to catch on to and interpret, but a mass of behaviour which becomes meaningful to him in one way or another and which is all part of the form of social life into which he is being initiated and in which he comes to share. There is no question of his having to decide what language is all about unaided, any more than he has to reach all by himself the conclusion that some

145

mobile bodies in his vicinity are people and that the movements that they make are actions.

I make this last point in view of Chomsky's remark, noted earlier, about the problem, parallel to that of the acquisition of the idea of language, of the acquisition of the idea of human action, so that just as generative grammar provides a theory relevant to language acquisition so there might be a theory of how people acquire an 'implicit theory of human action'. This in effect foists the other minds problem on to the child, since action is attributable in the primary sense only to things that have minds, and the question whether something is acting in the primary sense is therefore tantamount to the question whether it has a mind. Thus Chomsky's suggestion is that we have to explain how a child comes to understand that some things have minds and how he comes to attribute minds to the right things and not to others. But the child's relations to his mother and thereafter to other people are not so academic as this. Given the care and love that a mother devotes to her child (or if not this, at least *some* attitude which is appropriate to a person), how could there even be a problem for the child about the difference between people and things? Indeed one might expect that if there were a problem it would be how it can be, in effect, that things are not people. Consider in this connection the animism of children that Piaget and others have emphasized.

At all events, in the various ways that a child may have his attention drawn and in which he may draw the attention of others, in the various mutual responses, in what happens in the context of everyday life, there is much that prefigures the essential functions of language (functions, for example, such as reference and description, to which are tied the grammatical categories of subject and predicate). We should, however, expect that the original development of linguistic competence will be a very different thing from either the development of such a competence later in life or the application of the originally acquired competence to the learning of new languages with different surface structure. Every indication is that such expectations are correct. Such cases of 'wolf-boys' that have been recorded indicate that the acquisition of language at a later than ordinary age and where the usual mother-child relationship has been lacking (or at any rate some personal relationship) is extremely difficult if not impossible; while cases like that of Helen Keller reveal the difficulties for those for whom ordinary means of communication in similar or analogous personal contexts are drastically curtailed. This goes together with the claim that I have been making from the beginning that what learning consists in and how it takes place varies considerably according to what it is that has to be learned, who it is that is doing the learning, and in what circumstances. If an analysis of the task to be performed may make it possible to work backwards setting out the steps to be followed rationally in order to reach the goal, the application of such a construction to any educational context must involve making vast assumptions which may or may not be fulfilled to any appreciable extent. Any teacher must make such assumptions in applying his knowledge of what has to be taught; but they are assumptions nevertheless and teaching must for that reason remain an art. It is perhaps fortunate that so much comes out in the wash.

What I am left with is what I suggested at the outset – there are a number of differing kinds of learning process which are more or less fitted to the differing kinds of knowledge, competence, skill, or what have you, that may be required of human beings. Careful analysis of the goal to be attained and the circumstances in which the attempt to reach it is to be carried out may provide guidance on what form of learning is appropriate when. Consideration of the abilities, personality and character of those doing the learning may provide extra guidance on the ways in which the principles obtained by the analysis may be applied to given individuals. But in the end, as I have said, it is likely to be a matter of compromise and art, and this inevitably imposes limits on education as a discipline in its own right.

## NOTES

1 C. Taylor, *The Explanation of Behaviour*, London, Routledge & Kegan Paul, 1964, p. 143.
2 Cf. e.g. A.E. Seabourne and R. Borger, *The Psychology of Learning*, Harmondsworth, Penguin Books, 1966, p. 14ff.
3 D.W. Hamlyn, 'Conditioning and Behaviour' in R. Borger and F. Cioffi (eds), *Explanation in the Behavioural Sciences*, Cambridge University Press, 1970, p. 149 (this volume, p. 102).
4 The objection has been made to me by Mr J.M. Cohen.
5 D.W. Hamlyn, 'The Logical and Psychological Aspects of Learning', in R.S. Peters (ed.), *The Concept of Education*, London, Routledge & Kegan Paul, 1967, pp. 24-43 (this volume, pp. 71-90).
6 Cf. N. Chomsky, *Language and Mind*, New York, Harcourt Brace, 1968, p. 74, where he speaks about the problems involved in the idea of the grammar of a language being discovered by the child

'from the data presented to him'; his point is that the idea of language itself with its deep structure could not be so discovered.

7 D.W. Hamlyn, *ibid.* and 'Epistemology and Conceptual Development' in T. Mischel (ed.), *Cognitive Development and Epistemology*, New York, Academic Press, (this volume, pp. 107-31).

8 N. Chomsky, *ibid.*

9 Cf. e.g. G.E.M. Anscombe, *Intention*, Oxford, Blackwell, 1957, p. 67. See now this volume, chapter 3.

10 L. Wittgenstein, *Philosophical Investigations*, Oxford, Blackwell, 1953, I, s. 242.

11 D.O. Hebb, *The Organization of Behavior*, New York, Wiley, 1949.

12 Cf. the learning that not all men are Daddy.

# 9

# THE CONCEPT OF DEVELOPMENT

A seedling develops into a full-grown plant, an embryo develops into an independent living animal, a child develops into a man. In each of these cases I might have said 'grows' rather than 'develops'. There is a single identifiable subject throughout the process of development or growth, and we can, given relevant knowledge, in principle say something about what process that subject has to undergo in order to develop into the state which is the final one. That final state is also identifiable, or if not the final state at least some state along the road of development from the initial state. The development may be subject to certain conditions without the satisfaction of which no development will take place; but the thing that so develops contains already in some sense the possibilities of its subsequent development if the conditions are satisfied. Or in other words, given the developed state one is able in principle to see why the thing in question has got there from its initial state. The other conditions are conditions that merely make possible the actualization of the potentiality that was initially there; they are not so much independent and direct causes of what happens. The original state must be in some sense generative of subsequent ones, even if the generation still depends on the satisfaction of other conditions.

What has all this to do with the philosophy of education? Just this, that if taken seriously developmental psychology would have to be interpreted as an account of a similar unfolding of the mind or of the adult personality given the satisfaction of certain conditions, and it would naturally be interesting to know what the conditions were. The important question is whether the term 'developmental' does have to be taken seriously in this context. I had better say at the beginning that the immediate context for my concern with the question was the paper 'Education and Human Being' that Professor R.K. Elliott gave to the Exeter conference on the Philosophy of Education in 1973.[1] In his reply on that occasion Mr S.G. Langford was to some extent sceptical about the use of the notion of development in that context, but Professor Elliott took it very seriously indeed. Moreover he distinguished between the notion of development which has an internal norm and that which has an external norm, putting for his part a great deal of weight upon the former in his view of education. There is in this talk of norms, and indeed in other things that Professor Elliott says, the suggestion that the notion of development involves reference to that of value in some way. I am not sure whether this suggestion is true. (Similar things have sometimes been said with reference to the notion of 'function' and I am not convinced of *their* truth either). I am not sure, that is, that the notion of development should be limited in its application to those situations in which, where X develops into Y, either the change or Y itself is something on which we put a value. I would not like here to put a great deal of weight on the facts of ordinary English usage, but it is perhaps worth noting that to say of someone that he has developed into an empty and worthless person is not obvious nonsense, to say the least.

In the examples that I gave right at the beginning of this paper, the seedling, the embryo, the child, I said that I might, where I spoke of development, equally have spoken of growth. But even given a sufficiently non-literal use of the term 'growth', development cannot simply be equated with growth. It is at the least a species of growth, not growth itself. That growth of an organ may in some cases as in the growth of a cancer, be the result of malfunctioning, in such a way that to speak of development might seem out of place. This is not simply because the growth is in some sense a bad thing; for, as I have already said, I do not think that the process or its end has to be valued for it to constitute a development. It is because the growth, the mere increase in size, is not part of a pattern which can be seen in functional terms. Growth constitutes development, I suggest, only when it is part of such a pattern. If we saw the growth of a seedling into a full-grown plant merely as an increase in size, which is all that growth might be, it could be properly said of us that we had no adequate conception of it as a plant. In other words, as I said earlier, the original state must be seen as generative of subsequent ones, according to a principle of organization; and these conditions are satisfied by something's being a plant. Its being a plant gives a sense to the growth that takes place. We might indeed explain the growth in teleological terms, since growing in this way fulfils a function in the life of the plant and in relation to the wider function of the propagation and preservation of the species.

One can see the same thing by approaching the matter in another way — through the question what conditions have to be satisfied if a series of states which a thing undergoes is to be construed in terms of the development of that thing. Von Wright in his book *Explanation and Understanding*[2] tries to explain both functional or teleological explanation and historical or developmental explanation in terms of the items in a series being such that each one is a necessary condition of the one that succeeds and Professor Elliott also mentions this possibility. I do not think that this is adequate for functional or teleological explanation (what Von Wright calls 'quasi-teleology'), over which I think that Charles Taylor[3] is right in demanding that a teleological explanation should be such that, given certain background conditions, the fact that an event is a necessary condition of a subsequent event is itself a sufficient condition of that event's occurrence. And this whole thing implies the existence of a system within which the events occur so that the type of explanation involved might be elucidated in terms of general systems theory. As far as development is concerned, Von Wright seems to think that studying a series of historical events of the kind such that each one is necessary for its successor is itself the study of development, and he speaks of the history and development of natural events and processes together. Certain considerations will show that this will not do. Suppose, for instance, that British Rail employees are on strike and that this coincides with strikes in all forms of public road transport but not the underground. In that situation a necessary condition of getting to my college from my home, given that I cannot fly or walk all the way, is that I should catch an underground train. In the circumstances in question a necessary condition of my doing that is that I should drive to an underground station, and a necessary condition of doing that may be that I should put some petrol in my petrol tank. If I were to do all that, the series of events — putting petrol in my tank, driving to the underground station, catching an underground train — would constitute an historical series in which each of the first two members of the series were such that their occurrence was a necessary condition of the next occurring. It is clear, however, that there are no grounds for thinking that the series is a developing one or constitutes a development.[4] Why is this?

One thing that is relevant here is that in so far as it is right to speak of the account of the series of events as a history, it is a history only in the sense of a chronicle. It simply lists what took place in order. If the condition that each event is a necessary condition of the following means anything very much in this context, it is because the events form part of a series that is intentional. Hence they have a principle of organization in my intentions, given the circumstances that obtain. One could dignify the account by speaking of it as a history only when those intentions, etc., have been made plain. Even so not all history is the story of a development — unless of course one takes a Hegelian view of the matter, and that it is necessary to do so for that end to be achieved is significant in itself. For Hegel there *is* a principle of organization in the ordering of all events in history, and he tries to see the details in that light. Those concerned with the more specific details of the business might well be less willing to see things in this kind of light, and it is hard to see all historical events as part of a developing process. Yet an account of past events might be dignified by the title of 'history' rather than a chronicle if some attempt was made to make sense of those events, perhaps in terms of various human intentions in complex ways. This however would not be sufficient for us to say that some process of development had gone on. Hence it is that my mini-history of a hypothetical series of events affecting myself is not an account of a process of development. In saying this, however, I have not yet made clear what else is required for this purpose.

One thing that is required is that there should be some principle of identity to the series of events or states. It is tempting to say more than this — that there should be throughout an identical object whose states they are or to which the events are to be attached, as was the case with my opening examples. But this would rule out, for example, the development involved in a series of numbers which converge to a limit, a series specifiable perhaps by an equation, which in the context provides the principle of identity. It might be that a series of actual events might be capable of being looked at in a similar way. It will remain true that in most ordinary cases there *will* be a single thing that develops and there will be a similar progression in a given direction. Yet this is not enough, for in my mini-history the events occurred to a single thing — myself — and there was a progression in a given direction, specifiable in this case by my purpose. Yet I still think it wrong to speak of development in that connection.

In this context Piaget, in explaining his own theory of the development of intelligence and the theory of stages that goes with it, often refers to C.H. Waddington's notion of epigenesis, a process of development in a given direction which is governed by what Waddington calls 'homeorhesis' and follows 'chreods' or necessary paths if the development is to ensue.[5] And he criticizes other theories of stages, e.g. Freud's, because they do not answer to these conditions. Homeorhesis differs from homeostasis in that in the latter it is deviations from a normal state that are corrected so that there is a constant tendency for a return to and preservation of that state; in homeorhesis the deviations that are corrected are deviations from a steady progression in a certain direction, a progression the principles of which are in part laid down in the organization of the organism but which depend also upon interaction with the environment. Homeorhesis also entails that these interactive processes should lead to the setting up of states at given times which are a necessary condition of the attainment of states further on in the developmental process. Hence the idea of necessary paths or chreods. It is easy to see why this set of ideas appeals to Piaget as a framework for his own theoretical ideas. But I think that still more needs to be said in order to make clear the notion of development.

Let us for the sake of argument accept the general principles of Piaget's developmental psychology and agree that progression through the stages that he lays down is the pattern of human intellectual development. More particularly let us accept that 'development' is the right word to use here. Given this, it has to be said that it is not the right word simply because, say, passing through the stage of concrete operations is a necessary condition of attaining the stage of formal operations. Looking back over a given individual's intellectual history one might say that this ordering had a certain sense and that one can see why it had to be so, in a way in which, if one shares Piaget's doubts, one could not say that one can see why the Freudian account of a person's normal affective history is one of something that had to be so. But if one adds the word 'development' here one is saying something more. The principle of identity for the series of events exists; it is the same person who goes through them all. So that is not what is missing. Moreover the ordering can be given a sense; so that again is not the point at issue. The real point is surely one that is in a way obvious, that each stage must be seen as in some sense leading to the next so that the later stage, as one might put it, grows out of the earlier one, and the earlier one is seen in terms of its contribution to the later one. Thus if the stage of concrete operations is to be seen as part of a process of development it must be seen not merely as something that has to be gone through if the individual is to engage in formal operations, but as something such that its being a necessary condition of engaging in formal operations is, in some sense, its rationale.

It may seem odd to say *that*, since it may seem that whether or not something engages in concrete operations is a matter of fact, and if it is to be explained must it not be explained in terms of whatever has gone on before, not in terms of what is yet to come? However, in my mini-history of my journey to college could it not be said that driving my car to an underground station is something that indeed has as its rationale something to come, what ever else is to be explained in it by reference to what has already happened? Let me take the second question first; answering it may cast some light on the first question. It is perfectly true that the rationale of my driving my car to the underground station lies in something that follows, my getting to college, but only via the intention that I have, the intention to get to college in the circumstances in question where getting to college has driving to the underground station as its necessary condition. The sequence of events is in no sense a natural one; it does not arise in any way out of my own nature. It is simply that given the contingent fact that I have the intention that I do it can be fulfilled in the circumstances in question only by this necessary sequence of events. Hence the rationale of any one stage is to be found in a future event only via the preceding but forward-looking event of my having or forming an intention. This suggests that if we were to be able to see the sequence of events as a process of development we should have to see them as in some sense natural and not dependent on the contingent fact of intention. But in that case we should have to look elsewhere for the forward-looking element that intention provides in my examples. And surely what will come will come; it is simply contingent that any particular event will or will not occur. As Russell said about memory, there can be no logical connection between events at particular times.[6]

But against Russell it can be said that there can be logical connections between events at different times if they are seen under relevant descriptions. Thus under the description 'recollection of X' there can be a more than contingent relation between the recollection event and the X which occurred in the past. It is similarly under the description 'intended result' that my getting to college explains my driving to the underground station. In an analogous way, but without reference to the contingent fact of an intention, the flowering of a plant may be explained in terms of its future propagation of its offspring. But that is possible only if we can see a flower not simply as a product of the previous plant growth or as a beautiful phenomenon in itself but as a kind of instrument with a certain function. The point that I am making here is akin to the one that Charles Taylor makes over teleological explanation,[7] when he says that his account of this form of explanation entails a rejection of atomism in favour of a certain holism. To see a state of a thing as a stage in its development we must be able to see it as connected essentially in some way with an end-state which is some way the rationale of the thing itself. We must be able to see the acorn not just as a lump of vegetable matter but as, given the fulfilment of certain conditions, a future oak tree. This it will become naturally if those other conditions are fulfilled. This implies a kind of essentialism based not simply on the implications of principles of classification *simpliciter*, but on the implications of principles of classification which take in view what things naturally become as well as what they naturally are. It is an essentialism which is in tune with much of what Aristotle has to say on biological matters at least, and in this respect Aristotle seems to me right, not as he has often been thought, wrong.[8] It is, we might say, the natural function of an acorn to grow into an oak-tree if certain conditions are satisfied. It is not my natural function to get to college provided that certain conditions are satisfied: but it may be my intention and once given this other parallel features may manifest themselves – the sequence of events may, given background circumstances, be invariant, it presupposes an end and it presupposes a pre-existent structure which makes the sequence of events possible.

I mention these last features because they are considered in this context by Professor R.S. Peters in considering development in his paper 'Education and Human Development'.[9] He takes them from a previous discussion of the concept of development by E. Nagel. I find his discussion unsatisfactory, however, for several reasons. One is his willingness to adduce as evidence in the context our talk of e.g. the development of a photograph, the development of a musical theme, and industrial development, where, as it seems to me, what is in question is the development of something by someone and not the development of something *per se*. Industry does not, I hope, just develop even with the help that the satisfaction of other conditions provides: but organisms may do so. A second and much more important point is that I find his totting up of various criteria too piecemeal. For, as I hope that I have made clear, it is the interrelationship between pre-existing conditions, necessary sequence and end-states within a pattern which we see as natural to a given kind of thing that is important for an understanding of the notion of development. Within this pattern it is quite feasible for us to view the fact that something is a necessary condition of some later state as a sufficient condition of its occurrence, and this enables us to bring the explanation of events which constitute stages of a developmental process under the general heading of functional or teleological explanation as Charles Taylor rightly sees it. Moreover, as Taylor also points out,[10] there is no necessity that what is so explained should be explained, more fundamentally perhaps, in terms of pre-existent causes also — though nothing logically rules out that possibility either. If there have to be background conditions under which the event to be explained can be seen as necessary for some future state of affairs, nothing entails that the event should also have a straightforward causal aetiology in such conditions, though it may have.

Now given all this, what application does it have to any issue of the philosophy of education? Professor Peters[11] tries to draw some distinctions between mental and biological development, and says *inter alia* that few would now support an inner ripening or unfolding theory in application to education. Yet it seems to me that this to some extent at least is what Professor Elliott was suggesting, in so far as he presented the picture of the human being as possessing a set of mental powers the stimulus for the development of which it is the function of education to provide. And in this he seemed to set himself over against a theory of education which lays weight on an initiation into public forms of knowledge. I have in this a slight feeling of a 'plague on both your houses'. I wish in what remains not to attempt to adjudicate between these views or approaches but to underline what seems to me some of the implications of what I have said about development in general for our very natural talk of mental, intellectual, and other forms of non-physical development in human beings. I want to emphasize that word 'natural' for it is not part of my purpose to suggest that talk of development in these contexts is contrived or even mistaken. On the other hand there may be limits to its proper use or to its use with the kind of implications that I have outlined and I think that it would not be to the point to look for attenuated or extended uses of the term so that it may have application where the implications that I have mentioned are missing.

There are no problems in speaking of physical development in that we have a relatively clear idea of what a fully developed human body amounts to; and more than this, we have some idea of the contribution that various stages of growth make to the final stage, so that we can view them in functional terms as making that contribution. We can equally speak unproblematically about the development of the child's power of or ability for muscular co-ordination and the like. But can we speak so unproblematically about intellectual or moral development in the light of anything like a clear idea of what a fully developed person is on the intellectual or moral plane? Can we speak unproblematically of the development of a person's power of or ability for reasoning, moral judgment, creativity and the like? If we feel that these things are problematic (as indeed *I* do) it is not simply because they depend on factors that lie outside the person himself so that there is no simple actualization of the pre-existent potentiality. Development in the ordinary sense depends on the satisfaction of conditions some of which are external to the thing that develops, in the way that the growth of a plant depends on food, water and adequate sunshine. Not even Aristotle thought that a potentiality could receive actualization without a cause, which for the most part was external to the things whose potentiality is being actualized. But we might say that food, water, etc., *enable* a plant to grow in that the process of growth itself follows principles that are laid down in the genetic nature of the plant. That is to say that the notion of the actualization of a *potentiality* must be taken seriously, in a way that we may well feel it is not being taken seriously if someone says that a block of marble has the potentiality for becoming a statue. It is true that the nature of the marble sets limits on what kind of statue a sculptor can get out of it: it may be for example that it can be cut satisfactorily only in certain directions. But these conditions that the nature of the marble imposes are negative, while we would surely want to say that the genetic structure of a seed determines in a positive way *certain* lines of growth at least, even if external conditions have to be satisfied for those lines to be followed.

But where learning is involved the lines are necessarily determined by something external, and the external factors do not merely prompt or make possible the following of lines the potentiality for which the

157

thing already has. This is, of course, not to say that the ability to learn and thus take in things from elsewhere may not presuppose the development of powers in the individual in the ordinary sense; but the learning itself is not development in any ordinary sense. And this applies wherever the individual has to come to act in a way that presupposes independent standards of, say, truth, rationality, rightness and the like. I put the matter in this clumsy way, since it is not true that whenever one learns one learns what is true, or what is the rational or right way of proceeding. One can learn things that are wrong or mistaken, even ways of behaving that are by other standards irrational: but these facts are intelligible only if seen against the fact that truth, rationality, rightness and the like imply standards that are independent of the individual, and to the extent that they presuppose forms of agreement are social. It would be utterly wrong to equate truth with what is socially agreed upon, but it would be equally wrong not to recognize a connection between truth and what is capable of being agreed upon; truth must be public in the sense that a merely personal truth makes no sense. The same applies to a private rationality and a private rightness. In this sense an understanding of truth, and an acceptance of standards of rationality and rightness have to come from outside the individual. To that extent they are logically incapable of development properly speaking, even if their acquisition does depend upon the development in us of powers necessary for their understanding and acceptance.

When children are said to be, say, intellectually, emotionally or morally immature or undeveloped, one has the sense of there being involved a moral judgment, in a way that is not so of the statement that someone is physically immature or undeveloped. I think that that feeling is right since the supposed notion of intellectual, emotional or moral maturity presupposes a judgment about the proper way of thinking or of responding to circumstances. Let there be no mistake about it; it is no straightforward factual statement to say of someone that he or she is immature or undeveloped intellectually, emotionally or morally. It may, though it need not necessarily do so, be a way of signifying a lack of conformity with socially accepted standards. The radicals who have seen a sort of conservatism in an emphasis on human development in an approach to education may thus have a kind of justification, whether or not the conservatism is intended.

I said at the beginning of this paper that the immediate stimulus for my thinking about this subject was Professor Elliott's paper on 'Education and Human Being'. One paradox that now emerges from his emphasis on development in the light of the considerations that I have brought forward is that the emphasis may point in a direction very different from the one that he clearly intends. For his central concern is clearly with creativity and the need for an education that allows for and promotes this rather than a straightforward initiation into forms of knowledge and understanding with their external and publicly imposed standards. But if what I have said is correct, it is wrong to equate an emphasis on creativity with an emphasis on the development of powers of a non-physical kind that individuals may possess. I doubt whether in fact education can do much for creativity except to allow it to flourish and grow where it can and not set things in its way that may stifle it. As for the mental and other powers that people may have, education can develop them by as it were giving them exercise, but, as I said before in this paper, to speak of developing something is not the same as to speak of it developing.

Where then is there room for speaking of development on the mental side of a person? I have allowed for the possibility of the development of powers necessary for learning and the acquisition of understanding and insight; there are also things like sensitivity and awareness which may be necessary to other activities which we think important, whether or not we think them of any importance in themselves. But it is the fact that they may be necessary to other things that makes talk of their development appropriate, and in a sense of 'development' that answers to the conditions that I have elucidated. For the fact enables us to view them if we so choose, in a functional light, and to think of their necessity to those other things as in some sense the reason for their existence, just as we view a stage in the development of a plant or other organism as both necessary to some final state and such that this fact is the reason for the intermediate stage's existence. Thus we might speak appropriately of the development of the power of thought in so far as we could think of its growth as having as its function the promotion of learning. But we do not, properly speaking, *develop* the power of thinking, say, critically. We learn to think critically, and critical thinking is not something that we might call a 'type of functioning'.[12] Similarly being creative is not a type of functioning that human beings undergo, but we may speak of people developing in respect of their creative powers to the extent that we can think of creativity having a function in relation to other things that they do, so that its growth can be viewed in that context as development. Again, a person's general understanding may develop and he may be said to develop in understanding; but he cannot properly be said to develop in his understanding of quantum physics. For, quantum physics is something that has to be learnt. Knowledge of quantum physics may be a means to other knowledge or even to power but it cannot reasonably be thought of as having that function. But understanding in general may be thought of in functional terms; and it is for that reason that it is appropriate to speak of its development.

Education, then, has little to do with development except as something that may make it possible by providing the right conditions, just as physical education may provide some of the right conditions for physical development. But I suspect that protagonists of physical education think of themselves as doing more than fulfilling a parallel function to that which food and water do for plants. To the extent that they think of themselves as promoting physical powers they are in the same position as those who promote mental powers; it would not be right to think of them as concerned with development except in so far as those powers have a function in relation to other things. As for moral development, I do not think that there is any such thing. People may develop in personality and character, as well as in their mode of thinking, but how to be moral is something that we have to learn. To speak of development in that context would be to misconstrue both morality and moral education. But I hope that I have shown the limitations of the notion of development for education in general, and if so this is a point of some importance for contemporary discussions of the subject.

## NOTES

1   In *Philosophers Discuss Education*, S.C. Brown (ed.), London, Macmillan, 1975.
2   Von Wright, G., *Explanation and Understanding*, London, Routledge & Kegan Paul, 1971, ch. 2, sec. 6.
3   Taylor, C., *The Explanation of Behaviour*, London, Routledge & Kegan Paul, 1964, ch. 1.
4   It might also be objected that it is wrong to speak of a *particular* event as constituting a necessary condition for the occurrence of another. I do not think that this is an important objection. In any case, one is given an adequate spelling out of the background

conditions, thinking of the particular events as tokens of specific types.

5 See e.g. Piaget, J., *Biology and Knowledge*, Edinburgh University Press, 1971, sec. 2.
6 Russell, B., *Analysis of Mind*, London, Allen & Unwin, 1921, ch. 9.
7 Taylor, C., *ibid.*
8 See e.g. Balme, D., 'Aristotle's Use of Teleological Explanation', Inaugural Lecture at Queen Mary College, University of London, 1965.
9 Peters, R.S., 'Education and Human Development', in Dearden, R.F., Hirst, P.H., and Peters, R.S., (eds) *Education and the Development of Reason*, London, Routledge & Kegan Paul, 1972.
10 Taylor, C., *ibid.*
11 Peters, R.S., *ibid.*, pp. 503ff.
12 Cf. Peters, R.S., *ibid.*, p. 511.

# 10

# WHAT EXACTLY IS SOCIAL ABOUT THE ORIGINS OF UNDERSTANDING?

As I see it, the question in my title is a philosophical one. An answer to it would involve being clear about how the origins of understanding are to be construed — how, that is, they are to be conceived even as possible, and what makes them possible. I emphasize that point because it seems to me that one of my main concerns — perhaps *the* main concern — ought to be to explain why a philosopher may justifiably stray into this territory, despite all the appearances, perhaps, of trespassing. I have no claim to any expertise about how in fact understanding comes about in individuals, but will argue that this essentially psychological question presupposes an answer, whether explicit or implicit, to the question of how this is even to be construed as possible. My concern is therefore with the concepts involved in the formulations of the problem, the concepts of knowledge and understanding, and with the problems that they entail for a construal of the origins of these things. I am not primarily concerned with the nature of human beings as such.

That leads me to two caveats that I should like to make at the outset. First, if, as I believe, there must be something social about the origins of understanding in the individual, it will clearly be impossible to construe that 'something social' in the sort of terms that may be quite appropriate once the individual participants in the social context have understanding both of each other and of the rest of the world in which they exist. The 'something social' must not be construed in terms of an interactionism which presupposes the very forms of understanding that we are trying to explain through a reference to the 'something social'. That is not to say interaction of some other kind may not be an appropriate thing to invoke.

162

Second, it is, I think, possible to construe the opposition between Piaget and Vygotsky, where it exists, as reflecting a difference between two ideologies — individualism versus collectivism. Whether or not that is an exaggerated way of putting it, Piaget's way of considering the origins and growth of understanding in the individual is very much in terms of the relationship that exists between that individual and the environment in which he or she finds him- or herself. That, as I understand the matter, is not the case with Vygotsky. When, however, I refer to the social aspects of the origins of understanding, I do not have it in mind to press the cause of Vygotsky against that of Piaget in that respect. We are, after all, concerned with the origins of knowledge and understanding in the *individual*, and whether or not human beings are fundamentally social creatures, perhaps even in some respects social products, my problem is still one of how it is possible for knowledge and understanding to come about in *individuals*. For it is to individuals that knowledge and understanding primarily belong, however much it may then exist independently of them. (And since understanding involves knowledge, let me say again, as I have done elsewhere (Hamlyn 1978, p. 12), that nothing in this depends on whether one speaks of understanding or of knowledge.)

Nevertheless, as I said earlier, the philosophical problems about the origins of understanding stem from, and lie in, not what sort of creatures human beings are, but the very concepts of knowledge and understanding. One can bring out the issues by means of an argument-schema expressed in terms of a number of logical connections or chains of presupposition involving knowledge. If the connections hold they do so irrespective of the nature of the thing to which the concept of knowledge may be applied. Moreover, the presuppositions or implications in question are all meant to be logical or conceptual in nature and do not entail a similar temporal ordering.

The argument-schema is as follows:

(1) To understand anything one has, as I have already said, to have knowledge about it in some respect. I do not believe that this is controversial (at least I hope not).

(2) To know something in this way is to know it as true (or as right or correct). Nothing very much turns on the use of the word 'true' as opposed to 'right' or 'correct'. Since truth is normally attributed to propositions, I do not mean to be taken as implying that knowledge is for that reason restricted to language-users.[1] It is sufficient

163

that what one knows something *as* should possess the same formal
properties as truth has. That is why I am just as happy to speak of
knowing something as right, correct, etc. as I am to speak of knowing it as true, as long as the same conformity to a standard of
correctness is conveyed.

(3) To know something as true presupposes knowing what it is for
something to be true (correct, right, etc.) in some sense of those
words and to some degree or other. To say that is simply to point
to the fact that someone could not be said to know something as
X if he had no idea at all of what X consisted in. Moreover, knowing
something as true is not knowing it as any old X; it is knowing it
as something essential for it to constitute knowledge at all. One
might put the point to be made under this heading by saying that
knowing something as true presupposes possession of the concept
of truth or something like it to some degree or other. (That can
be as indefinite as one likes, provided that it holds good in *some*
way.)

(4) The possession of the concept of truth even in this indefinite
sense involves in effect the appreciation of the force of a norm or
the idea that there are or can be standards of correctness. We cannot conceive of that being the case except in creatures which have
been got to see certain ways of doing (or thinking) things as right
and others as wrong. It is at this point that the part played by the
social becomes evident. I cannot see any way in which the concept
of a norm (note that I do not say the norm itself) could be other
than social in its origins. To appreciate the force of a norm (and the
idea of force in this sense is something involved in the very concept
of a norm) is to appreciate whatever it is as, so to speak, imposed,
however willingly that imposition is accepted. One who had no form
of contact with others could have no conception of a norm, and
*a fortiori* no conception of truth or correctness.

(5) To be got to see certain ways of doing (or thinking) things as
right (correct or true) or wrong (incorrect or false) thus implies
something like correction by others, and more specifically and more
importantly, the individual in question seeing that *as* correction.

(6) To see something as correction implies seeing the source of whatever is done as a corrector. Whatever else that involves it certainly
involves seeing that something as a being with certain intentions,
and thus normally with desires, interests, etc — in other words as
a person or as something person-like. That in turn implies a context

of personal relations. It would be unintelligible that someone should come to see another as a corrector except in a context of that sort, however minimal. What is required is an appreciation of the significance of the act of correction, and that implies seeing the place that the correction has in the relationship with the corrector. It has sometimes been suggested that a machine could perform the correcting role. But any machine complex enough to do the job would in effect be a proxy or substitute person. The correction would still have to be seen as motivated in person-like ways. Personal relations themselves depend on the participants in the relation seeing each other in certain ways. Hence to appeal to personal relations in attempting to explain someone's coming to see another as a corrector is not to appeal to something independent of ways of seeing things. One would nevertheless expect all this to emerge out of natural ways of responding to persons when treated by them in a personal way. Indeed only such a context could provide the conditions necessary for coming to see persons as persons, and thereby make possible the other things connected with that which I have set out. It is, however, important to note that such conditions are not in themselves sufficient for this purpose. Social relations are not sufficient for knowledge even if they are necessary.

What all this implies is, among other things, that knowing any one thing involves knowing a great deal more. For the kinds of seeing-as that I have invoked at the various stages of the argument all imply knowledge. To see X as Y, whatever X and Y are, is not in itself necessarily to know something about X, but it does presuppose a knowledge of some kind and to some degree of what it is for something to be Y. I have not attempted at any stage of my argument, therefore, to derive knowledge logically from something that does not involve knowledge. I have not tried in any way to show that knowing something, or anything presupposing knowledge, could be reduced to something not involving knowledge, which could thereby constitute an independent but logically sufficient condition for the individual concerned having knowledge. On the other hand, at more than one stage of the argument I made reference to what I may as well now call 'non-epistemic factors' as necessary conditions for the existence of the kind of knowledge in question. Thus I said that knowing what it is for something to be true presupposes a social context, and I tried to spell this out in more detail in relation to the other items of knowledge that this in turn implies. I said, for example, that seeing something as correction pre-supposes seeing another as a corrector, and that has as a necessary con-dition standing to the other either in a personal relation or in a relation that could become that.

There are therefore in the argument-schema that I set out two kinds of dependence of one thing on another. There is a form of logical or conceptual dependence that one kind of knowledge may have on another — something that I believe to be true of all knowledge, although not always in quite the same way as seems relevant in the present context. There is also the dependence of a kind of knowledge on certain kinds of necessary condition without which it would be un-intelligible that such knowledge should exist. In the present context the first kind of dependence is exemplified by the dependence of the knowledge that something is the case on the knowledge of what it is for something to be the case or true. That is a logical or conceptual dependence, since if someone did not know what it was for some-thing to be the case or true he could not, logically could not, be said in any proper sense to know anything. The second kind of dependence is exemplified by the dependence of the knowledge of what it is for something to have the force of a norm on the person who so knows standing in relations to others. This kind of dependence is not simply a contingent or matter of fact dependence. It is not that simply as a matter of fact appreciation of the force of a norm is usually depen-dent on the existence of a social context. I have claimed that it would be unintelligible for it to be thought to exist if that social context did not exist as well. There is nevertheless a difference between the non-contingency that attaches to this kind of dependence and that which attaches to the first.

One might express the difference by saying that the first turns on certain necessary features of the *content* of knowledge. What I mean by this is that if it is a necessary feature of what is known (the content of knowledge in that sense) that it is true (and given what knowledge is it *is* such a necessary feature if the knowledge is 'knowledge that') then knowledge of anything necessarily presupposes knowledge of what it is for something to be true; and the reason for that could be simply expressed by saying that knowing that *p* implies knowing *p* as true, and one cannot know something as true without knowing what it is for something to be true. That exemplifies, although in a very special way, a principle that I have already hinted at — that one cannot know one thing without knowing other things.

166

By contrast, it is not the relation between knowledge and features of its content that produces the non-contingency of the second kind of dependence, or at any rate not just that. It is true that the argument for a connection between knowledge and social context works through the link between knowledge that $p$ and knowledge of what it is for $p$ to be true. The crucial step, however, is made in the claim that the latter presupposes in any intelligible application that the knower should have been subject to correction and therefore should have shared in a social context. That claim turns on the sort of thing that truth is and what knowledge of what it is for something to be true must therefore entail.

I would emphasize again, however, that such participation in a social context is merely a necessary condition of being a knower in any intelligible sense; it is not in any way a sufficient condition. Hence, while participation in such a social context — standing in relation to others — will itself inevitably presuppose for its possibility non-epistemic factors such as natural reactions and natural responses through feeling, it is the knowledge that these mediate that is important for other knowledge. For that reason it is seeing correction *as* correction that is important for the acquisition of the concept of truth, not merely response to whatever it is that is done under the name of correction, although the former (seeing correction *as* correction) will not be possible unless there is the latter (action performed by others as correction and response to that).

What all this comes to in relation to my initial question is that there cannot be knowledge (nor *a fortiori* understanding) in an individual unless and until that individual is in an important sense social, and unless and until that knowledge includes knowledge of what is in an important sense social. It might be thought that in saying that I am generating a regress in which the possession of one item of knowledge is dependent on the possession of an item of knowledge of a different kind, and so on. It is perfectly true that it is part of the scheme that I have presented that someone cannot be properly said to have one item of knowledge unless and until he has a great deal more. On that, however, I should like to emphasize a point that I have made a great deal of in other things that I have written in this area (e.g. Hamlyn 1978). The kind of conceptual dependences with which I have been concerned have no implications for any temporal ordering of items of knowledge, and for the same reason they generate no temporal regress. There was not meant to be any suggestion in what I said that one first comes to see others as people, then as correctors, and then that one comes to see thereby what it is for something to be true, and so on. The negative way in which I put the point just now, when I said that someone cannot properly be said to have one item of knowledge unless and until he knows a great deal more, should be taken seriously. What it means is that if we can properly describe someone as knowing that *p* it must also be appropriate to describe him as knowing other things — and that is all.

The point is, however, quite general. While my argument-schema may suggest that the chain of dependence is one way in ordering, that is not strictly the case as far as knowledge is concerned, although it may be so in relation to non-epistemic factors. It would make no sense to suppose that someone might know what it is for something to be correct without knowing anything of how that is exemplified. Hence, if it is right to say that someone cannot know that *p* unless he knows, among other things, what it is for something to constitute correction, the relation can just as easily hold the other way round too. If that is the case, a person cannot know what it is for something to constitute correction unless he knows that *p*, *for some value of p*; that is to say unless he knows *some* other fact. There can be no logical objection to that; the relation of logical presupposition can well be reciprocal. Involved in the claim that I am making are: (a) the thesis of the non-atomicity of knowledge — knowledge does not come in independent but addable items or lumps which could exist by themselves; and (b) the thesis that something about the social must be included among those things that an individual must be said to know if he is to be said to know *anything*.

Of these theses, the first, as I have already said, seems very plausible in itself, and it may be made even more plausible *via* the consideration that its opposite — the thesis that atomic items of knowledge are indeed possible — faces extreme difficulties over the question how those atomic items of knowledge are to be individuated. After all, when we say of someone that he knows that *p*, it is in terms of *our* understanding of *p* that we so describe him. Such a description is compatible with a whole range of different possibilities as far as the individual in question is concerned. It is a great mistake to suppose that when we have decided that someone knows something or other we have determined just by that anything very precise as far as that person is concerned. There is *no* precise answer to the question what someone knows when he knows that nothing travels faster than the speed of light, that the earth is round, that Henry VIII had several wives, that men are different from women, that yellow is a bright colour – just to give a few, disparate examples.

If, therefore, it cannot be said exactly what someone knows when he knows that *p* (except of course that he knows that *p*), it cannot be objected that it cannot be a condition of knowing one thing that he knows other things. For the description 'knowing one thing' has no definite sense such that that condition might be ruled out by it. For that same reason there is no logical problem about the claim that when someone knows that *p* he also knows what correction is. For him, knowing that *p* may indeed involve all sorts of things, but it may nevertheless remain true that he cannot know anything, let alone *p*, unless he knows, among other things, what correction is. For that reason there is nothing wrong in *our* saying just that – that his knowing that *p* must presuppose his knowing what correction is (if, that is, my argument is valid).

Knowledge is always a matter of degree, in the sense that, while two people may both be said to know that *p*, one of them may know more than the other of what is relevant to *p* or may know that better. The thesis of the non-atomicity of knowledge has, as a corollary, that there is a certain but indefinite minimum to what a person must know if he is to know *anything*. The second thesis, that there must be something social in what he knows if he is to know anything, points to certain directions in which what he knows must be taken to go. Just what form seeing others as correctors takes in an individual is, for the reasons which I have been spelling out over knowledge that *p*, impossible to say. If my argument is valid, what we are entitled to say is that whatever an individual has it is not knowledge unless other epistemic factors apply to him in some way, e.g. unless in some way he sees others as persons. The words 'in some way' in that formulation have to carry a great deal of weight. It remains true that, if it is true of someone that he knows that *p* at all, it must also be true of him that he knows something of what persons are – and *vice versa* – for some value of *p* (that is, that if he knows something of what persons are he must know some other fact, and the same applies to animals to the extent that anything approaching the concept of a person gets application).

If someone were still to object to what I have said, complaining that it seems very odd at least to claim that a condition of knowing one thing is that the person concerned must know a great deal more, it could be replied, first, that the only oddity is in accepting that

169

description of the situation at its face value; for it presupposes that 'knowing one thing' is a clear and definite description, which it is not. Second, none of this undermines the thesis that whenever knowledge is ascribable to an individual in one set of terms it must always be possible to ascribe knowledge in some other set of terms. If that general possibility is accepted, nothing remains but to take my initial argument on its merits.

I can imagine a further objection which may seem more pertinent to psychology than the rather abstract considerations that I have been concerned with so far. I have insisted that what I have had to say has no positive implications for any temporal ordering of events, and thus *a fortiori* no genetic implications either. There is nothing that a philosopher, *qua* philosopher, can say about what must happen first, and so on. More than that, there is *nothing to be said* on this matter in terms that have anything to do with knowledge. The idea of a first item of knowledge has, if what I have said is right, no content. It might be said, however, that it seems fairly obvious that getting to the point at which ascription of knowledge, even in a minimal sense, is possible in relation to a child must nevertheless take some time. What are we to say of the child and its 'cognitive state' during that interval of time, however long or short it may be? On that question seems to turn the possibility of a genetic epistemology, at any rate with regard to the beginnings of understanding (for we ought not to assume that what holds good with respect to the beginnings of knowledge and under-standing necessarily applies to the later stages too — I shall return to that later).

I implied in what I said earlier that as long as the possibility of knowledge is not ruled out altogether there must be some sense in which understanding of truth and its conditions is ascribable to the person concerned. We may well want to say that at this stage there is not much on these matters that the child knows, that its knowledge is inchoate to say the least, but that speaking of his or her knowledge of these things has nevertheless a certain sense, however definite. Is there not, however, a stage at which not even that can be said, and what marks the transition? One thing is quite certain. It is of no use to say that if we cannot ascribe knowledge we may be able to ascribe belief. That view is implicit in some of the interactional views that I men-tioned at the beginning, and that indeed is one crucial thing that is wrong with them. They presuppose something like the idea that the child approaches the world and everything in it, including other persons, with beliefs that serve as hypotheses for corroboration or refutation, and that other persons may play an important role in that process. There is much that is wrong in such a view that I have discussed elsewhere (Hamlyn 1978), and I shall not repeat my criticisms here. It is in any case clear that only a knower can have beliefs; to believe something one must know at least what is involved in the belief, whether or not the belief itself can be said to amount to knowledge.

A view at the other extreme is that we do not even know what we are asking in asking these questions.[2] What we are seeking thereby is to describe a state in which the conditions under which alone our adult use of language has sense and application are *ex hypothesi* missing. To ask for a description of a state of mind (if that is the right word) before knowledge has come about is to ask for the impossible when the whole of our language presupposes for its application the existence of that very thing — knowledge — which is being supposed as absent. The question is, however, whether it really is like that, such that there is an incoherence in even asking for a description of the state of mind of a pre-knowledge child, or whether we are not simply being asked to apply language beyond the area of its usual application — a situation in which we have to have recourse, as we commonly do, to metaphor and analogy. I am inclined to think that it is the latter which really holds good, but that there is a sense in which it does not matter which it is for present purposes. For we may know that the states of mind of a very young child may admit in principle of description involving serial ordering in time culminating in something meriting the title 'knowledge' without necessarily being able to provide adequate descriptions of the earlier stages. Moreover, we may know something of the conditions that have to be satisfied before the title of 'knowledge' can properly be bestowed. At the same time, it has to be recognized that, since knowledge is for any individual a matter of degree, and since the items of knowledge in the complex that has to exist if knowledge is to exist at all can vary in degree relative to each other, it is not an all or none matter whether and when the title of 'knowledge' can in fact be properly bestowed. Hence it will be impossible to say at what moment knowledge first exists, and equally impossible to say anything definite about the ordering of that knowledge or what immediately precedes it.[3]

Does that mean that, whatever is or is not possible with respect to later stages in the growth of knowledge and understanding, there is no place for genetic epistemology at this stage — at the beginnings? No, for it is not the task of genetic epistemology to set out the ordering of knowledge and its preconditions in time, at least not as I understand what genetic epistemology should be on the analogy of ordinary epistemology. For just as ordinary epistemology has as its concern the *possibility* of knowledge and understanding in general, or of the knowledge and understanding of this and that, so genetic epistemology should have as its concern the *possibility* of the growth and origins of knowledge and understanding. Into both these concerns will enter an interest in the question what knowledge and understanding actually are, since in order to show the possibility of X it is necessary to be at least relatively clear about what X actually is. That, however, – what is sometimes, although in my opinion mistakenly, called the 'analysis of knowledge' – cannot exhaust all that epistemology should have as its concern. Furthermore, there is a difference between the questions what makes knowledge in general possible or what makes knowledge of this or that possible, and what makes knowledge, of whatever kind, possible in the individual. The latter kind of question will inevitably demand in the end some account of the conditions that have to be satisfied as regards that individual if he is to have knowledge. Some of those conditions will have to do with the various individual capacities that make knowledge possible – perception, memory, conceptual understanding, etc. That account will clearly have implications for genetic epistemology also, since, if such and such conditions have to be satisfied if the possession of knowledge is to be possible, their coming to be satisfied is necessary for the acquisition of knowledge, let alone its subsequent growth.

It will be seen from all this that I interpret genetic epistemology as a kind of extension of ordinary epistemology, the problem being what makes it possible for knowledge to come about in the individual and for subsequent learning to take place on its basis. Obviously the preconditions for the possibility of having knowledge apply equally to the possibility of acquiring knowledge, but not *vice versa*. I am not sure that there is very much to be said about the conditions for the possibility of later learning, although I have tried to make clear certain things about it elsewhere (Hamlyn 1978, ch. 9). The restricted nature of that discussion may (and has) come under criticism for ignoring much empirical material about the conditions under which such learning may best go on. It seems to me, however, that such considerations are in a genuine sense psychological and are not part of genetic epistemology as I have defined the term. Thus although there are some things to be said within genetic epistemology about later stages of cognitive growth the crucial issues are those that arise over the early stages, particularly those over the very beginning. That is why it is so important to try to sort out the issues with which I have been concerned.

It may be suggested, however, that I have offered a prescriptive definition of 'genetic epistemology'. Piaget does not after all define it in that way; nor does Baldwin from whom the term was derived. I am not competent to speak of Baldwin.[4] What Piaget means by 'genetic epistemology' is a very obscure matter. It is not, in his view, to be identified with developmental psychology; for him it is a philosophical discipline, at any rate in some sense of those words. Some of the things that he says suggest that he views the relationship between genetic epistemology and developmental psychology as rather like that between theoretical physics and experimental physics, i.e. as the relationship between the body of theory in terms of which the facts are to be viewed and those facts themselves. At other times he seems to see the difference between the two disciplines as one in the scope of the inquiries involved. There may also be differences in the traditions to which the two disciplines belong. That is why, in the context of genetic epistemology as he sees it, Piaget can, and perhaps rightly, oppose his position to empiricism and what he calls 'apriorism' (although the latter involves a confusion as to what 'a priori' means — it does *not* mean 'innate'). All this may suggest that in his view genetic epistemology is just something fitting in with a wide-ranging and abstract way of thinking about the growth of knowledge.

There is also the fact that the concept of knowledge is in a certain sense a normative concept — at any rate in the sense that, as I have tried to point out, it presupposes an appreciation of the force of a norm. Piaget says that knowledge involves norms of validity, which are the business of the logician to adjudicate. Since, however, this validity has to be purely formal it is to be the province of the logician, there are required also those who are able to adjudicate, as he puts it in an essay entitled 'Developmental Epistemology' (in Piaget 1972), the appropriate relations between subject and object — and this turns out to mean the specialist in the field of the science in question. Looked at in this light, genetic epistemology would appear to be a co-operative inquiry involving psychologists, logicians and specialist scientists, plus anyone else who might be useful. How they are to proceed remains less than clear.

I suggest that the only helpful way of seeing whether there is a distinct discipline here, and if so how it is to be identified, is to sort out the questions that are at stake. Curiously enough, in the essay which I have mentioned (it is not clear when it was written), Piaget is on the fringe of doing just that. For he begins by giving as the question with which classicial theories of knowledge have been concerned 'How is knowledge possible?'; and he elaborates one or two other questions along the same lines. What he finds wrong with classical epistemology is not that philosophers have asked these questions, but that they have assumed that knowledge is a state, whereas it is really, he says, a process. On that last point he is just wrong; the acquisition of knowledge may be a process, but not knowledge itself. That, however, is of no great importance for present purposes. He might just as well have said that epistemologists ought to address themselves to the acquisition of knowledge as well as to its possession. The question with which they would then be concerned would be 'How is the acquisition of knowledge possible?', as long as that question is construed as being concerned with what gives the concept of the acquisition of knowledge a coherent sense (perhaps against sceptical suggestions that it does not have such a sense). It must not be construed as asking how it actually happens in practice. It seems to me that the crucial problem in understanding the possibility of acquiring knowledge in this sense is the problem of how it gets off the ground, so to speak. To understand that we need to take into account what sort of thing in general human beings are, what sort of thing a human consciousness is, and in what sort of capacities that consciousness is manifested; we need, that is, to take into account what a human form of life is.

The difficulties on which I have concentrated do not, however, lie there, but in the very implications of the concept of knowledge itself (something to which Piaget pays insufficient attention). Hence, if, for example, and to return to my original question, the possibility of knowledge in an individual demands some kind of social existence as far as that individual is concerned, the acquisition of knowledge also demands the acquistition of a social existence of that kind. The knowledge cannot exist before the social existence of the latter is its precondition; but that is the only temporal fact — a negative one — that is entailed by what I have said. It is nevertheless an important fact in itself that any story about the origins of knowledge and understanding in the individual must have as a theme something about the individual's acquisition of a social existence (for there is no adequate sense, I take it, in which children could be said to be born as

174

social beings). Finally, it is important to see in just what respect that theme is a necessary part of the story – and that has been my concern. I shall end with a little more on that subject.

I have emphasized in other things that I have written in this area (especially perhaps in Hamlyn 1978) the extent to which a child's growth of knowledge must be seen in terms of an initiation into a public and accepted body of understanding, and the extent to which that depends upon the child's attention being drawn to things and his being put in the way of things by adults. For that to happen it is no doubt important that the child should be treated as a potential member of a community of knowers and thus to an increasingly great extent as a person. That, I know, fits in with some things that some psychologists have said, sometimes for other reasons. It is not quite what I have said here. It is certainly not a necessary condition of the possibility of knowing that *p* that a child should have been put *by others* in the position of seeing that *p*. He might, given the satisfaction of other conditions, get to see this for himself (though not, I suggest, if he knew nothing else at all). It is inconceivable, however, that a child should be got to see the force of truth and falsity without at the same time and along with that being got to see something as true or false. That is to say that the appreciation of the force of a norm is bound to come along with an appreciation of some content of that norm, i.e. something to the effect that such and such is the case, correct or right; it is inconceivable that it should be otherwise, given what a human consciousness (or indeed any other consciousness that we could understand) is. Hence, while it is certainly not the case that the truth is simply what others tell us or impress upon us, even when we are babies, the paramount importance of what others believe and want for the beginnings of a child's understanding must be obvious. It is only against that background that there can be any subsequent independence on the part of the individual in the acquisition of knowledge and understanding.

I would like to emphasize again, however, that in any adequate account of the origins of understanding in the individual it is not enough simply to make reference to what the role of others is. An account must be offered of the child's response to that of sufficient adequacy to explain how the child comes to see the force of a norm. It must therefore see what it is for others to have wants and concerns, and that is possible only in a context where those concerns colour, so to speak, the behaviour of those involved. To say that is to say that the relations between those concerned, e.g. mother and child, must be in a genuine sense such as turn on affect or emotion — love being of course the most obvious example. It is quite hopeless to attempt to construe the relations in question in terms of stimulus and response in the ordinarily accepted sense of those terms. Relations so construed provide no foundation for seeing the force of anything, whereas there is an obvious connection between a relation involving love and concern (or indeed the antitheses of these, if it comes to that) and an appreciation of the force of something that may have importance, as a norm normally has and is seen as having.

It is only in a social context of that kind that there can be any intelligibility in the idea of the emergence of the appreciation of the force of a norm. Only with that can one properly speak of knowledge and understanding. Only on the basis of that can one conceive of the possibility of subsequent learning. That is the conceptual ordering of these matters. Let me repeat, however, that except for the fact that learning implies prior knowledge, there are no positive temporal implications in what I have said. It remains true that even if it is quite impossible to say when knowledge first comes into existence, and even if when it does it will be a matter of degree, it will not be knowledge (nor *a fortiori* understanding) unless the person concerned has the kind of social existence that a relationship with other human beings involves. That, I suggest is what provides the answer to my initial question 'What exactly is social about the origins of understanding?'

## NOTES

1 On this see further Hamlyn 1980.
2 Something like that was said by J. Nammour 1973.
3 It equally follows, although it is not my immediate concern here, that there is nothing to be said about how knowledge comes about and that certain conditions have to be satisfied if it is to do so, as my subsequent remarks on genetic epistemology indicate.
4 On whom see Russell 1978.

## REFERENCES

Hamlyn, D.W., *Experience and the Growth of Understanding*, London, Routledge & Kegan Paul, 1978.
Hamlyn, D.W., 'Experience and the Growth of Understanding: A

Reply to Mr Cooper', *British Journal for the Philosophy of Education*, vol. 14, no. 1 (1980), pp. 105-8.

Nammour, J., 'Resemblances and Universals', *Mind*, vol. LXXXII, no. 329, October 1973, pp. 516-24.

Piaget, J., *Psychology and Epistemology*, B.M. Foss (ed.), London, Allen Lane, The Penguin Press, 1972.

Russell, J., *The Acquisition of Knowledge*, London, Macmillan, 1978.

# PART III

# THE SELF AND INTERPERSONAL UNDERSTANDING

# 11

# UNCONSCIOUS INTENTIONS

Is it possible to do something intentionally and yet be unconscious of so doing? Many philosophers would answer 'No' to this question on the grounds that it is of the essence of intention that if we do something intentionally we do it knowing what we are doing.

Yet there *appear* to be cases where a man does something intentionally or apparently so and yet is *not* aware of what he is doing. It may be that he thinks that he is doing something else, or at least claims that he is doing something else, to all appearance with sincerity; or it may be that he seems not to be aware of doing anything at all. In the first category of cases falls that, for example, in which a man behaves consistently brutally towards another person yet maintains with apparent sincerity that he is giving him his deserts. This kind of case is to be explained, it might be suggested, by saying that the person concerned is just insensitive. Yet, if he is not generally insensitive, if to every other person he behaves with great sensitivity, we should perhaps be forced to seek another explanation for the case in question; we *might* feel constrained to say that his brutality is intentional even though he is not aware of this. In the second category of cases fall all those in which, if the man in question is aware of what happens at all, he describes it as a mere happening or accident; it is not, according to him, that he *does* anything. To this category belong all those cases which Freud describes in the *Psychopathology of Everyday Life* — the slips of the tongue, the cases of forgetfulness, etc., which, perhaps, happen too frequently to our mind to be mere accidents. There is probably a wealth of cases in both these categories — or at least so we have come to believe since Freud. But here, I believe, Freud has merely drawn our attention to something that was always known, at any rate by the more percipient observers of humanity.

I make this last point because it has sometimes been said that Freud stretched concepts, like that of *motive,* in terms of which we ordinarily explain actions. This was, for example, maintained by A.G.N. Flew in 'Motives and the Unconscious' (*Minnesota Studies in the Philosophy of Science*, vol. 1) and it was specifically in view of the fact that Freud made use of the notion of *unconscious* motives that the stretching of the concept was said to take place. It has been maintained by Peters (e.g. *The Concept of Motivation*, pp. 62ff) that Freud did not speak of motives at all, but rather of wishes. This, I imagine, is technically correct. It is, however, somehow beside the point. Apart from the incoherence in Freud's own use of the concept of a wish, a great deal of what he wanted to say could be expressed in terms of motives, and this for a good reason. The point may be expressed as follows.

In my view, more or less anything can figure as a motive for an action, provided that it plays a certain role in a pattern in terms of which we explain and interpret actions. It has been maintained by Kenny (*Action, Emotion and Will*, p. 90) that the pattern in question is the following: there is (1) a state of affairs of which the subject disapproves, (2) an action, and (3) a state of affairs of which the subject approves. This pattern seems to be built upon Anscombe's distinction (*Intention*, pp. 18ff) between motives which are backward-looking, e.g. revenge, interpretative, e.g. 'out of friendship', and intention for the future, e.g. 'in order to . . .', for these three kinds of motive-explanations make reference respectively to a previous state of affairs, the action in question, and a future state of affairs. But if Kenny's account is in fact built upon this distinction it makes it over-rigid, since not all backward-looking motives have reference to a state of affairs *disapproved* of (cf. 'He did it out of gratitude', or 'He did it from sheer joy at what had happened'). Anscombe says that backward-looking motives involve reference to good and evil – and there may be something in this – but that is not to say that all motives explain action against a pattern in which there is a state of affairs which the subject disapproves of. Rather, as it seems to me, since an action may involve an attitude or attitudes to past events, present circumstances or future states of affairs, it is therefore possible to see the action in the light of any of these things – though not necessarily of course *all*. It is indeed possible to characterize the action itself in terms of these attitudes. Something that is done in order to get even for past injustices may be characterized as an act of revenge; something that is done out of friendship may be characterized as an act of friendship; and something that is done for gain may be termed an acquisitive act.

Thus to give the motive for an action is to put it in a certain light. We need first to recognize the action as intentional; and with unintentional actions the question of motive does not arise. It is furthermore enough that the action should be simply intentional; it is not necessary that it should be performed with any further intention, with any further aim in view. It follows from this that it is wrong to hold that motive-ascriptions are always coincident with explanations of the form 'He did X in order to . . .', i.e. explanations which make reference to goals. Yet, given that the action is intentional, we may well need to see it as an intentional action of a certain sort; we may need to make it intelligible to ourselves *as* an intentional action. This is what the motive explanation does; it draws attention to some factor in the past, present or future circumstances of the action which makes it so intelligible. In the light of that circumstance, we may, as I have already indicated, recharacterize the action in its terms. A.R. White has maintained (*Mind* 1958) that motives are themselves explanations and must be distinguished from the things or factors which serve as explanations of this kind. The claim that motives are themselves kinds of explanations, however, is a mistake. Rather, reference to motives presupposes the context of a demand for explanation, a demand that an action should be made intelligible as an intentional action of a certain sort. It remains true that a great variety of things can make an action intelligible in this way; for it is in terms of what they mean to the person concerned that they reflect upon the action. What the person does he does in relation to them, and they make the action intelligible by way of his attitude to them. Sometimes indeed, in giving the motive for an action we make clear that very attitude itself, e.g. when we speak of an action done out of anger.

But it is just this point which makes the idea of an unconscious motive difficult. For if the factor to which we make reference in giving the motive is one of which the agent is apparently unaware, it is difficult to see how his attitude towards it can explain the action. We should be saying in effect that what the person is doing is performing an intentional action of a certain sort, and he will thus be doing something knowing what he is doing, yet apparently unaware that this is what he is doing. Just because when we explain an action in terms of a certain motive, we could also recharacterize the action, given that it is intentional, as one of a certain kind, it follows that, if the motive from which an action is done is one of which the agent is unconscious, then the agent must also be unconscious of the fact that he is performing an intentional action of the given kind or that what he does in this way is intentionally done. I say 'in this way' because the agent *may* quite well be aware of doing *something*, as I indicated earlier, although there are equally cases in which he may not be aware of *doing* anything.

What I have said is relevant to Freud, because whether or not he spoke of motives Freud certainly supposed that people intentionally do various things without being aware of so doing. And one point, though only one point, of psychoanalysis is to bring home to people not only that certain things that they do are interpretable in specific ways but also that they really intend them in that spirit even if they are not aware of so doing; e.g. constant hand-washing is not only inter-pretable by others as a sign of feelings of guilt but is really meant by the patient as an attempt to get rid of guilt. Alternatively, certain things that seem to happen to people, e.g. slips of the tongue, are not merely *signs* of certain attitudes on their part but are to be construed as actions performed by these people even if they are not aware of anything of the kind. Given that we are concerned with an intentional action at all — as we clearly are in the first kind of case, and may be, if Freud's hypothesis is right, in the second — then to say that in doing this the person concerned was really doing something else, whether or not he was aware of so doing, is in effect to explain what he is doing. To say that constant hand-washing is really an attempt at getting rid of guilt is in effect to say that this is why the constant hand-washing takes place. Redescription or recharacterization of something as an inten-tional action is the other side of the coin to giving an explanation of the original action by reference to motives. The concepts of motive and intention are thus intimately related and it is for this reason that it is not inappropriate to say that Freud was concerned with uncon-scious motives, whether or not he explicitly used that term.

However, we need not base everything on an acceptance of Freudian theory; we need not, that is, rely on Freudian theory in all its detail to substantiate the claim that sometimes people, whatever they think that they are doing, are really doing something else, even if they are not aware of doing so. There are cases, I suggest, in which the very repeti-tion of an apparent action without the agent being aware of it as that action makes the hypothesis that the person concerned really intends to do this the only plausible one. This is important, as there are some philosophers who would consider the difficulty involved in the notion of an unconscious intention enough to warrant the rejection of that part of Freudian theory which presupposes the notion, or at any rate enough to warrant its re-interpretation in other terms. But if there are quite ordinary cases where the only plausible interpretation is that the person is intentionally doing something without being aware of the fact this course cannot be adopted. Freud, as is well known, came to accept the fact that the symptoms of hysteria have an intentional basis (he uses in one place in the early writings the phrase 'act of will' in this connection). He did so because those symptoms conformed not to the facts of anatomy but to popular conceptions of anatomy. He thus came to the conclusion that the symptoms had some connection with certain ideas in the patient's mind. This is one kind of consideration and one that was particularly relevant to the clinical problem with which Freud was concerned. But repeated actions of which the agent claims sincerely to be unaware provide another kind of consideration; and these actions may be ones of which the person is not aware at all as actions, or alternatively ones of which he is not aware as actions of a certain kind.

I have already mentioned a case of the second sort — that in which a man is consistently brutal to another person and yet is apparently quite unaware of this, believing with every apparent sincerity that he is giving him his deserts. It might be maintained that because of the difficulties presented in this case by the possibility of insensitivity either in general or in a particular instance of personal relationships, we ought to look for a more perspicuous case. For the possibilities of insensitivity introduce the further possibility that what the man does is really unintentional, and not intentional at all; and it might be difficult to rule this out. Another possibility, though not perhaps one that is very plausible in the present case, is that what is done is done out of habit. If we were to take the case, for example, of someone who suddenly and out of character took to pouring all his available money into a beggar's hat, who did this constantly whenever he saw a beggar, and yet denied with every apparent sincerity all pretentions to generosity, it might not be immediately obvious what we should say of him. There might be considerations that would lead us to say that what he did was mere habit. This would take some explaining, but it is not beyond the bounds of intelligibility that such a man might have come to develop a habit of doing this sort of thing out of, perhaps, a desire or tendency for public display without any generous motives whatever.

185

Then, whenever he saw a beggar he emptied his pockets without thinking, without even being fully aware of what he was doing at all. This
would be a strange case, but I mention it merely to underline the point
that explanations like those of insensitivity and habit are possible ones
when a person constantly does something in a certain situation without
apparently being aware of doing so. They have to be ruled out if we are
to attribute intention with any certainty; and there may be other
explanations to be excluded as well.

We might exclude habit if the action in question was too complex
or involved too high a degree of skill; we might exclude insensitivity
if the person showed every other sign of being sensitive not only in
general but also in relation to this particular man or in this particular
situation. I think that there would remain cases in which the most
plausible explanation was that the person in question meant to do what
he did, without apparently being aware of it. Let me use and perhaps
adapt a case which I owe in a somewhat different form to Mr Christo-
pher Olsen. Let us suppose a man driving a car who, whenever a cat
crosses the road in front of him, turns the wheel so as to roll over the
animal. Let us suppose, furthermore, that he does this constantly and
that after, say, the fifty-seventh time, his wife who is a woman of
remarkable patience, says to him 'Why did you do that?' to which he
replies 'Do what?' Now there are various things that he might have
said — 'It was only a cat' (insensitivity) or 'I am sorry, I just seem to do
that these days' (habit) and so on. Saying what he did is not absolutely
incompatible with other explanations but, there are at least two ways
in which it might transpire that the most plausible explanation of his
behaviour is that he turned the wheel intentionally — most plausible
in the sense that other explanations seem ruled out.

First, it might transpire that he thought that he always tried to avoid
the cat and that his hitting the cat was always an accident. But of
course after the constant repetition of a supposed accident it becomes
implausible to suppose that it was really an accident at all; it is too
regular for that. Still, it might be due merely to a defect of skill, just
like the accidents which result from a failure to steer into a skid, where
the natural reaction is not to. Perhaps the man's incompetence was
such that his avoiding action always produced collision with the object.
It might of course be so, though not if in other similar circumstances
where a cat was not involved he showed no such incompetence. Perhaps he had a thing about cats — but it is not clear from this alone
whether his attitude is such as to produce incompetence in avoiding

cats or a kind of super-skill at hitting them. The point in all this is that his awareness of the cats makes it possible to construe his relationship to them in different ways, and even if we come in the end to the conclusion that he intended to kill the cats, much has to be ruled out on the way. But in the second case perhaps the choice is more limited. This is where the words 'Do what?' have to be taken quite literally. It is for him, apparently, as if nothing happened at all, or at least as if he did nothing at all out of the ordinary; he was just driving along in a straightforward way. Such gross unawareness of what was happening might be excused on one or two occasions; but on fifty-seven occasions? Even habit presupposes the possibility that he might reflect back on his action and see that he did it. The regular carrying out of what is after all a rather skilled operation without any apparent awareness of doing so demands an explanation, and just because it is a skilled operation it may be that the only really plausible explanation is that he really meant to perform it. In other words, where the action of which the agent is apparently unaware is complex and skilled enough for it to be implausible that it should be carried out unintentionally or by accident, and where the apparent ignorance on the part of the agent of what he is doing is so absolute that it is implausible that the action should be the result of incompetence or mere habit, it may well seem from the regularity of the behaviour that the only remaining explanation is that the agent intends to perform this action on each occasion, but does not know that he does.

My point in all this is the simple one that surprising regularities, wherever and however they occur, require explanation, and explanation in terms appropriate to what has to be explained. Surprising regularities in action require explanation in terms appropriate to action. What we have to be sure of is that it is an action that has taken place and an action of a given kind. Otherwise the person concerned can say, as I have already indicated, that he did not *do* anything that required explanation or that what he did was not of the required kind. Then, in the first case we should have to look for explanations other than those appropriate to action in order to explain the regularity of what takes place, and in the second case we should have to explain his regularly doing what he did in such terms as those of incompetence or lack of foresight. There remain, however, a residue of possible cases where, I suggest, unconscious intention is a plausible explanation and perhaps the only plausible explanation.

I embarked on this discussion because I wished to consider cases where it might be appropriate to speak of unconscious intention and where the grounds for doing so are not explicitly psychoanalytic. For, as I said earlier, if we bring into consideration psychoanalytic theory, there are other considerations such as those which Freud adduced in his early studies in hysteria — that the phenomena have some connection with beliefs that the patient has about his body. Similar things might be said of compulsions such as that exhibited in repeated and apparently unnecessary hand-washing. It could be said that these too make sense only in connection with beliefs that the person has about the point of his actions. It might, furthermore, be argued that the phenomena which I have been discussing are essentially one of the same kind and that I have not therefore escaped from the necessity of making reference to psychoanalytic considerations. I can reply to this only by saying that *on this point*, this general point that some human phenomena can be explained only in terms of the person's meaning something without apparently being aware of the fact, Freud was not an innovator. His innovations came in the details, in views about the range of phenomena to which this idea could be applied and in what way. As Ernest Jones has pointed out in his biography of Freud, the notion of unconscious mental processes was commonplace before Freud; what was new was the nature of those processes according to Freudian theory. What I have therefore been concerned with is the underpinning of psychoanalytic theory, something that can stand in independence from that theory itself and therefore something that does not presuppose it.

However, it might also be said that what is essential to psychoanalytic phenomena is something like self-deception and that this applies also to the cases which I have been discussing. The refusal on the part of the man who apparently tries to hit cats to admit that he is doing this or indeed doing anything at all out of the ordinary is mere self-deception, and the same applies to the other cases which I have mentioned. Self-deception is not mere ignorance, nor is it simple lack of knowledge. I suspect that all this is true. What is essential to what I have been trying to argue for is that the people concerned must both know and yet somehow not know what they are doing; if a person is to do something intentionally, and thus in some sense do it knowing what he is doing, without apparently knowing what he is doing, this must not amount to a straightforward contradiction. To say that what happens is that the person in these cases deceives himself is to remove the apparent contradiction, since in self-deception there is not simple

188

ignorance. Self-deception is itself an intentional activity.

Unfortunately this by itself does not remove every difficulty since by this token self-deception itself is an example of the same kind of phenomenon as that with which we have been concerned. To deceive himself a person must, while having a certain kind of knowledge, obscure from himself that he has this, and thus know and apparently not know at the same time. It is for this reason that doubt has sometimes been cast on the possibility of self-deception in any full sense; and it is for the same reason as that for which doubt has been cast upon the possibility of unconscious intention. They are indeed connected phenomena, if not aspects of the same phenomenon. If I hesitate to say that they are in fact two sides of the same phenomenon it is because there may be doubt whether, in all cases where one can intend something without knowing it, the explanation *is* self-deception. I shall not argue the point here, but it seems to me that just as it is possible for us to know things without knowing that we know, so it may be possible for us to do things knowingly without our knowing this. A man might, for example, be got to do things unintentionally in a way that he could hardly prevent (such as screaming by way of reaction to intense pain) and he might be told to do the same thing in the same circumstances intentionally. In this situation there might come a time when he was not really sure, and might not know, whether he did it intentionally or not.

If this is so, there may conceivably be cases in which one can be said to do something intentionally without knowing it, and yet these are cases in which self-deception seems ruled out. Thus people can intend things without knowing it *simpliciter*. It might be held as a corollary of this that, if it follows from the fact that a man does not know something that he cannot be conscious of it (and this *does* seem to follow), then I have shown that there is unconscious intention. Hence, my paper might come to an end. I think, however, that this conclusion would be premature, since, as I have said, the cases which I have mentioned are cases in which self-deception is ruled out. I suggest that where self-deception does occur we might want to say that the person does after all know that he knows what he is doing; only he does not know it consciously. This is a consequence of my claim that self-deception is itself an intentional activity; it is, if you like, something that involves a strategy, and for this to be possible the agent must have at least some knowledge of what he is up to. How this can be so is our problem. At all events, unconscious intention in this sense (and I shall in future use the phrase 'unconscious intention' to refer to this kind of phenomenon alone) is not a simple ignorance of, or *any* kind of failure to know, the fact that one knows what one is doing. In those cases of a failure to know that one knows which I have mentioned but not discussed there is involved a simple ignorance, due to the special features of the situation in question. The range of cases in which this sort of thing is possible is probably limited. But the range of cases in which unconscious intention seems possible is very much wider, and if they have to be explained they receive their explanation not from the special features of the situation but by reference to further intentions of the person concerned.

What I have said here could be put by saying that in appealing to simple ignorance of the fact that one knows what one is doing in doing something, we invoke by negation, in speaking of that ignorance, a concept of knowledge different from that involved in speaking of knowing what one is doing in the *full* sense. The knowledge which one lacks in being ignorant in this way is not the kind of knowledge which one has when one does something knowing what one is doing in the full sense. This latter kind of knowledge might better be termed a *consciousness* of what one is doing. When one lacks that consciousness of what one is doing it is still possible *in some sense* to know what one is doing. This is possible either when one does not know (or is ignorant of) the fact that one knows what one is doing or when one is unconscious of what one is doing. I wish to suggest that when one is unconscious of what one is doing one may still know what one is doing and indeed know *this* in turn.

There may, however, be different ways of being conscious of what one is doing. In trying to specify the kind of consciousness which is involved in knowing what one is doing in the full sense it is necessary to use expressions like 'consciousness of what one is doing, in doing it'. The phrase 'in doing it' is important; it serves to rule out any form of detached or depersonalized consciousness of what one is doing. I would also distinguish consciousness of what one is doing from awareness of what one is doing. It may be that we can speak of awareness of what one is doing in doing it, but a phrase of this kind suggests to me much more of an awareness of the *point* or *significance* of what one is doing. To become aware of what one is doing is often to become aware of the point, significance, or consequential importance of one's action. This is not true of consciousness of what one is doing, and the addition of the words 'in doing it' underlines that fact, since they

190

attempt to specify just what kind of consciousness of action is involved.

It is of course true that in speaking simply of *knowing* what one is doing, in the sense implied generally in intention, that sense should similarly be specified by using expressions such as 'knowing what one is doing, *in doing it*'. In this respect knowledge and consciousness of action are parallel. But there could be no valid suggestion that knowing X necessarily implies being conscious of X. There are many, many cases of knowledge where it would not even be in point to speak of consciousness – knowledge of the date of the Battle of Hastings, of how to ride a bicycle, etc. Hence, there is in cases such as these no reason at all why being unconscious of something precludes knowing it. Is there any reason why this should not be true specifically of intention also? Intentional action seems to imply at least knowing what one is doing, and, more particularly, knowing what one is doing in doing it. It cannot for that very reason be analysed or unpacked into action plus knowledge, since the knowledge is not independent of the action. The knowledge required is not merely knowledge of facts about the surroundings of the action, e.g. in the case of the cat-hitter, that there is a cat there, that his car is going in a certain direction; it is knowledge of what the action is *in doing it*.

But where one is not conscious of what one is doing and this is not due to simple ignorance of the fact that one knows what one is doing, we need some further explanation of the situation. Simple inattention is hardly plausible, except where the person performs the action from habit – and there is a sense in which it might well be said that a person who does something from habit knows what he is doing, in that he may be able to say what he is doing if asked or challenged. But where habit is excluded as I presumed that it was in the cases discussed earlier, it seems that the only possible explanation is that the inattention is itself intentional. This itself could be explained only by reference to a further end of which the person is in some way conscious. In that case it could be said that in unconscious intention the person does in some sense know that he knows what he is doing, although the story which would make clear the sense in question may be a very complicated one.

In other words, there is, in unconscious intention, *a* sense in which the agent does what he does knowingly, without knowing this. That is so to the extent that he is unconscious of doing it knowingly. That is unobjectionable, since if there is no objection to the idea that he need

191

not know that he is doing it knowingly, there can be no objection to his being unconscious of doing it knowingly. But if it is part of unconscious intention that it involves self-deception, we may want also to say that he knows that he knows what he is doing. For if he is self-deceived he has brought about the situation that he is unconscious of the fact that he knows what he is doing as a result of a strategy which is itself intentional. Hence, if we are inclined to say that he does not know that he knows, it is so merely in the sense that he has made himself unconscious of what he in fact knows. This differs from cases of a man simply not knowing that he is doing something knowingly, because in the present case the ignorance, if one can speak of it in that way, is in a special way due to the man himself, not to other things external to himself. This is possible because he has a further intention of which he is conscious, and which is related to his present intentional action in some way. This present intentional action can always be redescribed in terms of the further intention (i.e. if he does X for the further intention Y, he can be said to be performing an action which can be specified in some way in terms of Y). The action so specified is certainly intentional. In so far as the action so redescribed contains the original action as a component, and if the pattern of what takes place is such that we would be justified in saying that he must know that he is performing the component action if he is to perform the whole knowingly and consciously, then we may say that he knows what he is doing even if he is not conscious of it. Thus, *in a way* he both knows and does not know that he does what he does knowingly. But there is no contradiction here, because the sense in which he knows that he does what he does knowingly is different from that in which he does not know this. In the latter case we mean simply that he is unconscious of doing what he does; in the former we imply knowledge through a further and wider intention.

In sum, in order to perform an action intentionally the agent must know what he is doing *in some sense*; the general course of his actions must make it intelligible for us to say that he does what he does knowingly. This is most plausible, of course, if there is some point to what is done, if his doing this would satisfy some further intention which there is reason to believe that he has. But what has to be made sure of first of all is that he is *doing* anything at all; and once again only the general pattern of his other actions in the same context can make a decision on this possible. I tried to indicate earlier that in some contexts we should almost inevitably be forced to the conclusion that the person concerned was acting intentionally without being conscious of this. I have in the sequel tried to show that there is no logical objection to this, since the case is not strictly one of knowing and not knowing at the same time and in the same sense, and hence no contradiction arises from it. Ignorance of the fact that one knows what one is doing is also possible and similarly involves no contradiction; but the cases in which I have been primarily interested have not been cases of simple ignorance, as it revealed by the fact that it is normally possible in such cases to go on to ask for the further intention which explains why the person does what he does although he is unconscious of what he is doing. This suggests also that this kind of unconsciousness in action is something brought about by the person concerned. For it makes little sense to suppose that someone might do something for some further end without being conscious of that further end. Hence, if someone definitely appears to do something for some further end and yet seems to be unconscious of what he is doing, we can properly say that he *does* know what he is doing, though by intentional inattention or something of the sort he has made himself unconscious of what he is doing. That is why it is so plausible to speak of self-deception in these contexts, even in the invocation of this concept does so little towards showing how unconscious intention is possible. But granted that it *is* possible, self-deception sets the pattern of what is involved, for the reasons which I have given.

# 12

# SELF-DECEPTION

In an interview published in *The Times* just before she died Ivy Compton-Burnett said that she thought that there was no such thing as self-deception and that people generally knew what they were up to. My view is that she was wrong on the first point but that there is a sense in which she was right on the second. That is to say that while self-deception is a genuine enough phenomenon it need not be taken as implying ignorance on the part of the deceiver about his actions, beliefs, desires or whatever it is. To say that self-deception is a genuine phenomenon presupposes a certain assessment of a variety of human beings and it presupposes that certain empirical facts hold good about them. A philosopher can only use his judgment on these matters, but it is my belief that any philosophical treatment of self-deception must meet the phenomenon head on. Certain facts about a number of human beings make it plausible to describe what they are engaged in as self-deception. The philosopher's task is, given the plausibility of that description, to examine the question how, if at all, that description can be a possible one. If there is a contradiction in the notion of self-deception then the plausibility of this description of the phenomenon will be an illusion. Is there a contradiction of that kind involved in it? One suggestion to this effect is that if a person deceives himself he must know that he is doing so: he must therefore know the facts in question. On the other hand, the task of self-deception seems to involve the goal of making himself ignorant of those facts. How can he both know and not know the facts?

My answer to that question, as I have already hinted, is that the self-deceiver does not really make himself ignorant of what he knows,

194

and that the state of self-deception is not incompatible with knowing what one is up to and therefore with knowing the facts in question. The ignorance is in effect an as-it-were-ignorance. I do not wish to suggest by this that ignorance may not come about as a result of self-deception. By putting something out of his mind repeatedly a man may come as a result to forget that very thing. But the ignorance that thus comes about is an indirect and causal effect of what he does; it is not a constituent part of what he does. Indeed the idea that a man might directly make himself ignorant of something, as opposed to doing something that has ignorance as an indirect effect, does have an air of paradox about it. It might be suggested that the solution lies in the fact that self-deception does not involve the state of both knowing and not knowing the facts about oneself, but rather that of knowing facts about oneself while not knowing that one does. This however, does not get rid of all paradox at one fell swoop, since it seems to be the case that self-deception is, on some occasions at least, an intentional phenomenon, and that the self-deceiver for that reason and on those occasions deceives himself knowingly. (I add the qualification with respect to 'some occasions' because I do not wish to exclude the possibility of self-deception taking place unintentionally.) If that is so, he must after all surely know that he knows the facts in question about himself. And if he knows that he knows these facts, then *a fortiori* he knows the facts. If a man deceives himself, he does not make himself ignorant either of the facts about himself or of the fact that he knows these facts (at least not, as I have already indicated, directly).

If this is so, it may seem to follow that deceiving oneself is not a bit like deceiving others, and for that reason it may be suggested that 'self-deception' is a misnomer or at least misleading as a characterization of what goes on. Surely deceiving others does involve making or keeping them ignorant of certain facts. If that is so, there is an asymmetry between self-deception and other-deception. Is this a correct account of the situation? In fact, I do not think that other-deception is quite so clear cut as this suggestion makes out.[1] It is true that certain forms of deception of others may involve the intention or attempt to produce in them false beliefs or ignorance of the facts, but it is not at all obvious that this is universally so. A man may deceive his wife without meaning to keep her in ignorance of his relationships with other women, and whether or not she is ignorant he has still deceived her. It may be suggested that this is a very special kind of deception and that we ought not to draw any inferences from it. It is perfectly true that we cannot draw from it any inferences about what it is to be deceived in general. But we are not concerned with the nature of deception in general. It would be impossible to think of a man deceiving himself on a certain issue except in terms of more general attitudes that he has towards himself. (Moreover, though I shall not argue this here, it may be that a man's attitudes towards himself presuppose some conception of their significance for others.) That is to say that self-deception, as we typically understand it, cannot be construed on the parallel of those forms of deception in which we deceive someone by, for example, giving him by mistake erroneous information. Hence, it may seem reasonable to attempt to construe self-deception on the pattern of deception of others when this involves, as we might put it, being false to them.

To be false to another person involves a failure to conform to what is appropriate to the relationship that we have with them. This need not entail betraying them. In order to betray someone we need to do something more positive than failing to conform to whatever is appropriate to the relationship that exists between us. But if a man deceives his wife in the way that I have already mentioned he is certainly false to her whether or not he is betraying her, and in the way that I have just specified. What of being false to oneself? Polonius told Laertes that if he were true to himself he could not be false to any man. This could not be taken to mean quite generally that if he did not deceive himself he could not deceive others. Whether or not what Polonius said is necessarily to be taken as true, what he *meant* was presumably something fairly simple, such as that if Laertes did not pretend to be what he was not he would not treat others dishonestly. But pretending to be what one is not need by no means be a case of self-deception, and would not usually be this. Hence if to be false to oneself is taken to be the opposite of being true to oneself, it would seem that it need not entail self-deception, and that an understanding of the latter is not therefore to be found by a consideration of the former.

Another possible suggestion is that self-deception is closer to being dishonest with oneself and involves being false to oneself in *that* sense only. A man who deceives his wife may of course be quite honest with her about it, in one sense of those words. On the other hand, there is a sense of the words in which in certain circumstances he would not be honest with her. This would be the case when, although he is open and above board about what he is up to, he still claims that it makes no difference to their relationship, and in particular that it makes no difference to their marriage; and he goes on behaving as if it did make no difference. I think that in these circumstances it might well be feasible for someone else to say that he is not being honest with his wife. He is not, as it were, treating her honestly. Could self-deception be construed in any analogous way? Normally, perhaps, when we speak of a man not being honest with himself, we mean that he does not admit to himself how he stands with regard to a certain situation. That would constitute not being honest with himself in a way that a man is not honest to his wife if he is not open and above board with her. But is a situation possible in which a man admits to himself how he stands on a given issue but behaves as if it made no difference and perhaps claims that it makes no such difference? I think that such a situation *is* possible and that it may in a way be typical of some forms of self-deception.

I say 'some forms of self-deception' to emphasize the point that I do not think that self-deception always follows the same pattern. It is of course possible for a man to be dishonest with himself in the sense that he is not open and above board with himself. He may refuse to believe what is staring him in the face and insist on construing it or the situation in which he finds himself in misleading terms. We should certainly say of such a person that he is not honest with himself, if there is some evidence that he *is* refusing to believe the facts and intentionally misconstruing them. And we might well say that if he refuses to see how things are and insists on construing them in this way he is deceiving himself. I take it that this picture of the situation is close to the one offered by Fingarette in his book *Self-deception*, when he describes the self-deceiver as not spelling out his engagement in the world. According to this account the self-deceiver does not make explicit to himself how he stands. I suppose that it might equally be the case that he spells out the engagement wrongly. To refuse to face the facts might be described as not spelling out one's engagement; to misconstrue them is to spell them out wrongly. But Fingarette offers this as a new model of consciousness, and it seems to fall short of this in at least two ways. First, and this is a point to which I shall return, it seems to me less a new model of consciousness in general than an account of one way in which a conscious being may deal with practical situations; it is none the less necessary to say something about what it is for a conscious being to be conscious of something. Second, even construed as an account of how a conscious being may deal with certain practical situations it seems to me too limited in scope. That is why I wish to consider also that form of being dishonest with oneself in which there is apparently no question of a man not spelling out his engagement in the world, or even perhaps of his misconstruing it in any straightforward sense.

A man who is unfaithful to his wife and who is quite honest about it in the sense that he tells her the truth may, I have said, be dishonest with her in a different and perhaps more fundamental sense. This may be so if he claims that, and behaves as if, his conduct in this respect has no particular bearing upon and can be isolated from other aspects of their relationship. (It should be noted that I say that it may be so, not that it will be so, but I believe that it will usually be so, and that suppositions to the contrary rest upon misconceptions about what is and can be involved in a human relationship.) Behaviour of this kind need not always involve self-deception; it may be a product of ignorance, false belief or simple lack of thought. But sometimes it may involve self-deception and in these cases it is feasible to say that he is not being honest with his wife because he is not being honest with himself. But however it happens, the crucial point is that even if there is a sense in which he is quite open and above board about what he is doing, that openness may constitute a form of dishonesty if it involves a misconstrual of what is appropriate either to that relationship between two human beings or to the relationship to that particular human being, especially given the reciprocity that such a relationship entails. The apparent openness and rationality of it all may, for example, involve a blocking of natural human feelings on which human relationships depend. I have already said that this may involve self-deception on his part; hence I have already begun to indicate how the same sort of thing may be true of a man in relation to himself, as well as in relation to others. Indeed it may be true that self-deception of this kind arises specially in contexts of spurious relations with others, and if this is so then here at least it is true that there is an intimate connection between self-deception and deception of others.

What I have been leading up to is the idea that one form of self-deception, one form of being dishonest with oneself, may involve not just a failure to spell out correctly one's engagement with the world, as Fingarette suggests, but something that is in a way the reverse of this. The falsity lies in what is to all appearances a super-honesty with oneself; it is false because it involves employing 'rationality' and 'sweet reasonableness' where and in a way in which these may, in a sense, be inappropriate. If I may continue to use Fingarette's terms, the person concerned may be so intent upon spelling out his engagement with the world that he ceases to be truly so engaged. The way in which I put this may seem to have some superficial resemblance to the hypothetical case of the young woman which Sartre discusses in chapter 2 of Part I of *Being and Nothingness*, but the kind of case that I have in mind is in fact the inverse of his. His woman, he says, leaves her hand in that of the man with whom she has consented to go out because 'it happens by chance that she is at this moment all intellect'. This is a case of bad faith because in her intellectual involvement she becomes split off from her physical involvement. If I were to adapt this case to the one that I have in mind it would involve her being only too conscious of her physical involvement, but that physical involvement would be rationalized and so in a way isolated from her real feelings and attitudes. I do not mean by this to suggest that Sartre's case is not a genuine one also (though, like other examples that Sartre uses in other contexts, it seems to me too under-described to enable one to draw any general conclusions from it with any certainty). It is simply that I do not believe that self-deception is always of one pattern and can be reduced to the kind of formula that Fingarette invokes. And Fingarette claims in the introduction to his book that his account and that of Sartre have a 'remarkable parallelism'.

Whether self-deception comes about through not being honest with oneself or by being, in a sense, too honest with oneself, the self-deceiver seems to employ a curious kind of rationality. It is the same kind of rationality that is involved in what Freud calls 'mechanisms of defence', to the extent that these can be construed as devices that the person uses to protect himself from his true nature. Perhaps the clearest and most overt account along these lines which is to be found in Freud is that provided in *Inhibitions, Symptoms and Anxiety* and it is noteworthy that he there refers to 'isolation' as one device of this kind. Thus when I spoke earlier of a person's isolating his or her physical involvement from his or her true feelings I had something of what Freud has to say in mind, though I do not pretend that what I have said fits what he has to say in its entirety. Nevertheless it remains true that to employ devices of this kind, whatever their exact nature, is to employ a curious kind of rationality. Of course, when the devices used in this way have drastic effects upon the person's life, as is the case frequently enough in the neurotic, there is good reason to refuse to speak of the behaviour in question as rational. The rationality involved in the employment of such devices is, to say the least, a perverted rationality. (We might sometimes say that it is only too rational.) Hence when the behaviour is put in its proper context and seen as a whole, it must become apparent that it would be quite wrong to speak of it as rational without qualification. Yet when taken in isolation from other aspects of life there is certainly something very intelligent, even clever, about it; the behaviour in question is certainly such that only a rational being could engage in it, and it would be quite wrong to speak of it as irrational, since this term would suggest that there is nothing calculating about it. The truth is that it is quite possible to use rational means towards irrational purposes, though even this is too simple a way of putting what is often the case with the neurotic.

However one is to construe this blend of rationality and irrationality, it is important to recognize that it exists. Otherwise there will be difficulty in accepting the possibility that a man may know something well enough but refuse to accept it; and, moreover, that, at least to all appearances, he may take every step to ensure that he does not accept it. Another reason for stressing this point is that it affects further diagnoses of the self-deceiver's state of mind. Fingarette, for example, maintains rightly enough that to be rid of self-deception one has not only to acknowledge one's engagements but also accept responsibility for them, but he seems to think that what makes this difficult for the self-deceiver is a lack of courage. Thus he says (p. 143), 'What the self-deceiver specifically lacks is not concern or integrity but some combination of courage and a way of seeing how to approach his dilemma without probable disaster to himself.' Insight is certainly one strand in the recipe, and this has always been recognized by psychoanalysis – but only as *one* strand. It is not so clear that another strand is always courage, for it is not clear that the motivation of the self-deceiver *must* be fear or something of that kind. While being honest with oneself may indeed require effort or determination, it is another matter to maintain that it always requires courage. Self-deception may sometimes come about, for example, not through fear of a dilemma, but as the result of taking the easy way out of a difficulty. It is possible to allow oneself to believe something because it is too much of an effort to correct oneself. Self-deception is then like the deception of others which results from simply allowing them to believe things which they are inclined to believe any way. A person who in this way becomes entrenched in a certain attitude as a result of allowing himself to persist in it may then adopt various 'rational' procedures to achieve this irrational end, because any other policy would require more effort. Such a person may require an incentive towards the appropriate effort, but a jolt may sometimes be more appropriate to this end than the instilling of courage.

Nevertheless, it is certainly true that to be rid of self-deception one needs more than self-knowledge, even if the self-knowledge in question is itself more than just an explicit awareness of one's immediate actions — something, that, as I tried to indicate earlier in discussing the idea of being dishonest with oneself, could be compatible with self-deception on a grander scale. Indeed, as I suggested at the beginning of the paper, I think that there is a sense in which the self-deceiver does have self-knowledge, and this is a suggestion to which I must now return. The opposite of self-knowledge is ignorance of self and self-deception is a more subtle phenomenon than that. I think that the situation with regard to self-deception in general is like that which holds good more specifically with regard to psychoanalytic phenomena. (Nor is this surprising since the notion of repression, which, as Freud said, is central to psychoanalytic theory, is very close to that of self-deception. Freud defined repression as putting something out of consciousness, and this is essentially what self-deception is.) Freud's discovery that the symptoms of hysteria — paralyses, anaesthesias, etc. — tended to extend over those parts of the body which conformed to popular conceptions of anatomy rather than the true anatomical facts, led him to the view that hysterical symptoms had some connection with ideas or beliefs in the patient's mind. My view is that the only way in which such a connection can be made intelligible is by a reassessment of the symptoms. One way of putting this is to say that the symptoms must be construed less as something that happens to a man, as would be the natural characterization of, say, paralysis, than as something that he does. A belief is a quite intelligible component in the explanation of an action. But the only possible action that seems to be pertinent in this context is the man's general course of behaviour, which can itself be described in terms of the belief. Thus instead of characterizing the symptoms as those of, say, paralysis, a better account might be to characterize them as consisting of a form of behaviour to be described as 'acting in the belief that one is paralysed'. If there are grounds for saying that the person who behaves in this fashion knows that he is not really paralysed (and such grounds might be available from various sources and in various ways), then there are clear grounds for saying that he is self-deceived — a point which serves once again to reinforce the view that there is a connection between psychoanalytic phenomena and self-deception. Such a view is possible only on the premise that the person concerned does know about himself.

It might be said that we have no real grounds for accepting this premise but that it is possible to admit nevertheless that the phenomena are what I have said they are. That is to say that it may be possible to construe an apparent paralysis in a man as his acting in the belief that he is paralysed. The person in question may simply want to believe this and he may be sufficiently motivated to come to accept it; there need be no question of his knowing this in turn. On this account there would be motivated belief only, and why should not self-deception in general be construed in this way? The only answer that I can give is that it would not in that case *be* self-deception, or, if there is a danger of this reducing itself to a point of terminology, that there are phenomena, properly describable as self-deception, which are more complex than this. As I said at the beginning of this paper, a philosopher must on an issue of this kind use his judgment. Where there is an overt symptom or apparent symptom it may be possible to get behind it, so to speak; the behaviour may be such that it is possible to show it to be inconsistent. An apparently blind man may, for example, fail to be blind in certain contexts or with respect to certain people or things. Where there are no such overt symptoms it may be much more difficult to show that there is more than motivated belief — something that is quite compatible with a real and genuine ignorance of the facts. Only the general pattern of a man's behaviour could show this. Nevertheless there do seem to be occasions on which we have reason to say, 'If he believes that he is deceiving himself' and on which we mean more than that he just wants to believe it, let alone that he is just mistaken. These are the occasions on which we can say with some justification that he *must* know the facts; it is impossible for him to avoid knowing them.

But the fact that a man cannot avoid knowing certain things does not entail that he is aware or conscious of them or of knowing them. It is this distinction between knowledge and consciousness that makes possible an intelligible account of self-deception in a full-blooded sense which involves no reduction to a state of motivated belief only. Sartre also makes a distinction between knowledge and consciousness, but it is one that works in the opposite direction from the distinction as I should make it. He says (*Being and Nothingness*, trans. Barnes p. lii): 'Not all consciousness is knowledge (there are states of affective consciousness, for example), but all knowing consciousness can be knowledge only of its object. However, the necessary and sufficient condition for a knowing consciousness to be knowledge of its object, is that it be consciousness of itself as being that knowledge.' And he goes on to say that if this were not so 'it would be a consciousness ignorant of itself, an unconscious – which is absurd.' I find it difficult to come to a firm conclusion on the first part of this statement – on whether all consciousness is knowledge; it depends so much on how one is using the terms involved. Certainly Sartre seems to adopt an over-intellectual and restricted concept of knowledge; I do not myself see why an emotional awareness should not be spoken of as knowledge. But in the present connection, when we are concerned with self-deception, it seems hardly deniable that if a man is conscious of certain facts about himself he must know them. Hence whatever the status of a claim for a general implication between consciousness and knowledge, the implication seems to hold where it matters, in this case. It would still not follow, however, that there could be knowledge without consciousness, and with this we must turn to the second part of Sartre's statement.

Sartre's opposition to the notion of the unconscious is notorious. Yet it is not clear what is its basis other than something that is implicit in the quotation that I have given – that the idea of an unconscious consciousness is an absurdity, presumably because it involves a contradiction. So it does, when it is put in those terms. But why put it in those terms, rather than by asking whether a conscious being, i.e., a being capable of being conscious, can be unconscious? The reasons for Sartre's having put the matter in these terms doubtless lie in his general metaphysics, in his division of the universe between the two categories of the '*pour soi*' and the '*en soi*'. There just *is* an exhaustive distinction between beings which are conscious and beings that are not, between conscious and non-conscious things. If this is not how it is for Sartre, it is difficult to see what *is* the justification for his attitude towards the possibility of unconscious knowledge. Indeed on his terms a person's becoming unconscious must be something of a betrayal of his nature.

There are many common or garden examples of a person knowing something without being conscious of this, without indeed even knowing this. (See, e.g., A.P. Griffiths's introduction to his collection of papers on *Knowledge and Belief.* Even discounting the cases in which the knowledge is dispositional and where not being conscious of the knowledge means merely not being conscious of it on a given occasion there remains a residue of cases which are to the point.) Not all of these cases will count as self-deception, since often when we speak of someone knowing something but add that he is not conscious of knowing it, the failure to be conscious of it may not be in any relevant sense his responsibility. (Consider, for example, the case of someone investigating something, when an observer can say that he has clearly got the answer though the person concerned is not at all aware of this being so. This, I take it, was the state of mind of the boy in Plato's *Meno* after 'solving' the geometrical problem. Plato describes him as being in a dreamlike state.) For self-deception it is required that the person concerned make himself unconscious of what he knows and it is in this sense that he is responsible for the fact that he is not conscious of knowing this thing. As I have already suggested, it would be wrong to take this as meaning simply that he does not make explicit to himself what he knows, although I have no doubt that this is one way in which self-deception may come about. That is why I would reject Fingarette's notion of spelling out one's engagement as a model of consciousness, while accepting it as one, but only one, account of how self-deception may come about. Indeed the idea of a 'model of consciousness' is in many ways an odd one. I take it that what is required here is some illuminating account of what consciousness is, a philosophical elucidation of the concept. To speak of a model suggests that what is being provided is a reduction of the concept to something else, or at least that we are being asked to consider the concept in terms of an analogy with some other concept. I do not wish to suggest that it is philosophically unhelpful in all cases to look for such an analogy. Fingarette suggests that we have been hampered by concentrating on a perception-model for consciousness; that is to say that we have been hampered by concentrating on the analogy between perception in particular and consciousness in general. I do not really believe that this is true. At the same time it is not easy to see what a philosophical elucidation of being conscious of something could consist in, although there may be much to say about the differences between possible objects of consciousness and what is presupposed in consciousness of them. (To ask what consciousness is has some affinity to asking what time is, and the well-known difficulties that St Augustine expressed over the latter question apply equally well to the former.)

However this may be, the self-deceiver has to make himself unconscious or unaware of what he really knows. How is *this* possible? Such a question may be taken in different ways. It may be taken as a transcendental question, akin to Kant's 'How are *a priori* synthetic judgments possible?' To answer it, it is necessary to undertake an investigation into the concept, showing under what conditions it can have a possible application, and that nothing in the way of an incoherence in it rules out such a possible application. Another way of taking the question, and one which is not entirely without a bearing on the former way of taking it, is as asking for some account of the forms which the application of the concept might take. How, that is, can a man set out to make himself unconscious of what he knows? What should his procedure, strategy or policy be in this connection? If there are ways in which a man may intentionally deceive himself, I take it that there is no difficulty in the idea that he may do so unintentionally. Indeed some may find this latter an easier idea to accept, since it seems reasonably clear that a man may unintentionally or by mistake put himself in a position where he is not able to have a clear view of the facts, and in that sense deceive himself without meaning to do so. For such a man need not know that his view of the facts is wrong, while the man who does the same thing intentionally must surely know at least of the possibility that his view of the facts is wrong.

If, then, the question 'How is self-deception possible?' is taken in its transcendental sense, it should be said first that I have tried to make it clear that the concept is not an incoherent one, and that there is, as far as that goes, no obstacle to its possible application. For it is not true of the self-deceiver that he knows and does not know the same thing in the same respect; he knows certain facts but has made himself unconscious of this in turn. For this to be possible he has to be a conscious being with intentions. Such a being can concentrate his attention on certain things to the exclusion of others, he can take a certain view of things to the extent that he becomes convinced of it and by it, he can make certain things explicit to himself rather than other things, and so on. To point to these techniques is, however, to have concern with our question in its other, more practical sense. I said that what is involved in this sense of the question is not without its bearing on the other sense of it, and this now becomes clear. For the possibility of a human being having the capacity for self-deception depends on his having intentions and an awareness of what he is doing complex enough to make possible the application of techniques such as I have referred to. The human mind is not capable of giving everything equal attention, and people may be inclined for reasons which may differ from case to case to accept what is most close at hand and most nearly the object of attention. It is indeed the fact that people are not purely rational that makes it possible to apply rational or quasi-rational techniques to irrational ends. But though the techniques in question may depend on the kind of general factors that I have mentioned, they may differ greatly in detail, and some people may be better at them, or at some of them, than others. That is why I emphasized earlier the differences between different forms of self-deception. Moreover awareness of what is at issue may be a matter of degree both in clarity and detail, so that a man may at differing stages have different degrees of awareness of the fact that he is deceiving himself. If there comes a time when we are inclined to say that he is totally self-deceived and imply by this that he is totally unaware of the truth about himself, it must be remembered that he has probably passed through stages involving differing degrees of partial awareness. Nevertheless I am inclined to think that as long as we speak of his being self-deceived at all, as opposed to saying that he is ignorant about himself, we imply that he really knows the truth, even if he will not allow himself to be aware of the fact. And he may prevent that awareness, as I have indicated, as easily by being too aware of part of the truth as by being inattentive to the truth in general.

We are naturally inclined to think that self-deception is a bad thing, and the last question that I wish to raise (though I can hardly discuss it in anything like the proper detail) is whether we are always right to do so. I think that our attitude to this question is likely to be determined by our conception of what a human being is and therefore to some extent by our moral point of view. A possibly extreme point of view, and one obviously influenced by religious considerations and by a conception of man in tune with these, is that represented by Kierkegaard's strictures on double-mindedness in *Purity of Heart*, and his allied claim that to will the good is to will one thing. A whole host of philosophers from Socrates onwards have maintained that a divided self is in one sense or another wrong. Apart from religious considerations it is not easy to see what could be the foundation for this belief. It cannot, for example, be maintained that to deceive oneself is necessarily and of itself to betray oneself, any more than, as I indicated earlier, deceiving others always involves betraying them. Moreover, there is a sense in which self-deception may sometimes be the right policy, in that it may be the only way of maintaining a viable human life. If to err is human, the same is true of self-deception, especially given the complexities of social life and the complexities of interpersonal relationships. It would be absurd to recommend as a moral *policy* something that does not do justice to what human beings are, even if there may sometimes be point in setting out the same thing as a moral *ideal*. But it is absurd to recommend even as a moral ideal something that makes no sense in application to human beings. Many philosophers have taken as such an ideal the idea of a purely rational being. I do not think that I can make sense of this notion at all, but it certainly has no sense in application to human beings. Nevertheless, if we tend to think that 'double-mindedness' is *necessarily* a bad thing, and not merely that is bad in some contexts and on some occasions, it is, I believe, because we have some such idea at the back of our minds. In the context of self-deception it is as if we suppose that respect for and recognition of the truth about ourselves must be paramount and above all other considerations. But there is clearly no reason why this should be necessarily so. And to suppose that it must be so may have its evil consequences. Too vivid a consciousness of oneself, too much of a concern for the truth about ourselves, may lead to the inhibition of the feelings on which personal relationships thrive. As I said earlier in Fingarette's terms, too much of a preoccupation with the nature of our engagement may lead to a failure to be properly engaged. Thus while I entirely accept the position that self-deception is sometimes a bad thing, I cannot accept that it must necessarily be so. Or am I grossly self-deceived?

## NOTES

1 I owe this point and the example that follows to Mr J.M. Cohen.

# 13

# PERSON-PERCEPTION AND OUR UNDERSTANDING OF OTHERS

## I

The term 'person-perception' which has come to be used to mark off one province of social psychology must seem an odd one to the layman. Why should people, *qua* objects of perception, raise any questions that do not arise in considering perception in general? Some of the problems here arise from the familiar internal/external, or private/public distinction — from the fact that not all or even much that is the case about a person may show on his face or even be evident in his external behaviour. Much of the work discussed in the psychological literature about the recognition of emotions or attitudes in people on the basis of such things as facial expressions bears this out. But to put this kind of thing at the centre of any investigation of what it is to know or understand another person seems a strangely intellectual, not to say artificial, way of construing the situation. We may in our everyday lives have to form judgments about other people on this kind of basis to some considerable extent, but we should surely admit that when we do so we are not in the position of knowing much about the person concerned. If we have to have resort to such 'external judgments' it is because we really do not know the person concerned. If we did, those very externals might take on quite another appearance, we might be able to see things in a quite different light. For this reason it seems to me a useful prolegomenon for any attempt to investigate person-perception so-called to inquire also into what is entailed by knowing a person.

What I have been saying in effect could be put by saying that the cases in which we derive knowledge or understanding of another person through what we see of external expressions, whatever form these may take, are to be viewed as degenerate cases and not the basis for a general understanding of our knowledge and understanding of other people. They are degenerate in the sense that if those expressions make sense to us they normally do so on the basis of further knowledge of what a person is; the expressions are not to be taken as data on which all the rest of our knowledge of people is built. Nor is that knowledge to be construed as the response to the stimuli provided by those external expressions. If the external manifestations were such data we should in effect be confronted with the classical 'other minds problem', so well known to philosophers, but in a way that makes the problem impossible to solve. For the data, construed as data on which knowledge of the other person is to be constructed, would be totally inadequate for the purpose. In order to construe a facial expression as one, say, of joy one would have to know first that the expression was one manifested by something that could indeed manifest joy — by, that is, a person. And that fact could not be derived from the data themselves. The same applies even to the construal of bodily movements as actions; for them to be taken as actions we have already to know that we have before us a person.[1] (The inadequacies of the so-called argument from analogy here are well known to philosophers; the argument fails for similar reasons. To use an analogy between ourselves and others we have to presuppose that those others are fitting recipients for the analogy — and that is the whole point at issue.) Thus a classical empiricism that tries to derive knowledge of other persons from perceptible data must fail, and short of an appeal to innate ideas of persons (a suggestion which certain remarks of Chomsky in *Language and Mind* (1968) might lead one to assume he would espouse) one must seek another approach.

But all this is, as I hinted earlier, a curiously intellectual approach to the problem, a curiously intellectual attitude to what is involved in interpersonal understanding. Let me for a moment try to approach the matter as it were from the other end. If I am asked to try to understand another person with whom I am confronted the best way to start may well be for me to attempt to put myself in his place. This requires imagination, so that some people are better at it than others; but in any case it may be that in many situations there is little enough on which imagination may get a purchase. What of course may help it to get a purchase is knowledge about the person concerned. And putting oneself in his place is not necessarily a sufficient condition of getting the understanding in question, however much it may be necessary. What I have in mind here is the point that people do not always see themselves aright, so that even if we manage to get ourselves into the position of seeing things and them as they do we may not have got all the way. That is why I would not wish to repudiate in any way that form of knowledge of people which may be obtained by general inquiries into, for example, the motives that people have in certain sorts of circumstances. There is plenty of knowledge of people, their motives, their behaviour in certain sorts of circumstances, and so on, to be obtained by purely empirical inquiries. That is not in the least in dispute; nor is the fact that such knowledge may be of considerable use in the attempt of one individual to understand another. The question is simply *how* it gets a use, *how* the general knowledge of people gains an application to one man's understanding of another. It may be that, in some instances at least, this kind of knowledge may be another necessary condition of getting such understanding. But this does not entail that putting oneself in the other person's place may not be just as necessary. It is just that in some cases, if not all, I shall not be able to put myself in the other person's place without some knowledge at least of this other kind. Alternatively or in addition, my putting myself in his place may be insufficient for a true understanding of him; where I fail may be just where he fails in understanding himself. This may be due to an inability to get a proper perspective, and this in turn may be due to my not knowing sufficient facts about him, just as he may know insufficient facts about himself. Failure to understand oneself may come about in many ways and for many reasons; another may acquire a better understanding because he knows more about me than I do or because he has a better view of the facts, a better perspective than I do. Hence, by putting myself in another's place in the imagination I may or may not obtain a better understanding of him. I wish to make no claim that such a procedure is sufficient, merely that it is necessary. If it fails it may be because of my ignorance of crucial facts, which may be of differing kinds. But it *may* be because I do not really know him, and for that reason cannot really put myself in his place.

There is a very subtle difference if any between really knowing someone and really understanding them. Some people might wish to claim that we cannot ever really know our fellows, and this point of view has been reflected in certain metaphysical theories that claim to present a view of the nature of man and his place in the world. I have in mind here, for example, the views of Sartre, in whose philosophy it is something of a necessary truth that one man cannot really know another. I do not want to go into this in detail here. It is however worth noting that the origins of Sartre's point of view are Cartesian in the sense that there is presupposed a radical division between consciousness and what is bodily. Hence one is confronted with the impossibility of getting to another's consciousness through his body. This is another version of what I have already described as a curiously intellectual approach to the issues. Is the attempt to understand or know another adequately represented as an attempt to get at something between which and us there is necessarily a veil? Whatever the metaphysical basis of Sartre's view, the picture that results surely fails to fit the facts. If we fail to know or understand another person it is because the task is just too difficult, not because it was doomed to failure from the start through some kind of metaphysical necessity. Some people are no doubt inscrutable, and some people are no doubt impercipient, but whether they are or are not is a matter of empirical fact, not a necessity. There are certain philosophical models of human beings which, as we have begun to see in the Sartre case, turn this into a necessity. The Cartesian model is very much with us in one form or another, and the assumption that a person is fundamentally a centre of consciousness has its hold on many approaches to a variety of psychological issues. Certainly it generates the over-intellectual attitude to our present problem which I have already referred to, since it promotes the idea that in getting to know a person we have, as it were, to penetrate beyond the veil constituted by a person's bodily expressions to the inside him; or it promotes instead by reaction the idea that there is nothing but the outer expressions, the bodily movements, or whatever. And it is on one or other of these models that person-perception, so-called, tends often to be construed. But if, as I have suggested already, we are to have person-perception at all, we have to have some prior understanding of what a person is. If we are to understand person-perception therefore we must be clear about that understanding, an understanding which must surely be based upon what we might call natural reactions of persons to persons.

One way of doing this is to investigate the question what is conceptually necessary for a person's standing to us as an object of knowledge and therefore of understanding. I say '*therefore* of understanding' because the sense of 'object of knowledge' that is in question is one which implies the 'really knowing' that I have already mentioned. There is of course a sense of 'know' in which to know something is merely to recognize it or to be able to recognize it. Thus we might say 'You know Edward, well the girl I was talking about is the one sitting next to him'; and we may imply little else when we talk on occasion of knowing certain people. But we may accept such a usage without being concerned with it in the present context. For we might equally go on to say that we do not really know the people concerned; and we could not be said to know someone really if we did not have any understanding of him. If there are degrees possible in our knowledge of people there are equally degrees of understanding, though whether the two are correlated is another matter. It is possible and legitimate for us to say 'I know him very well, but I don't really understand him; indeed I doubt if I understand him at all.' If the last is probably an exaggeration it may not be totally false. Yet the conditions necessary for knowledge of a person in the sense in question overlap, if they are not identical with, those necessary for understanding that person. I wish at all events to approach the matter from the side of knowledge, and on the broadest front, by considering what is necessary for something to be an object of knowledge in general; in the course of my inquiry certain differences between knowledge of persons and knowledge of other sorts of thing will emerge. I wish to consider certain principles, viewed as conceptual principles, statements of what is necessary to something's being properly considered as an object of knowledge. I shall mention four principles in all, the first three of which I consider valid; the fourth, which is, I think, invalid, I mention because some things that I have to say may tempt people to think that it too is valid.

## II

(a) The first principle (which I shall call Principle A) is that *a necessary, but not sufficient, condition of our being said to know X is that we should understand what kind of relations can exist between X and ourselves.* This principle is by far the least problematic, except that in relation to a large number of possible objects of knowledge it hardly seems to arise and may therefore seem otiose. What I mean is this. The principle has its origin in what seems quite obvious — that in order to be said to know something we must at least understand what it is for something to be the thing in question, we must have the concept of that thing, or, if it is in one sense or another a complex object, the concepts involved in understanding what it is for it to be what it is. If I am to be said to know my car I have to understand what it is for something to be a car, and this will comprise a complex piece of understanding, which will involve knowing certain facts about cars, knowledge which will presuppose the understanding of other concepts and so I am not concerned here to set out the relationships between knowledge and concepts in detail, but that there is such a relationship is clear. Given this, the question that Principle A raises is whether, if knowing something involves having the concept or concepts in question should involve in turn an understanding of the relations that can exist between that thing and ourselves (and *a fortiori* the relations that cannot exist). I suggest that the answer to this question is 'Yes'. What this answer implies is that we cannot have a proper conception of a possible object of knowledge unless we understand what relations can and cannot exist between it and ourselves.

It might be asked why a conception of a thing should necessarily involve a conception of its possible relations with us. Whatever may be said about that issue it is not to the point in the present context, since we are concerned only with the conception of a thing as a possible object of knowledge. How could something be a possible object of knowledge if it stood in no relations to us? Indeed it seems reasonable that its status as an object of knowledge turns on what these relations may be or perhaps even are. The relations that can exist between myself and another person are quite different from those that can exist between me and physical things. The relevant considerations are the following. The relationship that exists between me and another person can be in a very real sense reciprocal; the relationship that I have with him may have a reflection in that which he has to me. It does not of course have to be so; there are such things as one-way relationships, though even here reciprocity must be possible. But nothing of this kind can be true of relationships to physical bodies except via the relationship of my body to them; there may be reciprocal spatial relationships, and causal relationships, between my body and other bodies, but does this amount to a relationship between me and other bodies? If it does, it is in some way a derivative sense. Being a person involves being more than just a physical thing; it involves having all that philosophers have come to speak of, rightly or wrongly, under the heading of 'privacy'. For present purposes, I think that the important thing to stress is the feelings that one person can have with another, since it is on these feelings that personal relationships are based, and these can clearly be reciprocal. Moreover, I suggest that these, in one way or another, provide the basis for moral relationships that can exist between one person and another, but not between a person and a thing as long as the latter is taken in independence of persons. To understand what a person is, therefore, involves understanding what sorts of relationships can exist between mere things or between persons and things.

One might ask how much of this applies equally to animals. It is not to be doubted that relations of some sort can exist between me and my dog; the dog can exert influences of one sort or another on me, and I on him, apart from the obvious spatial relations that exist between us. The question is whether these influences amount merely to the causal relations that can exist between material things and my body. I can have feelings towards my dog; can these be reciprocated or is the relationship necessarily one way only? To put the matter in another way, can animals share our form of life? Some philosophers would rule out of court an affirmative answer to this question, or say that to attribute to animals anything like the kind of things that we attribute to humans is, as it were, a courtesy attribution only (this presumably on the grounds that the ability of human beings to use language creates a great gulf between them and other creatures). My own view is that such a view flies in the face of the facts. Something like rudimentary personal relationships *can* exist between humans and certain animals. And it may be that to the extent that we are willing to contemplate such a possibility with an animal to that extent are we willing to consider it as a conscious being with states of mind in some way akin to ours. I say 'akin', since I do not of course wish to claim that animals can share all our states of mind. Yet when Wittgenstein (1953) asks the question whether an animal can hope, I think that the answer is 'Yes'. (Much of course depends on what the hope is; a quite different answer would be pertinent with regard to a hope for something 'the day after tomorrow' since this would imply complex temporal concepts presupposing ways of distinguishing temporal intervals, like a day.) In sum, I suggest that some animals can share our form of life in part, and that this makes them, as far as this goes, possible objects of knowledge in something like the sense in which other human beings are. (I should perhaps say finally on this matter, that this does not merely apply to those animals which we call domestic. Something like an embryo personal relationships can exist between a human and a wild animal, and in saying this I do not have in mind *Born Free* or anything of that kind. My point is that personal relationships are not based merely on feelings of, say, affection or respect, feelings that might be thought to exist in some rudimentary way between ourselves and domestic animals. Hatred is just as possible a foundation for a personal relationship, and it may be in some cases the only appropriate foundation. However that may be, an encounter between a human being and an animal which is in effect a moment of pure hatred can be construed as a personal encounter.)

What follows from all this is that knowing a human being, and in some cases an animal, may be a quite different matter from knowing a merely material object, to the extent that it is intelligible to speak of knowing merely material objects. To know a person (and an animal to the extent that an animal can have relations to us akin to those which we have to people) presupposes at least that we have a conception of what kind of relations can exist between us and him; if we have no conception of this we should not be in the position to have knowledge of him. But I have said very little so far of the relations in which we can stand to merely material objects of knowledge. The truth is, I take it, that there are many material objects in respect of which it would be very odd to say that we do or can know them. Is there any sense in which we might be said to know, for example, a pebble on the beach? I suppose that if we were on holiday somewhere and went regularly to a certain part of the beach we might be struck by the appearance of a certain pebble. On seeing it and recognizing it on the nth time we might say, 'I know that pebble.' Such a remark would be an expression of recognition of the familiar, but perhaps not just this; the pebble has also become an old friend, so to speak. The background story that I have provided gives sense to the remark 'I know that pebble', and a similar story might be given for remarks in the second and third persons. The story might suggest that knowing a thing is a kind of pseudo-case of knowing a person — that to know a thing we have to conceive it as capable of standing to us in ways which are reminiscent of personal relations. I do not think that this would be a correct conclusion. I do not in this wish to deny that people do sometimes treat things in ways which are akin to that in which they might treat people; the things are to them 'old friends' or even 'old enemies'. A gardener, for example, might treat a tree or a weed in this fashion, and if we say of him 'He knows that tree well' it might be this kind of thing that we have in mind. This applies particularly when the objects of knowledge have, as it were or indeed in truth, a life of their own. In that same sense I might know my car very well, and in a way that the garage mechanic does not know it; for he may not know what it is like to live with it.

Yet I may know things which do not have a life of their own in this way, e.g. my desk or my house. Yet these again are things that figure in my life; they are part of my life in a way that any old pebble on the beach is not, and they can for that reason stand as objects of knowledge in a way that the pebble never can unless, of course, it is made to do so for a special reason. So perhaps while it is not true that for a thing to be an object of knowledge it must be capable of standing in quasi-personal relations with us, it may yet be true that it must be capable of playing a part in our life in some way. There is thus an important sense in which for something to be an object of knowledge it must be capable of standing in relations to us, even if not personal or what I have called quasi-personal relations. And by the latter I mean the relations that things may have to us when we treat them as having a life of their own, so that we can view them as, say, old friends or old enemies. But of course to treat things in this way is not to treat them as they actually are, and one who insists on treating a material thing as a kind of person in all circumstances does not have a proper conception of that thing, whatever else may be said about him. Thus it would seem that the relations in which a thing can stand to us do enter into a conception of that thing, and a person does not have an adequate conception of a thing if he does not know what relations it can have with him. Thus he would not have an adequate conception of a material thing if he did not know that while he can in certain circumstances treat it as a person, he cannot without absurdity do so in all circumstances. Similarly, he would not have an adequate conception of a person, if he did not know that he cannot without absurdity always treat people as things.

It might be thought that I ought to have said something stronger here; that is, that a person would not have an adequate conception of a person if he did not know that he can *never* treat people as things, in the sense that it is morally inappropriate that he should do so. It might also be said that when I have in this context spoken of what a person can and cannot do in this connection I have really meant that it is appropriate and inappropriate *in this sense* that he should do. I do not think that this is correct, but it is well that I should go into this matter, since this is the first occasion in my discussion in which there has been reference to the notion of appropriateness, which figures to a considerable extent in my remaining principles. It would, I think, be correct to say that someone does not have an adequate conception of a person if he does not know that it is inappropriate to treat people in all circumstances as things. But to say this is to say simply that if he did do this his behaviour would not match his putative understanding. Such a person might still treat some people as things and the question whether this would be morally appropriate is a quite separate question. My question is concerned with how far he could go along these lines before we should say that his behaviour was not just morally wrong but crazy in the sense that he had no understanding of what he was up to. The point is that if a man is to have an adequate conception of, say, persons that conception must be reflected in his behaviour towards people in an adequate way. What will count as adequate it is impossible to lay down with any definiteness, but to speak of what it is appropriate that he should do is to speak of ways of behaving which are proper expressions of an adequate conception of a person; and whatever counts as appropriate it is certainly inappropriate to treat people as things in all circumstances. Furthermore, if a man is to act out of the conception in question and not merely conform to it he must know the sort of thing that is appropriate and inappropriate in this sense. This is to say that if he treats people as things in all circumstances, and in doing so acts out of his conception of a person it may be inferred that he does not know that it is inappropriate for one with a proper conception of a person so to behave and that he does not have such a proper conception. The inappropriateness of treating people in all circumstances as things that I have in mind, therefore, is an inappropriateness to one who has a proper conception of a person. Part of that proper conception must of course be the recognition that people are moral agents and therefore capable of standing in moral relationships with ourselves. But that does not entail that we must *never* treat people as things.

With this said, we can, I think, turn to my second principle, Principle B, which will in consequence of all this discussion of Principle A require a less extended treatment. I hope that I have shown that the claim that a necessary condition of our being said to know something is that we should understand what kind of relations can exist between ourselves and it can be justified in a way that leaves it fairly unproblematical. I hope that I have also shown the special relevance this has to knowledge of persons.

(b) Principle B states that *a necessary condition of being said to know X is that the one should know through experience what it is to stand in appropriate relations to things of the kind that X is*. This principle adds to what was stated in Principle A that we should have had experience of what it is to stand in relation to the objects of knowledge of the kind in question, and that our understanding of what it is so to stand is thus based on this experience. Given what has been said about Principle A, one might wonder how one could have such understanding in any other way. It might be argued, however, that we might deduce what it would be like to stand in certain relations with a certain kind of thing from our knowledge of those things, knowledge which was in no sense based on acquaintance with the kind of thing under consideration. Our knowledge of the kind of thing in question would then be something like the knowledge which we might have of a given individual person on the basis of a dossier of information about him, although we had never met him personally. In science fiction there sometimes occurs the conception of superior intelligences who acquire this kind of knowledge of human beings in general. They do not share much that is human, and in particular they do not share human feelings and emotions. While in consequence they have never had the experience of standing in relation to human beings in ways that one human being might stand to another, they are supposed to deduce what it is like so to stand from what they learn of human beings by watching them from outside. I think that such a conception is in fact nonsense. If we can make any sense of such a being — which is itself doubtful — it must be clear that he could not deduce what it is like for one human being to stand to another in characteristic human ways from a study of their behaviour. Or rather, that behaviour itself would make no sense to such a being, so that there would be nothing to deduce the requisite conclusion from.

Let us however look briefly at a case which does not involve knowledge of people. There may be people — indeed there presumably *are* people — who have had no experience of cities. Such a person might however acquire a lot of information about, say, London, from reading things about it, hearing accounts of it, and so on. Such information would not be entirely irrelevant to his own experience, which might be confined to life in villages or small towns. Such a person might come to feel that he knows London very well, and others might be surprised

218

that he had never been to London when hearing his accounts of the city. What he knows about London would certainly include things that he had inferred from what he had read and heard; yet in a very real sense he would have had no experience of the kind of thing that London is. All this is certainly possible, but it should be noted that there is no radical break between what he has had experience of and what he has come to know about, as there was between the knowledge possessed by the putative superior beings and the human beings whom they were supposed to come to know about by inference. There is at least an analogy between villages and cities, an analogy which is quite missing in the former case. It is this which makes it feasible to say of our villager that he knows from experience what it is to stand in relation to the kind of things that cities are.

I do not say that our villager does in fact know London. The principle which we are considering is concerned only with one necessary condition of being said to know something, not a sufficient condition. There might be some justification in saying of the villager that however much he feels that he knows London, he does not do so in fact. If he were brought to London, and if the difficulties of practical adjustment to new ways of life were surmounted with aplomb, someone might say of him that it was as if he had known London all his life. But one who did not know of his circumstances might say that he obviously knows London very well indeed, and I am not sure that the correct reaction on being told of the circumstances is to say that after all he did not really know London; it was only *as if* he did. Here much depends on what we expect of one who is supposed to know a city, and it should be noted that we do not expect the same knowledge of everyone. We do not expect of ordinary inhabitants of London who might justly be said to know London the kind of knowledge to be expected of, say, a civil engineer, any more than we expect of the driver of a car who may justly be said to know it knowledge of the kind possessed by his garage mechanic, or of the householder all the knowledge possessed by the builder of his house. To be said to know something a person need possess only that knowledge which is appropriate (in the sense already discussed) to the relation in which he stands to the thing — provided that he does stand in some relation of a pertinent kind. Thus perhaps our villager does have all the knowledge that is appropriate to the relation in which he stands to London, and might therefore justly be said to know London, before he has had any personal experience of it. If we feel some reluctance to agree to this it is because his case is an unusual one, it is not one that we normally feel obliged to allow for, not because there is any logical objection to the villager's being said to know London.

Whatever may be the right conclusion on this matter the case is very different, as I have already said, from the earlier one. It remains true that someone who has no relevant experience of something of a certain kind could not be said to know something else of that kind (and we can stretch the term 'kind' to cover experience of things only in a fairly remote way similar to the putative object of knowledge, as long as there is a relevant connection). The question that I have left open is whether it is a necessary condition of being said to know something that one should have had experience of *that* thing. It is a pertinent question whether I can be said to know a certain *person* if I have not had personal experience of him in some way, and not merely of people in some way like him. In other words, we may grant that we must have had experience of what it is to stand in appropriate relations to the kind of thing that X is if we are to be said to know X (and I have hinted at what is involved in the notion of 'appropriate relations' in what I have said above about what might be expected of ordinary inhabitants of London in relation to London etc.); but do we require another necessary condition — that we must have had experience of standing in appropriate relations to just this thing?

Whatever may be said about our villager in relation to London, can we properly be said to know people whom we have never met — even people whom we have seen much of, such as those who appear repeatedly on television? We can certainly feel that we know them, just as the villager felt that he knew London. But it may be that in this case it is a definite illusion, for knowing people seems to involve a reciprocal relationship, which does not apply to knowledge of cities. This fact may make all the difference between the two cases. With material things, even with such things as cities and cars, a reluctance to admit that we might be said to know a thing of this kind without having had experience of it itself may be due just to the rarity of such possible cases. We might find it difficult to imagine *how* a person could have come to know a city without having experience of it, and on this basis come to insist that such a person only has the feeling that he knows it, without actually knowing it in fact. In most cases there might be reason for such an insistence; but I still think that it would be wrong to elevate this into a point of logic, into something that follows from an aspect of the concept of knowledge. With knowing people, however, the situation seems different. If we had learnt an immense amount about a given person, so much that other people say in a surprised way that it is just as if we had known him all our life, there must still be an 'as if' about it if we had never in fact met him. This does not affect the truth of Principle B, since this gives a necessary condition for knowledge of people, not a sufficient condition. But the case suggests the need for an additional necessary condition, since in it the reason why there is not even the *possibility* of our knowing the person in question (let alone its actually *being* the case that we know him) is that we stand to him in no sort of personal relationship. This in effect takes us to Principle C.

(c) This says that it is *a necessary condition of being said to know X that we should actually stand to X in relations which are appropriate to the kind of thing that X is.* I have said earlier that there is not one way, nor indeed any one class of ways, in which a man should have stood to a car, a city, or a house in order to be said to know it — not, that is, *qua* man. And I took it to follow from this there is not one set of items of knowledge that a man, *qua* man, should know about if he is to know a car, a city, or a house. In cases of this kind much depends on the kind of role that he plays in relation to the object in question. These roles determine what has to be satisfied if he is to be said to know the thing in question. Once given this it may seem obvious that to know X a man must actually stand in relations to X which are appropriate to one conforming to such roles in relation to X. This, it might be said, is what I meant in specifying Principle C as saying that to know X we must actually stand to X in relations that are appropriate to the kind of thing that X is — appropriate, that is, for one of a certain kind playing a certain kind of role in relation to a thing of this kind. Thus, for a builder to know my house, he must stand in relations to it which are appropriate for a builder towards a house, i.e. he must have built it, or otherwise been involved in the details of its construction or reconstruction and repair. For me to know my house I do not need to stand to it in those relations, but what I know of it must be based on familiarity of another kind — from which it follows that I do not need to know all that my builder knows nor he all that I know. Here the roles determine the relationships, and these determine what must be known about X if X itself is to be known. If I do not stand towards my house in the kind of relationship appropriate to it as a building-construction (i.e. if I did not build it or repair

221

it, and am not interested in it as a building) then I cannot be said to know it as that; but the role that I do have in relationship to it does imply that I may know it as something else, e.g. as a home.

It is, I think, analytic that if a man's relation to a thing is determined by the sort of role that he plays in relation to it he must actually stand in that relation if he is to know it as the sort of thing that fulfils that role. Suppose, however, that a man's relation to a thing is such that it could never properly play the part that he gives it in the role that he plays. A man's relation to his car may, we are told, sometimes be like that of a man to his mistress. The question is 'How like?' 'Surely we may say that if it is really like that he does not really know his car. It cannot after all respond in all the appropriate ways. But if it were really like that as far as he is concerned, what sort of mistake would he have made? If a man treats his wife entirely as a mistress, then whatever else he is doing, he *is* making a mistake about his role in relation to her. But if he treated his car in this or some analogous way, the confusion would go well beyond anything that could be called a 'mistake'.

Two further points need to be made. The first is that the relationship of one person to another, to the extent that that relationship can be specified in terms of roles, must be one that is two-way if it is to be a condition of knowledge. This is the point about reciprocity that I have made before. The second point is that the relationship may go beyond any roles into which they have entered. This gives a vast complexity to the question of what counts as a mistake in this context. Neither of the points applies, however, to the relationship of the man with his car; for whatever one says about that relationship it depends ultimately on the fact that he stands in relation to it as user to used. And as I said earlier, one who thinks that he can stand in this relation to people in all circumstances does not have an adequate conception of a person. But conversely if a man really did treat his car as a mistress, he would not have an adequate conception of a car, and must therefore be at least confused. Thus if a man's relation to a thing is such that it could never properly play the part that he gives it in the role that he plays, he must lack an adequate knowledge of that thing in that he is confused about the sort of thing it is. He fails to stand to it in the relationship that is appropriate to the kind of thing that it is.

I spoke earlier when discussing Principle A of the point that for something to be a possible object of our knowledge it must be capable of figuring in our life in some way. This point is connected with the second point that I mentioned just now — the point about human relationships going beyond roles. One way in which something may figure in our life is, it is true, that it plays a part in connection with certain roles that we perform in relation to it. This could be applicable both to material things, and in some respects persons, as I have indicated. But as far as persons are concerned, it could not be the whole truth. For people do not figure in our lives simply in respect of the part that they play in connection with our performance of roles, nor simply in respect of the roles that they play in relation to us. Nor have we got very far when we attempt to construe our knowledge and understanding of people in terms of roles. For people are not just role players; they can feature as objects of more personal and emotional attitudes on our part, and the relationship can be reciprocal. Can it be maintained, therefore, that a necessary condition of our knowing people is that we should stand in this kind of relationship to them? For, after all, this is a relationship which is appropriate to things of this kind, i.e. to persons. I am not here saying that the relationship should be one of any specific attitude, not for example love. Hatred may be the appropriate attitude towards some people, although this would be a case of moral appropriateness and we are not here concerned with that. All that I am asking is whether if a man did not stand to another person in some relationship that involved one or other of those feelings which we might call 'personal' he could have any claim to be said to know that person. I am not asking, for example, whether the more involved he is with the other person the more he is entitled to claim knowledge of him. That might well not be the case. On the other hand the absence of any feeling towards the other person does seem to prejudice the possibility of knowing him; it prevents one getting close enough for the purpose, so to speak.

In connection with knowledge of persons, too much feeling is blinding, too little inhibits personal relationships, such that one is in danger of being concerned with externals only, and eventually perhaps in danger of treating people merely as things. I do not mean to imply by this that one might not having feelings towards things as distinct from people. Indeed some of them — pride, affection, dislike, boredom, for example — might be the same. But with people there must be the reciprocity that I have emphasized all along. I do not mean by this that they must have the same feelings towards you that you have towards them. This need not be so at all. But suppose someone had a passionate interest in another person in a personal way but received nothing of this kind at all in return, being treated if anything some-what as a thing. Would there be any possibility in this case of the person concerned being said to know the other in any real sense? For one thing, he would not have had experience of the other's personal side, as one might put it. But it might be argued that this merely reduces to the considerations adduced under Principle B — he must have had experience of the other's personal side, have had experience of standing in personal relations with him at some time; he need not so stand now. But it should be noted on the other side that we do tend to say things like 'I used to know him very well, but I haven't seen him for a long time; I cannot really claim to know him now, not personally at any rate.' It is the current relationship that is important in this respect; for people change in their attitude and relationships as much as in everything else. But the important point is that whether or not one has met a person lately and whatever feelings one has toward him currently one must have some attitude to him which is the sort of attitude one has to a person.

Some may think this something of a minimal claim, and I am happy to acknowledge this fact. Others may be worried that a story about attitudes, feelings, and the like should be thought to be part of an account of what knowledge consists of. What of this sort of thing is involved in an account of what is to be counted as knowledge of facts? Accounts of knowledge that something is the case in terms of such notions as justified true belief have come under considerable attack lately, and rightly. If knowledge of this kind implies belief, and I think that it does, the knowledge that $p$ will imply the belief that $p$ because $p$ is true and not for some other reason. I do not put this forward as a sufficient account of the place of belief in an account of the concept of knowledge, but it is sufficient for my purposes. For to believe that $p$ because $p$ is true implies a certain attitude towards truth or fact. Thus even in this case there is involved some attitude and relationship to the object of knowledge, which ought to be men-tioned in any adequate account of the knowledge in question. To be said to know a fact a person must stand in a relation to the fact that is appropriate to the kind of thing in question, i.e. to facts in general. The relationship is simply stated — it is appropriate that he should accept it as such. Thus knowledge of fact falls under my principles and is not to be thought of as an exception to my account of know-ledge. The man who knows that $p$ must stand to the fact that $p$ in the relation appropriate to facts — acceptance. When it comes to objects of knowledge of other kinds the relationship that is appropriate will depend on how the object is construed. If the object is construed in terms of the part that it plays in connection with roles that we perform in relation to it, then, as we have already seen, the relationship is prejudged. But where this is not so, as is the case with knowledge of persons as such, then the relationship has to be determined independently, and this I have been trying to indicate. It remains true that the relationship to the thing in question exists in virtue of its being a *kind* of thing, e.g. a fact or a person; and it is our understanding of what that kind of thing is that determines what relationship is appropriate to it. Indeed what is meant by an appropriate relationship here is simply one that is involved in an adequate understanding of the kind of thing in question. If Principle D were valid more would be suggested than this, and I must therefore turn, finally, to a brief consideration of this.

(d) Principle D, the invalid one, is that *a necessary condition of my being said to know X is that I should stand to X in relations which are appropriate to X*. This principle states that a condition of being said to know something is that I should stand in relations to that thing which are appropriate to it, i.e. that the relations that should exist between me and it should be of a kind that should exist between me and it independently of the fact of knowledge, and independently of the thing's being construed as an object of knowledge. It is perhaps difficult to know what that would mean in connection with a material thing. What relations should exist between me and a thing of that kind independently of its being construed as an object of knowledge of a certain kind for me? But the situation might be thought different in connection with knowledge of people. Could it be the case that for me to know my wife I must stand in relations to her which are appropriate not just to a person or to a wife, but to her? I think that if any sense can be given to this suggestion it will have to be in terms of *moral* relations. For it could certainly be maintained that certain moral relations are appropriate between me and my wife, and it might even be held, that the relations in question might go beyond anything that turns simply on the fact that she is a person or a person of a certain sort or kind, e.g. a wife. Again, to take a very different example, the moral relationships that would be appropriate between me and a man who was positively evil in a certain way might well go beyond anything that turned on the fact that he had other relationships with

225

me or that he was in other ways a person of a certain kind. Whatever be the case on this point, it would be very difficult to maintain that having appropriate relations of this kind is a necessary condition of being properly said to know the person in question.

Suppose for example that there were someone towards whom the only morally appropriate attitude for me to adopt was complete sympathy. Suppose also that I just could not bring myself to this attitude — something that might be due to certain factors in me. Would it be right in this case to say that I cannot then know that person — or at any rate not properly? I cannot think so, for I might know the person in question very well indeed and know that my attitude should be the sympathy in question, but still not be able to bring myself to that attitude. This kind of thing is a familiar occurrence with human beings, and must be reckoned with, in any account of them, as a possibility at least. We do sometimes say to someone 'You cannot really know him or you would not take that attitude towards him', and in some cases the remark may be quite just. But it need not always be so. Normally indeed we expect what a man knows to show in his behaviour; but this is not to say that one who knows someone cannot behave towards him in ways that we feel to be morally inappropriate. The behaviour may in such circumstances require explanation or justification and we may feel that the man in question is being unreasonable. But this does not amount to the claim that there is an absurdity in someone who knows another behaving towards him in ways that are morally inappropriate, let alone ways that we simply *feel* to be morally inappropriate.

The way in which knowledge of something has been connected with attitudes towards that thing, throughout all the principles until this last one, has been that the thing *construed as an object of knowledge* brings with it kinds of attitude towards it in being construed in that way. The attitudes that are morally appropriate to someone are not a function of how he is construed in the same way. My failure to take towards someone the appropriate moral attitude is not, or not necessarily, the result of a failure of understanding. Hence, I do not think that Principle D can stand. The other three principles remain, I think, valid.

## III

What are the implications of all this, perhaps boring, detail for our present concern? They are surely these: In order to know someone we must know what personal relations are, we must know from experience what it is to stand in personal relations, and we must stand in some kind of personal relationship to the person in question. It seems clear that in one sense of 'understanding' at least, the same applies to understanding a person. The question before us is 'How are we to conceptualize the processes through which one person comes to understand another?' If anything else emerges from my discussion it must be that we cannot conceptualize those processes as if the understanding of a person was no different from the understanding of any other kind of thing. Moreover it matters whether we stand in any kind of personal relationship to the person and this must be taken into account in an attempt to set out what it is for one person to understand another and how that understanding comes about. It might be said that we can sometimes stand outside any such relationship with another person and seek to understand him in an impersonal sort of way; indeed it might be maintained that just this must be involved in any scientific and objective attempt to understand people. My claim would be that if what I have said in discussing my third principle is right there are limits to what understanding of people can be derived in that way. For without standing in a personal relationship to the other person we cannot be said really to know him, and while some understanding of him may be possible without so knowing him, complete understanding, if this is in any sense feasible, is not possible. Hence the fundamental importance in any adequate treatment of interpersonal understanding of interpersonal dynamics.[2]

In the first two principles that I have discussed as giving necessary conditions of knowing another person, I have made reference to knowledge or understanding of other things — what relations can exist between the other person and ourselves, and what it is to stand in relations appropriate to a person. This could be put in other ways by saying that the two principles in question state the conceptual underpinning of knowledge of persons — what is involved in having the concept of a person. The third principle demands something more than this, and it is this principle which must be relaxed if we are to allow the impersonal knowledge and understanding of people to which

227

I made reference just now. I insist here only on the recognition that there are limits to what can be known or understood unless application is given in a particular case to this principle. But it may be that further questions arise in connection with the first two principles. If, as I said at the beginning of this paper, it is necessary in order to see what is in front of us as actions, behaviour which has sense,[3] that we should already understand that we are concerned with a person, and if a condition of this is that we should understand what it is to stand in personal relations with another, how does *this* understanding come about? From experience, yes, but how? Secondly, in what sort of ways do these necessary conditions get translated into sufficient conditions? In what sort of ways, in other words, does the actual understanding and knowledge of another develop? I spoke earlier of putting oneself in the other's place; but clearly much else must have gone on before this is possible at all.

I have said something on the former question elsewhere.[4] It would be wrong to think that a child comes to understand what a person is by asking himself what relations are appropriate between himself and other people. It cannot be, that is, a question of the child having to decide just what is the difference for him between people and other kinds of thing. The animism of children which Piaget and others have emphasized is more than understandable if one thinks of the child having to come to see what is *not* a suitable object for a personal relation rather than what *is* a suitable object. I have in the paper referred to spoken of the crucial role in the development of the child's understanding played by what it is put in the way of by others, and I have claimed that without so being put in the way of things there would be no possibility of there arising an objective understanding of an objective world (something that brings in social considerations). Whatever be the truth on that matter it remains a fact that the child's relationship with his mother (or in other cultures than our own whatever other human being is responsible for the child's nurture) takes up a considerable part of his early life. Such relationships are not to be construed as, so to speak, transactions between the child and adults, nor indeed a matter of stimulus and response unless this is viewed in a far from orthodox way. I mean by this that while it would be quite inadequate to think of the child reacting to stimuli provided by the mother in the usual mechanical way that is implied by talking of stimulus and response or reaction, it is more feasible and perhaps indeed vital to see how crucial emotional responses and attitudes are in this business. It is impossible to construe such attitudes and the responses to them merely as the presentation of, say, pleasurable stimuli which the child then reacts to in a positive way (with negative reactions to painful stimuli, of course). To adopt such a simple-minded hedonism does not do justice to what human beings, even very young ones, actually are. Hedonism of this kind, in which it is supposed that human behaviour is built up from positive and negative responses to what is pleasurable or the reverse have, in the history of thought, generally gone along with attempts to construe human beings along mechanist lines (cf. Hobbes). The idea that human beings are rather more complex than this does not imply a kind of mysticism; we need suppose only that certain emotional attitudes and reactions (by which I mean not simple mechanical reactions but complex forms of response to, e.g. love and concern) are part of our genetic inheritance, thus forming the basis of what I spoke of in section I as the natural reactions of person to person (cf. here, in opposition to my previous reference to Hobbes, Bishop Butler's view of man as something possessing a set of particular propensities, among which might be benevolence). What may be the physiological basis for such propensities is another matter, but we need not suppose that, on the psychological level, human beings are to be viewed simply as governed by hedonic pushes and pulls.

One might put the matter in other ways by saying that a personal relation is a natural thing for a person whether it is recognized as such or not. There is no need to find the notion of personal relations either puzzling or mystical. Rather, it would be more adequate to think of the child's view of the world around him developing out of what he is put in the way of in the course of relationships of this kind. Hence the animism; it is likely on these circumstances that the child will see personal agency in inappropriate places, since he will see all sorts of things as suitable recipients of personal attitudes and not just persons themselves. Hence it is no puzzle that the child should, to go back to my second principle, come to know through experience what it is to stand in relations which are appropriate to persons, since standing in such relations is what he is from the beginning and the fact is continually pressed upon him. It may well be doubted whether a baby could possibly stand in such relations to anyone from the beginning. I mean simply this. The possibility of being aware of other people as people and of oneself as a person among others depends on the ability to receive what is offered as, for example, love *as love*, and on the ability to respond with analogous expressions of affection. I do not mean by this that the child has to have any deep understanding

229

of what love is; I mean only that the child is genetically determined to respond with whole patterns of behaviour, emotional expression and feeling to certain forms of treatment. It learns what it is appropriate so to respond to in terms of whether the patterns of response so released fit in with subsequent treatment, whether the whole pattern of behaviour and response by others is one that fits in with its needs and interests. It is important to distinguish this sort of account from one which says that stimuli call out certain reactions which produce further stimuli, etc., such that those reactions which are rewarded are repeated, those which are not rewarded not repeated. If the child construed as a physiological mechanism can be thought of as subject to stimuli which produce physiological reactions (and whether a child can be so construed and so thought of is in the end an empirical matter of a kind) this is not the level at which I intend my account to apply. To receive a certain form of treatment as love involves engaging in a complex form of emotional and other kinds of behaviour, which may develop in certain ways according to what fits in with what happens. To learn what is appropriate to certain kinds of object of that behaviour is to learn what fits in this way. But in so far as the child, for genetic reasons, responds and can respond in a human way to human forms of treatment so it stands in embryo personal relations with others. It is only to be expected that it may stand in bogus or inappropriate relations of this kind to things that are not persons, and a proper development includes the recognition that this may be so. Hence the possibility of recognizing others and oneself as persons, and of acquiring the concept of a person proper, depends on the natural tendencies that a child has as a human being, on, to use Wittgenstein's phrase, what is part of its form of life. The understanding of what it is for something to be a person rests on what is in effect the facility for *being* a person and for reacting to the world in ways that are appropriate if this is to be encouraged. Without being treated personally and as a person by others no such development would be possible.

I have in this tried to say something (no doubt inadequately) about the conditions for the development of an understanding of what it is to stand in relations appropriate to persons. Once given this the child must be given *eo ipso* a rough knowledge of the sort of thing that counts as a person, an ability at least to distinguish in most cases between what is a person and what is not. This does not of course amount to any real understanding of people; it amounts only to that rough understanding which makes person-perception possible, which makes it possible to see certain things in the world in the light of what is to be expected from persons. In this light a facial expression, for example, is not just a pattern, a physiognomy, but a complex reaction from a person which may or may not fit in with whatever else that person is taken to be. I suspect that the negative results of many experiments on the recognition of facial expressions are due to the fact that the operation is divorced from the living context, so to speak. A physiognomy is just one aspect, and perhaps a minor aspect of a person, and it may not loom very large in a personal relationship. Within a personal relationship there may be much less uncertainty about the other's moods than the undoubted ambiguity of facial expressions might suggest.

This in effect takes me on to my second point – what else has to be added to the necessary conditions for knowledge of persons, of which I have spoken, to give the sufficient conditions? No *general* answer to this question can be given, since what will be sufficient will depend on the people concerned, the circumstances, and how deep the knowledge and understanding has to be. I wish here only to give some pointers, and some suggestions as to how it *cannot* be. Given what I have said it cannot be the case that we have to gain our understanding of others *via* inferences from their outer expressions in behaviour, etc. I mean here just what I say – it cannot be the case that we *have* to do this. I do not wish to deny that this is how it may sometimes be, although it would not be possible in this way did we not have other understandings of people, other understandings of what it is to be a person. But we do of course sometimes have to gain our understanding of a person from external observations. I doubt, as I have said before, that this can take us all that far, even if it may be in some cases essential as a basis for other kinds of knowledge. Nevertheless this cannot be the way it is in every case or even perhaps normally.

One other suggestion that might be made by way of reaction to the failure of inference from data as a general method of coming to know people is that our knowledge and understanding of others may be a matter of skill or knack. I do not think that this will do either. Such a suggestion would reduce our relationships to other people to one of craft. Once again this may be how it is on some occasions, but it cannot be how it is in general. To suppose that it might be would be to present a false, indeed a corrupt, picture of what humans are like. This is not to say that knacks or skills may not enter

231

into those transactions with others in which we seek understanding of them. A diagnostic session of whatever kind must involve such things. But to confine oneself to this entirely would be to stand outside a relationship with the other, and thus fail to fulfil the necessary conditions which I have stressed.

I spoke in section I of the place that a general knowledge of people and their motives, etc. can play in the understanding of a particular person: It also needs to be stressed that a direct experience of relationships with other people can also be vital for the understanding of one particular person. For what may be vital to such understanding may be the ability to see the person in a certain way in terms of relationships of this kind. In any account of understanding the notion of 'seeing' in an extended sense ought to play an important role. I say 'extended sense' though I am not at all sure that this is a correct way of putting it. How we see things can often enough have little to do with any properties of the strictly visual experience. One way, for example, to describe what is involved in the experience of being happy is to say that we can see the world as, say, a glittering place. That we see it in this way may be determined by our mood, our understanding of certain things, what we know to be the case, and so on, but our seeing things in this way is not to be identified simply with our mood, our understanding or our knowledge. Analogously, how we see a given person may be determined not simply by what we know of him in a way that we could express, but by various things that have entered into our experiences, including feelings that we may have towards him or that he may have towards us. Nevertheless the growth in our understanding of a person may be viewed as an increase in our vision of him; we may see him from a wider point of view, from more aspects. It is easy enough to see that closer relations with a person may well present us with more aspects, even if a too great degree of closeness may sometimes be blinding. We need sometimes to stand back and take a more detached view. The point might be put by saying that the only general thing that can be said about how knowledge and understanding of other people is to be attained is that it comes by way of increased experience, general knowledge of people, and above all perhaps by way of an imaginative approach to them. We could not do this without experience of and insight into the relationships that we have with others. Hence the concept of a personal relationship plays a crucial role in any conceptualization of what is involved in one person coming to understand another, and this is the central point that I wish to make.

232

IV

## POSTSCRIPT AND COMMENTARY

The principles that I have set out and discussed in section II are meant to be *conceptual* principles; they are meant to bring out factors which are involved in the concept of knowing something, and these factors have, I think, been overlooked or under-emphasized in philosophical accounts of knowledge. They seem to me to apply to knowledge of objects of all kinds, even facts, though they may assume a role which is more important in connection with certain objects than with others. With facts in general, for example, it is important to recognize that an understanding of what it is for something to be fact involves certain attitudes on our part to it. Someone who had no regard for and saw no reason to accept facts could scarcely be said to know what facts are. Here perhaps, however, the importance of what I have said about our relationship to the object of knowledge goes no further; but in the case of other objects of knowledge, particularly persons, there are further implications and ramifications.

The principles that I have discussed are progressive in the sense that starting from the proposition about the necessity for understanding the relations that can exist between a putative object of knowledge and ourselves, they move to the proposition that we must actually stand to that object in relations appropriate to things of that kind if it is really to be an object of knowledge. As far as concerns persons this means that the notion of something like personal relations enters into an account of what knowledge of persons involves. It may do so in different ways and to different degrees according to the context of the knowledge. Since understanding a person implies knowledge of him, or does so if that understanding is to be an adequate understanding or something approaching a complete understanding, the same principles apply here too. I have no wish to deny that there can be certain kinds or degrees of understanding of people which may be arrived at through a kind of impersonal observation or analysis of them and their behaviour. Even so I believe that such understanding presupposes the application of my principles A and B. But I also believe that there are limits to what is possible in this way. Hence for complete or fully adequate understanding and knowledge of people, for real knowledge of them, my principle C must be taken seriously and the point of principle

233

D is in effect to make clear the limits of principle C.

My concerns, when it comes to the application of my principles, are, therefore, fundamentally twofold — the conditions for *really* knowing and understanding another person, and the conditions for having knowledge and understanding of persons at all. The first concern brings in all three of principles A, B and C, the second principles A and B only, although it is scarcely conceivable that someone should have come to know what it is to stand in relation to persons without so standing to some person or persons. Thus in effect my concerns cover (a) person-perception so-called, and real interpersonal understanding, and (b) the genetics and development of such interpersonal understanding. In each case my concern is with necessary conditions, since I believe that little can be said of a *general* kind of what is sufficient for such knowledge and its development.

Over (a) I have already said enough. Over (b) what I have suggested is that we need to bring in something like the notion of personal relations at the beginning. Knowledge of others would then have for its foundation something like relations between the child and others based on feeling. This could be summed up by saying that the child comes to have understanding of others as persons if and only to the extent that it is itself treated as a person rather than a thing. It is the relations so established that are all important. I have tried to say something about this in section III of my paper, but I am conscious of the inadequacy of what is said there. The attempt to get back into the child's mind at the very beginning of its life is in one sense an impossibility since success would mean sloughing off all the features of adult understanding without which an *account* of the child's mind would be impossible anyway. Thus the very features that are necessary for such an account — the concepts and terms in which the account is and must be expressed — make the success of the account impossible. Here, however, as in some other contexts, I believe that there is every virtue in trying to do what is impossible.

I said something in section III about the inadequacy of trying to explain the way in which the child comes to behave to other human beings in terms of what it finds pleasurable and painful in the treatment that it receives, particularly, of course, from its mother. Satisfaction of hunger cannot, for example, consist merely in the receipt of what is pleasant to the child, the hunger itself being unpleasant or even painful. I do not think that this is an adequate account of what it must mean to the baby to have its hunger satisfied. In discussing this issue lately R.K. Elliott said to me that such satisfaction might be more like grace and salvation to it, and I am much indebted to him for this observation. Some may find such theologically-derived terms too high-flown for these purposes. But there is something apt about the description. It is not of course claimed that the child sees the food, the mother's breast, or what have you, in these terms; *that* would be an impossibility. It is that such terms do greater justice to what must inevitably be the child's experience on such an occasion. Indeed the process of development and learning about the world must involve learning that this satisfaction is not, as it were, a gift of heaven, but due to another human being who stands to him in a complex relationship within which love, it is to be hoped, figures prominently. I do not think that this is mere sentimentality; I think that such an account, if it could be developed, would be the only realistic one, even if it would require much imagination on the part of the theorist.

For these purposes, the child must be granted a fairly rich genetic equipment, and a consciousness which can be educated by experience. Such an education will involve the turning of an awareness which has a formal object only (an awareness, perhaps, of everything in general and nothing in particular) into an awareness of different and particular things. For this to happen the child must be able to come to see things as belonging together and other things as different, if and to the extent that things are brought before the focus of its attention. That is why, again, it is so important how the child is treated and what it is put in the way of. But to think of the child as a simple classifier and distinguisher would be far from doing justice to the facts; for this would be to confine one's attention, once again, to the purely cognitive aspects of its life, and I think that these would be nothing without the background of feeling and emotion which constitutes the foundation of the relationships with others within which alone its development could thrive.

That is why the fact that the child stands in relations to other persons is so important for a general account of how it comes to have an understanding of the world. But it might be thought that this presupposes than an answer has been given to a prior question — 'How does the child come to recognize persons as such?' For how can the child stand in relation to persons without having some idea of what it is standing in relation to? And how does it come to have that idea? It is perhaps interesting that Chomsky (1968, p. 64) includes human action under suggested topics for a theory akin to his generative theory of linguistic competence. The point, I take it, is that just as there is, given his premises, a problem how the child comes to recognize the noises made by other humans in its presence as language unless it already has the idea of what language is, so there is a problem how it comes to recognize the movements of certain bodies as actions. Those movements would, of course, be in the running for identification as actions only if they were made by persons. Hence the problem specified amounts to the problem how the child recognizes certain things as persons unless it already has the idea of what a person is. I do not think than an appeal to a putative innate idea of a person will do, although I cannot discuss this issue here (I have discussed it in a general way in Hamlyn 1973 and in this volume, pp. 132-47). But I do not think that we have a need for such a solution any way, for what is really wrong lies in the premises of the argument. It is not a question of the child having to come to recognize persons as such in this way. The child could come to have the idea of what a person is only *via* and in the context of *being* a person; and for this to have any real sense the child must, as I have said, be treated as a person. Thus when I said in section III that the child must stand in personal relations from the beginning, I did not mean that the child had from the beginning to be aware of this as the case. *That would* presuppose an understanding of what a person is and the problem that I have been discussing would immediately ensue. Rather the child must be thought of as being the recipient and progressively the source of attitudes and behaviour which is of the kind appropriate to persons, whether or not the child is initially aware of this as such; all this is the product of what I have spoken of as natural reactions of person to person. It is this human context which provides a basis for, and eventual substance to, the understanding of what it is both to *be* a person and to take other persons *as* persons. For this is the sort of concept that the concept of a person is. (It is perhaps worth noting that, although they may not provide exact parallels, there are numerous concepts the acquisition of which is dependent on participation in activities and possible relations; consider — to take what some may think a highfaluting example, but one which may well have some pertinence in the present connection in the light of the theological conception of a personal God — the concept of prayer and the correlative concept of a God to whom prayers may be addressed.) At all events, to think of the child's recognition of persons as merely a function of its classification of some things as persons and other things as non-persons in virtue of characteristics possessed by the first and not by the second is a most unrealistic account of the situation, and one which fails to take proper account of what sort of concept that of a person is. If what I have been saying is right it is no surprise at all that knowing what a person is implies knowledge of what it is to stand in personal relations, and hence that understanding people implies this too. Such a conclusion indeed seems inescapable. Hence my answer to the question 'How does the child come to recognize persons?'

Let me return finally and by way of summary to the general thesis of my paper. My position could be put as follows:

(1) Any understanding of other people, any person-perception, presupposes an understanding of what people *are*. This implies knowing what it is to stand in relations to people, and implies also, if I am really to understand another person, standing in a personal relation to him or her. The child has somehow to enter into relations of this kind, if only in a rudimentary way, if he is to develop any understanding of what persons are.

(2) There is, even without the 'real understanding' which I have mentioned under (1), the possibility of *some* degree of understanding of people. Coming to understand people in this way may, *provided that one has a prior knowledge of persons in general*, involve such things as (a) putting oneself in their place, (b) inferring things about them from 'externals', (c) applying to them knowledge that one has about what makes people tick in general, and other things of this kind.

(3) Hence, what I have had to say implies limits at two ends of a scale, so to speak.

(a) Complete or full understanding of a person is impossible without standing in a personal relationship to him (and to say this is not *merely* to say that without this I should not have sufficient information about him, if that information is construed in an impersonal way, nor is it to say that without this I should not have the tacit knowledge how to cope with him and things of that kind).

(b) Understanding of people is impossible altogether without knowledge of what a person is, and this implies a foundation in what Wittgenstein would have called features of our form of life, and what I have referred to as 'natural reactions of person to person'. It is on this basis, as I see it, that interpersonal understanding develops, and without it it would never get off the ground.

One final and dogmatic point: I argued in relation to my Principle C that one cannot fully know or understand another solely in terms of the role that either of us plays. The view that a human being can be summed up in terms of a collection of roles seems to me not only an inadequate view of human beings, but, if I may so put it, a corrupt one. It leaves out of account those features of human beings which give morality a real content and reduces personal relations to something at the best artificial and at the worst inhuman.

## NOTES

1 Cf. J. Cook (1969).
2 I was interested to see that in Philip Vernon's book *Personality Assessment* (1964), person-perception and the like is discussed under the heading 'naive interpretations' of personality. This categorization is right if person-perception is thought of independently of personal relationships.
3 Cf. for this way of putting it Franz From (1971).
4 In my paper 'Human Learning' which was a contribution to the Royal Institute of Philosophy Conference on the Philosophy of Psychology, at Canterbury, Kent, September 1971 (in *Philosophy of Psychology*, ed. S.C. Brown and this volume, pp. 132-48).

## REFERENCES

Chomsky, N., *Language and Mind*, New York, Harcourt, Brace and World, 1968.
Cook, J., 'Human Beings' in *Studies in the Philosophy of Wittgenstein*, P.G. Winch (ed.), London, Routledge & Kegan Paul, 1969.
From, F., *Perception of Other People*, trans. by B.A. Maher and E. Kvan, New York, Columbia University Press, 1971.
Hamlyn, D.W., 'Human Learning' in *Philosophy of Psychology*, S.C. Brown (ed.), London, Macmillan, 1973 (this volume, pp. 132-48).
Sartre, J-P., *Being and Nothingness*, trans. by Hazel E. Barnes, New York, Barnes and Noble, 1956.
Vernon, P.E., *Personality Assessment*, London, Methuen, 1964.
Wittgenstein, L., *Philosophical Investigations*, Oxford, Blackwell, 1953.

# 14

# SELF-KNOWLEDGE

I have the impression that someone who wished to sum up recent philosophical and psychological work in the area of self-knowledge and understanding might justly say that those investigating this area have had much to say about various aspects of our knowledge *about* ourselves, but comparatively little about self-knowledge proper. Let me explain what I mean by this. First the philosophers. I shall have something to say directly about the historical philosophical traditions that have thrown up problems about the self. In recent times, at least within what might be called the broadly analytical tradition of philosophy, there has been almost an obsession, if an understandable one, with problems stemming from Cartesian privacy. I mean by the last roughly what Descartes maintained when he said that we have a clearer and more distinct idea of our own states of mind than we have of our bodies, let alone other things. Wittgenstein's concern (Wittgenstein 1953) with the conditions for a public understanding of the concepts of states of mind which are in a certain sense private — concepts such as that of pain or other sensations — has led to a preoccupation with the conditions for speaking, if we *may* so speak, of knowledge of those states of mind. Thus one of the few books in this tradition of philosophy in recent times which has the words 'self-knowledge' in its title — Sydney Shoemaker's *Self-knowledge and Self-identity* — is, to the extent that it is concerned with self-knowledge at all, concerned with this aspect of knowledge about ourselves. Yet, even if considered at the level of knowledge *about* ourselves, this might well seem to psychologists a rather minor aspect of that knowledge, even granted the point that in self-characterization, as opposed to the characterization of others, a good deal of weight is put upon personal experiences and how things appear to us.

The fact that recent philosophical concerns with the self have been limited in scope should not necessarily, however, be taken as a criticism of those philosophers. Philosophical concerns, however minute they may seem at first sight, usually have at the back of them large-scale traditional issues. It might indeed be said that it is these alone which in the end mark off the more limited concerns as philosophical. By 'large-scale traditional issues' I mean and have in mind such matters as the place of man within nature in general, a philosophical concern that goes back almost to the beginnings of philosophical thought in Greece. I am inclined to say that the form of a philosophical problem can be set out as 'How is X possible?', and the possibility of man being construed either as a part of nature or as set apart in some way from the rest of nature is an issue which generates a whole mass of other problems which in one way or another provide a challenge to the understanding. A concern with one aspect of these large-scale issues is understandable if it provides a particularly pressing challenge to the understanding.

Apart from the Cartesian thesis of which I have spoken, together with various reactions against it, there have, however, been other philosophical issues that have affected such concern with self-knowledge as there has been. There has, for example, been a philosophical puzzlement about the status of the 'I', originating perhaps in Hume's inability to find an impression of the self, together with Kantian reactions which lay emphasis on the correlativeness of the ideas of the self and non-self. There is also the connected issue of the distinction between self and other which is to be found in, for example, Hegel. There may be other themes of this kind, and in some philosophers one can find amalgamations of more than one theme. There is thus in Ryle's discussion of the systematic elusiveness of the self in the *Concept of Mind* a blend of the Hume/Kant theme with an anti-Cartesianism; while in Sartre's claim in *Being and Nothingness* that consciousness is a nothingness and his doctrine of the transcendence of the ego one might also find the Hume/Kant theme together with certain preoccupations with questions about self and other. I think that it is generally true that philosophical treatments of self-knowledge have been overladen with concerns of this kind, concerns which are in a genuine sense metaphysical; and there has been little in the way of an attempt to get at self-knowledge pure, so to speak. Is it possible to do this, to divorce a philosophical treatment of self-knowledge from these more general metaphysical concerns? And if so, are recent inquiries by psychologists relevant, whether in themselves or in providing a stimulus towards a shift in point of view?

So, to the psychologists. I am no expert here, but a relatively casual survey of the literature seems to reveal a preoccupation with such things as the self-concept. (There is an ambiguity here that ought to be noted. Sometimes, perhaps even generally, what seems to be meant by the self-concept is not what philosophers have in mind when they speak of the concept of the self, as opposed to, say, that of others — not, that is, the conception of what it is for something to be a self at all — but rather the conception of oneself as a certain *kind* of person, the picture that people have of themselves.) Connected with this seems to be a concern with the attribution to oneself of various characteristics, its conditions and basis, and its relation to the attribution of similar characteristics to others. Finally, although by no means exhaustively, there is the matter of the presentation of oneself to others and the place of other people's attitudes in one's picture of oneself. The notion of something like the picture of oneself (even if this is not the term generally used) seems to have a large place in this. To be concerned with this, however, is in effect to be concerned with one's *beliefs* about oneself and about the way in which those beliefs are formed. Many, if not all, of those beliefs have to do with relationships with others, and that is particularly so in connection with the presentation of the self, where the notion of roles has a large part to play. One might say, therefore, that a good deal of the psychological literature in this area is concerned with the beliefs that people have about themselves in a social context, and the way in which the beliefs about the sort of person one is affects one's general behaviour. That does not amount to self-knowledge.

There is perhaps some tendency to invert what I have said and to see the beliefs as arising from the behaviour rather than vice versa. At the extreme that would amount to the thesis that our beliefs about the kind of person we are are the product of the interrelationships of behaviour that we are involved in; so that what we take ourselves to be is simply what interaction with others makes us believe. An even more extreme thesis would be that we *are* no more than that; we are not merely what society makes us but what society makes us believe ourselves to be. There are suggestions of this point of view in G.H. Mead, to whom references are often made in writings in this area.

Mead saw the notion of the self as social in origin, and what he called the 'me' he defined as 'the organized set of attitudes of others which one himself assumes' (Mead, 1934, p. 175). The assuming of these attitudes is what promotes self-consciousness. Hence as far as the 'me' is concerned 'that is the self that immediately exists for him in his consciousness' (ibid.). That is not perhaps the very extreme view that I have mentioned, but it is an easy step from it to that view, and I believe that others may have taken it under his inspiration. Mead in any case distinguished between the 'me' and the 'I' that reacts to it, although he did speak of the 'me' as a kind of 'censor' on the 'I', so setting limits to its expression (Mead, 1934, p. 210). I shall return to something of this issue later. It is sufficient for now to indicate that it is not a large step from this to the Goffmanesque position that what I am is determined by the set of roles that I take up and that these are determined by my interactions with others.

However all this may be, it is natural that a psychological concern with the self should be a concern with the beliefs that one has about oneself, how one sees oneself or thinks about oneself, and the relevance of all this to behaviour, particularly social behaviour. For how people see themselves has clearly a large bearing on our understanding of that behaviour. Yet it has to be said that an inquiry into the acquisition of the self-concept, into the attribution of characteristics to ourselves, or into the ways in which we see ourselves, is not as such an inquiry into self-*knowledge*. While it may be an inquiry into *a* way or *some* ways in which we understand ourselves, such understanding may not amount to knowledge. My concern in this paper is with *knowledge*; it is arguable whether such knowledge is commensurate with complete understanding, but I do not have to take a stand on that issue here. It is enough to indicate that the approaches that I have mentioned are concerned with our understanding of ourselves to the extent that, but only to the extent that, they are concerned with the beliefs, it may well be true beliefs, that we form about ourselves. Whatever more there is to complete understanding of ourselves, this must fall short of knowledge since true belief is never sufficient for knowledge. (I shall return to this point in the next section.) One might perhaps express my concern in this paper by putting the issues that I have mentioned so far alongside the Delphic saying that Socrates welcomed and insisted upon — 'Know thyself'. What was Socrates asking of us and what has it to do with any of the philosophical and psychological issues that I have mentioned? Was he indeed asking us to embark upon a wild-goose chase?

I do not think that the answers to these questions are at all obvious. Socrates clearly thought that the possession of self-knowledge would have moral consequences, and indeed that self-knowledge was a necessary condition of true virtue. I do not think, however, that he believed that the self-knowledge in question could come about by any kind of self-analysis or any kind of psychological inquiry into, say, the nature of one's personality, although it may well be unrealistic to suppose that we can have self-knowledge without *some* knowledge of that kind about ourselves. Indeed in some cases it may be necessary to know a great deal of that kind. It is equally clear, however, that too much attention to facts about oneself may lead, not to self-knowledge in any sense that Socrates can have been concerned with, but to self-consciousness in the colloquial sense that Laing describes as implying both an awareness of oneself by oneself and an awareness of oneself as an object of someone else's observation, if not more than this (Laing, 1965, p. 106). It might even be said that self-consciousness in this sense is antithetical to self-knowledge. Someone who has true insight into himself needs to be aware of what he is to others, but he does not need to be looking over his shoulder all the time to see how others are regarding him; to do so would inhibit a concern for and a commitment to what he is engaged in and thus one of the essential conditions of self-knowledge proper would be missing. To say this is, however, to anticipate what I have to say later. Let us first try to get clearer about the relationship between knowledge of self and knowledge about oneself by considering what we ordinarily mean by those words.

## KNOWLEDGE OF AND KNOWLEDGE ABOUT SELF

I said earlier that what is often discussed under the heading of the 'self-concept' is certain beliefs about oneself, in particular beliefs about the kind of person that one is. Such beliefs would of course be parasitical upon having the concept of a person in general and upon some kind of understanding of the notion of the self both as opposed to what is not oneself in general and as opposed to other persons in particular. These latter issues have, as I noted earlier, been of concern to philosophers in the past and are still with us as philosophical issues. But the issues that are of immediate concern are: what is the relationship, given my possession of those concepts, of the beliefs that I have

243

about the kind of person I am to knowlege about myself, and what is the relationship of this to self-knowledge?

The first of these questions is relatively easy to answer — formally at any rate. The relation between belief about oneself and knowledge about oneself is the same as that between belief and knowledge generally. I said that it was easy to answer the question formally because the exact relation between knowledge and belief has been the subject of much philosophical discussion lately. It is sufficient for present purposes to say, what is in any case true, that for a belief to amount to knowledge it must be true and it must be no accident that it is what is true that is believed. There is, however, a further point that is for present purposes more important — that if one's beliefs about oneself are to be considered rational they must be founded in some way on knowledge that one has about oneself. Moreover, it is implausible to suppose, perhaps even inconceivable, that one should have beliefs about oneself but no knowledge about oneself. People often have a false conception or picture of themselves, or so we say. But what we generally mean by this is that their beliefs about themselves are false in certain very important ways. It is perhaps rarer for people to have beliefs about themselves which are merely accidentally true, but similar considerations would apply. It would be impossible to say what proportion of people's beliefs about themselves are usually false or merely accidentally true; nor do I see any grounds for claiming that knowledge about oneself is in some sense the norm. The claim that I wish to make is a much weaker one — that a person could have no beliefs at all about himself if he knew *nothing* about himself; he must know, for example, that he is the sort of thing that can have beliefs.

The second question, about the relation between knowledge about oneself and self-knowledge is more difficult and more complex. It seems clear, for example, that to have self-knowledge it is not enough to have knowledge about oneself *of any kind whatever*. The notion of self-knowledge is more restricted in its application than that, and some kinds of knowledge that one may have about oneself seem irrelevant to the question whether one has self-knowledge proper. For example, knowledge about one's looks does not seem to the point in this context unless one's looks effect other things about oneself. Cyrano de Bergerac's long nose was rightly portrayed as affecting very considerably his character and personality, so that it had a considerable place in the pattern of his life; he could scarcely be said to have known himself at all if he did not know about his nose. The same would not be true of some much less prominent physical characteristic which had no appreciable affect on a person's life. Not any old facts about oneself are material to self-knowledge.

Can one, then, go straight to the character and personality of which I have spoken, and say that to have self-knowledge a man must know about these things as they affect himself? The answer depends to some extent on that 'as they affect himself'. If I know something about my character and personality I will know such things as that I am cheerful and honourable, or morose and unreliable. Suppose that I know a lot of things of this kind, to the extent that I can produce what is in effect a profile of my character and personality. It would not necessarily follow that it would be right for someone to say of me 'He knows himself all right.' Suppose that while I can indeed produce this profile of myself, a profile that seems to others accurate enough, I show no ability to apply this knowledge to the particular circumstances of life. Suppose, for example, that in particular exchanges with others I show no signs of recognizing that unreliability which I avow to in general and which in general holds good for me (I say 'Suppose'!); I behave on the contrary as if it is clear that I shall keep my promises, do what I say I shall, and so on. There will in that case be a gap between what I seem to know about myself in a general way and what I seem to know of myself in a more practical and particular way. I say 'seem to know' because the conflict of evidence might cast doubt on the extent to which it is appropriate to speak of knowledge proper in these circumstances. One way to put the matter might be to say that while I do indeed know a great deal about myself, including what kind of character and personality I have, I do not really know myself; the general knowledge about myself that I have is not somehow cashed in the ordinary course of my life. Hence, there certainly seems to be a sense in which I may know a great deal about myself, and attribute to myself characteristics that I undoubtedly have, without having self-knowledge; my conception of myself is in one sense quite right in these circumstances, but that is not enough.

There is also what might well be regarded as the opposite tendency. Suppose that certain person has a kind of knack in practical affairs and in intercourse with others, so that he seems to know exactly how far he is likely to go and can go, how seriously he should be taken, how reliable his faculties are, and so on. Thus, as far as concerns himself, all his affairs are conducted in what appears to be a well-oiled way; and in so far as failures occur they arise not from any inability to estimate his own potentialities properly, but from a simple failure to foresee what others may or may not do (and there are clearly limits to anyone's ability in that respect). Yet he is quite unable to produce any account of his general character and personality. It is not just that he is modest about it or that he cannot find the words; his success in practice simply has nothing to do with any general views of himself that he may have, if indeed he has any. His practical success in life is an extension of that kind of success which may be achieved by athletes who know just how far to push themselves and how far they can go in their efforts. If we are at all inclined to say that such a person knows himself, it is in the sense that we should say such things about the athlete – meaning that he has things nicely judged as far as concerns himself. This could not be in any full sense what we expect of self-knowledge, since he lacks any explicit self-insight. At the extreme such cases correspond to that of the so-called 'holy fool', the person who has a complete sense of right and wrong and of his position in that respect, but who is quite incapable of spelling out what is involved and appears in a certain sense not to know this.

It may be said that there is a certain artificiality in my procedure up to this point, in that I have been relying on intuitions which may not be shared by others, and on a sense of the ordinary use of words like 'self-knowledge' which may be idiosyncratic and may well not be relevant to our purposes. It may well be that in ordinary parlance we *would* say of the athlete 'He certainly knows himself', meaning that he knows the limits and extent of his physical capabilities. But our judgment would be confined to that particular context. If we wished to extend the scope of the judgment in asking what a man has to have in order to have self-knowledge in a fuller sense, would it be enough to add to the knowledge of the physical capabilities knowledge of potentialities and dispositions of other kinds – for example those already mentioned that go to make up a person's personality, temperament and character? It could not reasonably be denied that a successful athlete must know much of these things too in regard to himself. Yet if the knowledge in question still manifested itself simply in what he did and was disposed to do, it would amount at best to a knowledge of 'what he would do if . . .', and a knowledge that he might not be able to express to himself or others. Thus while we may sometimes limit our concerns in speaking of self-knowledge to one particular dimension of a person's life, e.g. his practical skills and concerns, it has to be admitted that there is more to a person, and therefore more

246

to the possibilities of self-knowledge, than that.

Earlier in this section I asked whether, in seeking what is required for self-knowledge, one could go straight to the knowledge that a man might have of his personality and character (and now one might add other capacities) as they affect himself. I said that the answer depended to some extent on what was involved in the words 'as they affect himself'. I have since then discussed two contrasting ways in which such knowledge might *not* affect the possessor, first in not carrying over into his practical life, and second in being in effect confined to this. Yet there is an asymmetry between the two cases, as was in effect indicated by the fact that there seemed to me some inclination to say that the second man did have self-knowledge if only in a limited way and with limited scope. A relevant point is that the first man undoubtedly had knowledge *about* himself, even if that knowledge did not carry over into his more practical life; the second man could not really be said to have knowledge *about* himself at all, or at least not to any great extent. His knowledge was of a quite different kind, that one might call 'practical' (it is not the only relevant sense of the term, as we shall see later). This does not necessarily suggest that knowledge about oneself is antithetical to self-knowledge, or knowledge of oneself, but it does suggest that knowledge *about* oneself is nothing if it has no relation to one's life in general – nothing, that is, as far as self-knowledge is concerned. That would suggest in turn that certain models of self-knowledge, which regard it in terms of information-getting are on the wrong track. We should not approach self-knowledge in the first place through the idea of getting knowledge about ourselves, or at any rate not through this to the extent that the knowledge is construed like that of other things – and that is what the story about information-getting suggests.

## BLINDNESS TO SELF

It does not seem quite right to say of the hypothetical persons whom I discussed in the last section that to the extent that they failed to have self-knowledge they revealed ignorance of self. The last phrase is not one, in any case, that is in common use. There is no problem about a person being ignorant about himself. To say that he is this is simply to say that he lacks knowledge of things about himself that he may or may not be in the position to know. Ignorance *of* oneself is another matter. We can be ignorant of other people, if they have never, so to speak, come within our ken; but that makes no sense in regard to ourselves, to the extent that we have a conception of ourselves at all. If we wish to speak of a failure of self-knowledge, if we wish to speak of that to which self-knowledge may be opposed, self-ignorance does not seem to be the right term, whether or not it is a term which is used in ordinary parlance. Moreover, even 'ignorance about oneself' suggests merely a failure of diagnosis that others have made or could make; someone who is ignorant about himself fails to know what others know or could know, and the knowledge that he lacks is thus a form of knowledge that others must be able to have in principle at least, such as a knowledge of general characteristics and the like. There are other forms of knowledge of himself that a person may lack. The failure to possess them may reveal itself in his behaviour and in the general conduct of his life, so that to speak of the failure as a failure of diagnosis may be quite wrong. An athlete who was the converse of the one whom I mentioned in the last section, an athlete who regularly failed to pull it off because of misjudgments of various kinds about himself need not have failed in any self-diagnosis; for he need never have made any diagnosis of himself at all, or felt it relevant to do so, preferring to rely on a kind of practical knowledge of himself – a knowledge that, as it turns out, he lacks.

One might speak of this kind of failing as a form of blindness to self. Blindness is what Aristotle called a 'privation' – the lack of a quality by something or someone which things or people of the kind in question normally have or may be expected to have. A successful athlete may be expected to have some sense of his own powers, if only on the practical level that I have mentioned. A failure to have that sense on the part of a practising athlete may therefore be set down as a privation, in the way that blindness in the literal sense is for ordinary human-beings (although not, Aristotle believed, for moles!). A blindness to self may, however, take many forms, not simply this impercipience in action which is reflected in a lack of skill. There is, for example, the blindness to self which comes from overriding attention to other things, with perhaps as a correlate a complete lack of concern for one's own position in the matter. There is also, though perhaps arguably, self-deception.

Let me take the latter first. I have argued elsewhere (Hamlyn, 1971b) that the self-deceiver does not really make himself ignorant of what he is or of what he is up to, but rather that he somehow prevents himself from being conscious of what he in fact knows. I have also argued that it is a mistake to think that the deception involved is always to be construed on the model of that form of deception of others in which we deceive them by giving them false information. Indeed false information need not necessarily constitute deception; the person receiving it has to take a certain attitude to it and to the person who gives it. Similarly, it is impossible to understand self-deception without taking into account other attitudes that a person may have to himself. All this obviously fits in with the strictures that I have put on construing self-knowledge in terms of getting information about oneself; that would, for one thing, leave out the place that that information might have in relation to the attitudes that we have to ourselves. I shall not argue these points again here, but it may be as well to point out some of their implications.

In the first place, the position that I have maintained about self-deception does not preclude the possibility that by putting out of consciousness something that he knows about himself a man may eventually come, even if he could not produce that result intentionally and directly, to be in a state equivalent to that of one who is ignorant of the same thing about himself. That is to say that by, so to speak, blinding himself to a certain point a man may with luck, if that is the right word, come to be in a state in which he is quite incapable of recognizing that point. He will be so incapable not simply because he will not allow himself to be capable of recognizing it, as may be the case during the initial stages of self-deception, but because he has become like one who has genuinely forgotten. The item has passed not only out of his consciousness, but out of, if we may speak, his knowledge. He began by blinding himself to the issue, and he has ended up as good as blind to it. If this comes about, however, it will be, as I have said, by 'luck' and not as a result of his direct and intentional agency. Unless and until this comes about, the self-deceiver may blind himself to certain things about himself, but the blindness is not a genuine and proper blindness; rather it is more like the hysterical blindness of one who cannot see something because he does not wish to do so, fears to do so, or cannot bear to do so. (I do not, of course, adduce the case of the hysteric as more than a parallel; in itself it raises as many problems as that of the self-deceiver, and may in fact be considered as a special case of that.)

A further point is whether there are any restrictions on the possible range of objects for self-deception, the things that one can possibly be deceived about. Can one be deceived about *anything* in regard to oneself? I think that the answer to this question is that nothing in logic restricts the range of possible objects of this kind, but that if something is to be such an object it has to satisfy certain conditions which would make it very implausible that certain things *should* be in the range in question. What I mean is the following. If it is the case that self-deception involves one's putting out of consciousness something that one in fact knows, it is inevitable that it should presuppose a certain conflict in oneself. For, suppose that one is self-deceived in believing $p$; then one must know that not-$p$ but one must have put that fact out of consciousness. Otherwise the belief that $p$ would amount to wishful thinking only and not self-deception proper. But to know that not-$p$ one must have some concern for the truth, while if one wishes to put the fact that not-$p$ out of consciousness one must have a concern of a different and opposing kind about the truth of not-$p$. Hence opposing concerns must be involved. This means in turn that it is possible to be deceived about something only if it is in one way or another the object of differing concerns, and that it is not possible to be self-deceived about something that cannot in any way be this.

The next question that arises is whether there are any restrictions in the range of things or of truths that can be a possible matter for concern. In this one is up against the kind of issue that Elizabeth Anscombe raised in asking whether it is possible to want a saucer of mud (and this simply, and not because, for example, one wanted to use it for some purpose) (Anscombe, 1951, p. 70). If it is asked whether anything at all could be a matter of concern for us, the answer must be that there comes a point at which we should find it unintelligible that the thing in question could be so — at least in the sense that if someone did claim to find it a matter for concern we should have to say that we did not understand *him*. Thus it seems to be the case that if in ceasing to be self-deceived one gains a kind of insight into oneself, that insight must have regard to what it is that is a matter for concern for oneself. The self-deception itself must involve an obscuring of that concern.

This suggests that what is important for self-knowledge, at least in the sense of this that is involved when we speak of freedom from self-deception, is what one puts value upon. The man who knows himself in this way, and who is not subject to self-deception, knows, without obscuring the fact from himself, where his values lie, what he truly wants, and where he stands in relation to those wants. I do not think that such knowledge can plausibly be construed in terms of knowledge of 'what he would do if . . .'. It is of course true that one way of finding out whether one wants a certain thing is to ask oneself what one would do if one were deprived of it or if one were presented with the opportunity of getting it but only at the cost of other sacrifices. Doing this, however, is really to employ a kind of heuristic device, an imaginative way of giving concreteness to a choice by putting oneself in the position of making a hypothetical decision. Nevertheless, what is demanded is a *decision*, not a prediction about onself. In such circumstances we should not be passing a judgment about ourselves as to what we should do in hypothetical situations; rather we should be using those hypothetical situations to give body to a decision. Moreover, in making the decision explicit to ourselves we should be gaining knowledge of ourselves that we did not previously possess. It is very often the case that it is only in the context of an actual decision that we become really conscious of where our values and true wants lie; for in those circumstances we may become aware of what really matters to us. In abstraction from contexts of decision, speculation about 'what we should do if . . .' may become idle because it is divorced from any real concern about the objects and matters in question.

What this means is that although I have been discussing the kind of blindness that is involved in self-deception in terms of the self-deceiver blinding himself to certain things *about* himself, there must inevitably lie behind this another kind of blindness to self. This latter blindness, or rather blinding of oneself, is more akin to a refusal to commit oneself to a line of action or perhaps even to make a decision on the course of one's life – or at any rate it must be seen in a context of that kind. A similar point emerges from a consideration of the other example of blindness to self that I instanced earlier – that which comes from an overriding attention to other things. I suggested at the outset that this might be correlated with a lack of concern for the person's own position in the matter. There are, of course, people with a genuine lack of concern for themselves in comparison with others, but what we expect of such people is really a concern for themselves which is limited to what is necessary for the promotion of the concerns of others. If someone had a completely overriding lack of concern for himself he would be likely to be thought of as a liability – his lack of concern for himself would certainly not be anything like a complete virtue. For it to be anything approaching this the lack of concern for self must

251

be both relative and positive, not the negative thing involved in a privation. It should be clear, however, that this blindness to self, to whatever
degree, is not a simple blindness about oneself and could not be construed simply in those terms. Whereas behind self-deception there lies
perhaps a refusal to commit oneself to one single course of action, a
refusal to recognize this as one's course, the blindness to self that I
have been concerned with now involves a failure to see oneself as having
a place in any course of action. The important thing in this is the
reference to action. One would expect of one who revealed any degree
of blindness to self that his life and course of action would lack a
continuous sense. I shall return to this point and its converse later.

## SELF-KNOWLEDGE AND SELF-INVOLVEMENT

The opposite of being blind to oneself would be something that corres-
ponded to having one's eyes open to oneself, a form of self-awareness,
but not one that amounts to self-consciousness in the colloquial sense
of which I spoke earlier. I said in an earlier paper ('Person-perception
and our understanding of others' in T. Mischel, ed., 1974) that a
condition of knowing something is that we should stand to the object
of knowledge in relations which are appropriate to things of that kind.
If that is true, how does it apply to self-knowledge? In what sort of
relations can one stand to oneself? One negative thing should be clear
from what I have said already — that one must be neither blind to
oneself nor in some sense standing back from or apart from oneself.
The failures of self-knowledge that I discussed in the last section
amount to these two alternatives. Indeed the self-deceiver, by standing
back and apart from himself, may well blind himself to himself and so
put himself in the position of the person who is blind to himself *simpliciter*. So much for the negative side of the problem. What, however,
can be said on the positive side about the attitudes appropriate to
oneself as a condition of self-knowledge.

The major problem here, as it often is in philosophy, seems to be
to find a form of words that sums up what is the case. To employ
the wrong words would be in effect to have recourse to a model which
would be misleading. In an earlier version of this paper I used the
notion of 'acceptance' to express the attitude to oneself that is a condition of self-knowledge. I do not think, however that that is quite right,
even apart from the conservatism and quietism that the notion suggests

252

in this context. There is, however, a tradition in the history of thought which connects self-knowledge and self-understanding with a freedom which itself involves an acceptance of oneself in one way or another. I should like to go into that tradition a little.

One strand of it – represented, for example, by the Greek atomists, the Stoics, and Spinoza, though in rather different ways – lays emphasis on the idea that freedom comes through an acceptance of oneself as part of nature and through an understanding of just how one is part of nature. (Those whom I have mentioned had different conceptions of nature, but that does not affect the general point.) There is another strand, however, which emphasizes the idea of knowledge of, commitment to and perhaps acceptance of whatever one is engaged in as a conscious agent. There is something of this, for example, in what Hegel has to say about the connection between self-consciousness and freedom (where of course 'self-consciousness' is *not* being used in the colloquial and pejorative sense). In modern Anglo-Saxon philosophy the idea is to be found in, if I understand them correctly, the writings of Stuart Hampshire, although he, I think, also connects what he has to say with Spinoza. For he puts a premium on a rational understanding of our actions, so that the more that we understand and know of what we are up to the greater our freedom. The self-knowledge that this involves is thus, in part at least, practical. As Hegel puts it, 'Actual free will is the unity of the theoretical and practical mind' (Hegel, ed. J.N. Findlay, 1971, p. 238, S. 481). For Hampshire, as I interpret him, self-knowledge and freedom equally depend upon an increased consciousness of the reasons for our actions, so that what we do becomes to the maximum extent intentional. This means that the increased consciousness in question must not be seen as external to the actions; it is correlative with increased involvement in what we are engaged in. If this is put together with the idea that it is possible to recognize more and more aspects of our life as involving intention, then the involvement of which I have spoken has acceptance of what we are as a natural corollary.

Freud has sometimes been seen as an ally in this, just as he has sometimes been seen as a preacher of self-knowledge.[1] I think that this is a wrong view on both counts. The 'historical' aspects of psychoanalysis, the suggestion that the analysis has to do with the past history of the patient, loom larger in Freud's early writings, or at any rate have a more obvious rationale there, than they do later. The views expressed in Freud's middle-period and later writings, after the 'discovery' of the fictitious nature of reports of infantile seductions, with the emphasis on instinct theory, the primary and secondary processes and the like, really amount to something like a theory of human nature. In the theory of analysis that goes with this the notion of 'transference' plays an all-important part, a fact which in itself makes it impossible to construe analysis as having self-knowledge as its primary goal. Indeed Freud sometimes speaks of analysis as a kind of education for life (e.g. *Introductory Lectures on Psychoanalysis*, ch. 27). Although changes in the theory of human nature that Freud brought forward changed the theory of analysis itself to some extent (the influences are evident in *Inhibitions, Symptoms and Anxiety*), analysis remained for him a kind of education for life in conformity with his conception of human nature. It is not at all clear that self-knowledge as such plays a central part in all this, and I think that to that extent one popular view of psychoanalysis is wrong. Indeed it might be argued that it is at least consistent with Freud's theory that too much self-consciousness is a bad thing.

The same is true of the more special view that psychoanalysis has as its aim the bringing to consciousness of the reasons for our actions in the light of the revelation that more of our life than had previously been supposed is governed by reasons. This view has been criticized on the grounds that what psychoanalysis reveals as governing our actions is not generally or strictly speaking reasons.[2] In one way at least this line of criticism seems to me correct. If Freud indicated that more than had previously been supposed is intentional, he also indicated that not all that is intentional is conscious and perhaps more importantly still for present purposes that it is not all rational or capable of being so. He was quite definite, at least in his mature years, that the irrational and unconscious parts of the mind, those corresponding to the primary process, are not as such capable of being made conscious and rational. What therefore has to be aimed at is a control, though often of necessity a tenuous control, of our irrational instincts on the part of the ego. This may involve a kind of 'know how', which may itself be based on some kind of insight into one's past self; but it is scarcely true that what it produces is an increased consciousness of the reasons for our actions. (I should perhaps add that I am not so much concerned here with the truth of what Freud had to say as with its bearing on considerations about self-knowledge).

Moreover, even if it were true that psychoanalysis was concerned to produce self-knowledge of the kind in question and that this is correlative with an increased freedom on our part, the notions of self-knowledge and freedom that this would involve would surely be severely limited ones. As far as freedom is concerned, it is important to recognize that one does not stand alone; there are of course other people. Thus Hegel, for example, says (1971, S. 431, *Zu*), 'I am only truly free when the other is free and is recognized by me as free', and he elaborates this conception in what he has to say about the master-slave relation, and the restrictions on the master's true freedom imposed by the relationship. Hegel's treatment of this in the *Phenomenology* has sometimes been looked at as a brilliant piece of social analysis. It is scarcely that, brilliant though it is; for it has no particular connection with any actual cases of human relationships. It is rather a metaphysical exposition of certain aspects of the concepts of a person and personal relationships as they arise from Hegel's view of the self and self-consciousness. This becomes clear from his parallel treatment of the matter in the *Encyclopaedia*, although that treatment is much less elaborate and brilliant. He does not simply say there that one cannot have a clear view of oneself without taking into account how one stands to others (although that is no doubt true); he says that 'in that other as ego I behold myself' (1971, S. 430), and in the accompanying *zusatz* he emphasizes the universality of the 'I'. Nevertheless, Hegel's conclusions may have considerable interest for us, irrespective of the grounds on which they rest. There would be, to say the least, an extreme artificiality in the claim that one can attain self-knowledge and thereby acquire a certain freedom by seeking an increased awareness of one's intentions in and reasons for action; for that would presuppose a view of oneself as cut off from all else. At the worst this would involve not merely an artificiality but an arrogance of attitude.

It would thus be quite wrong to think that how one stands to others had nothing to do with oneself or that knowledge of how one stands to others had nothing to do with self-knowledge. If self-knowledge involves some kind of involvement in what we are engaged in (a notion that is connected with the emphasis on intention that we have noted), it is also true that in very many aspects of life what we are engaged in cannot be separated from what we are to others and what they are to us. That is one important implication of Hegel's master-slave case; one cannot be a master and cannot be engaged in being a master without others being involved – a truistical point, perhaps a boring one, but an important one for present purposes all the same.

## SELF-KNOWLEDGE AND OTHERS

It might be said that the master-slave relation presents a very special case. Why should we extrapolate from it to the conclusion that self-knowledge inevitably presupposes something about how one stands to others? Does a hermit, for example, have no possibility of self-knowledge or do we have to treat an absence of relations to others as one kind of relation to others? There is some plausibility in the suggestion that the answer to the last question is 'Yes', but in order to get a clear view of the situation it is necessary to disentangle various different issues here. There are, first, issues concerning what is presupposed in the possibility of acquiring self-knowledge at all. And there are, second, issues concerning the extent to which someone who fulfils the conditions under the first head is capable of having self-knowledge without regard to others. It is the second set of issues to which the consideration about the master-slave relation belongs, and I shall return to it and similar issues later. For the time being I wish to concentrate on the first set of issues.

Negatively the moral of the considerations that I wish to raise under this first head is the same as one to which I drew attention earlier in the paper — the impossibility of construing self-knowledge or even self-understanding as coming about simply via the consideration of information about oneself. While it is the same in this respect, it is so, however, for different reasons. It is not just a matter of our being unable to come to an understanding of self-knowledge on this model alone because of the practical side to our lives and the practical nature of the knowledge that must be presupposed; the model is inadequate any way if treated as an account of how self-knowledge comes about or can come about in the first place. Roughly, it can be said that, if that were all that there was to it, it could never amount to knowledge, nor, since understanding involves knowledge, understanding either. The point is a familiar one to philosophers since Wittgenstein, and it is one that I have made use of elsewhere.[3] Simply put, the point is that if something is to count as knowledge it must be true (or in some sense correct), and if someone is to have knowledge he must know what it is for things to be true or what it is to be correct. But truth, though it is not identical with intersubjective agreement, depends on it in the sense that the concept of truth would get no intelligible application except through it. Hence anyone who knows what truth is must at

256

least know what it is to be in agreement with others. (The same applies analogously to correctness.) It follows therefore that the possession of knowledge implies this also, and if this is true of knowledge in general something like it must be true of self-knowledge. Self-knowledge is possible only for one who has stood to others in the kind of relation that makes agreement possible; for only by so standing could he understand what it is to do so. (This presentation of the argument is excessively brief, and for a longer version I must refer to the references given.)

Thus while someone could gain information about himself, given that the other conditions are satisfied, it would make no sense without that; for in that case self-consideration could not produce anything that could function as *information*. That is not to say that when a person does get information about himself it is *ipso facto* information about how he stands to others. It is rather to say that he could not be said to have knowledge unless he did stand in some way to others, and in particular in a way that gives application to the notion of agreement with them in some ways. I have argued elsewhere that such agreement must be founded ultimately on agreement in emotional attitudes or attitudes involving feeling. Once given this and the gradual acquisition of a set of concepts in terms of which knowledge of oneself is to be expressed, one can by attending to oneself in various ways come to acquire information about oneself that may amount to self-knowledge of a kind, if only of a kind. This too might take place under conditions of isolation from others, but could not take place unless there had been some initial contact with others. To this extent, but to this extent alone, self-knowledge must necessarily presuppose a social context. All this is in effect an extension of Wittgenstein's point that one could not gain an understanding of, say, pain simply by considering the sensation that one is now having (Wittgenstein, 1953, I. 314). A public, social context is presupposed in the understanding of any given concept, since the knowledge that is involved in having that concept is itself public. Without sharing in a public and shared form of life, or at least being in the position to do so, one could not have knowledge. Hence, much else has to be understood before one can begin to think of self-knowledge in terms of getting information about oneself.

The act of a hermit, therefore, in removing himself from society is clearly in one sense a social act, and it is quite fair to consider his consequent lack of relations with others as one kind of relation to them. To say this, however, is merely to say that his act of removing himself or keeping himself apart from others is, to the extent that he knows what he is doing, an intentional act under that description; and even if he does not construe his act as having anything to do with others, he could have knowledge of what he is doing only if he is one who once had things to do with others. Hence, his state as a hermit is a privation of one relationship with others, not a simple negation of all such relationships. Nevertheless, and this takes me to the second issue, if someone takes himself into the desert in isolation in order to seek self-knowledge through contemplation, he thereby deprives himself of certain possibilities of self-knowledge, or at least of knowledge about himself. He cannot see himself in other people's eyes any longer, and for this reason he cannot get those kinds of information about himself that are usually obtainable only through others — how he is to others. Nor can he reliably gain knowledge of what he would do and how he would be in a variety of social contexts and roles. Such knowledge would be of the kind 'what would be the case if . . .', and I tried to indicate earlier that this cannot be all that self-knowledge consists in. It may nevertheless be relevant. If knowledge about oneself is not entirely confined to what one is to others and the like, some part of it must have to do with this.

It is important, however, not to confuse the two points that I have discussed. The fact that self-knowledge, along with other knowledge, presupposes relationships with others, is not to be taken as implying that what one knows must be set out in terms of those relationships, even if some, perhaps much, of what one may come to know about oneself may be construable in those terms. To suppose that would be to confuse the conditions for a kind of knowledge with its content. I suspect that this mistake is made by Mead in his social view of the self. He says, for example (Mead, 1934, p. 138):

The individual experiences himself as such, not directly, but only indirectly, from the particular standpoints of other individual members of the same social group, or from the generalized standpoint of the social group as a whole to which he belongs. For he enters his own experience as a self or individual, not directly or immediately, not by becoming a subject to himself, but only insofar as he first becomes an object to himself just as other individuals are objects to him or in his experience; and he becomes an object to himself only by taking the attitudes of other individuals toward himself within a social environment or context of experience and behavior in which both he and they are involved.

258

Some of this might imply that all that there is to be known about oneself is what is available to others, and that one can acquire knowledge of oneself only by taking on the attitudes of others. That, however, does not seem to be true. It *is* true that the existence of a social context is necessary for the initial acquisition of knowledge about oneself, it may sometimes be true that one can get to know certain things about oneself only through the attitudes of others, and it may be true that our own attitudes to ourselves may be considerably influenced by the attitudes of others. None of that, however, adds up to the point that Mead seems to want to make — that knowledge of myself is simply the knowledge that others have of me. That does seem to involve a confusion of the conditions of knowledge with its content.

What I have been discussing, however, is in the main knowledge *about* oneself, and it is necessary to bring these considerations into relation with self-knowledge in the full sense. Before embarking on a discussion of the place of others in knowledge about oneself, I was concerned with the idea that self-knowledge can be connected with some kind of commitment to oneself. My initial reason for embarking on a discussion of our relations to others was to counter the suggestion that one could think of self-knowledge as concerned primarily with a knowledge of one's reasons for action and perhaps as connected thereby with the idea of a commitment to that line of conduct. I suggested that the idea would involve, as it stands, a kind of arrogance, to say the least, a lack of interest in or concern for others and what we are to them. My succeeding discussion was meant to provide a warning against going to the other extreme and suggesting that self-knowledge is entirely a matter of our relations with others in one way or another. Given this, let us return to the main theme.

## BEING ONESELF

One objection to a concentration on knowledge of one's own reasons for acting or what one is intentionally engaged in as a key to what self-knowledge involves is that such knowledge seems to be a one-sided diet. It might reasonably be held that a concentration on one's own doings and the reasons for them may be inhibitory of spontaneity; there would inevitably be an element of rationalization in the process, a rationalization that might well prevent natural and spontaneous reactions to situations. It does not seem to me at all obviously desirable that people should continually try to make explicit to themselves the reasons for their actions, and if this were what self-knowledge consisted in it might be said that it is not necessarily a good thing. To say that, however, would be to make a comment on the moral desirability of this kind of self-awareness, and while I believe that there are many interesting implications for ethics in this point, my present concern ought to be with its implications for self-knowledge. My main point is that a concentration on making explicit the reasons for our actions must inevitably involve a kind of detachment from oneself, which at the worst can produce that bad kind of self-consciousness which I referred to in connection with Laing. It would of course be wrong to imply that it *must* produce that kind of self-consciousness. It is, however, very likely that it will do so, and to the extent that it involves detachment from oneself it must in any case prevent one being oneself.

How then could it be supposed that concentration on the reasons for our actions and our intentions in acting is the paradigm of self-knowledge, and equally the key to the kind of freedom that this may produce? I indicated earlier that, as I understand him, Stuart Hampshire is one of the main proponents among Anglo-Saxon philosophers of this point of view. He might say that the kind of knowledge of reasons for actions that I have been considering is theoretical and not the practical knowledge that he has in mind. For he insists with some emphasis that the knowledge that he has in mind is practical. It is so in the sense that what we know in doing something intentionally is what we are doing *in doing it*; we do not have to watch ourselves in order to get the knowledge, or anything like that. To do something intentionally is to do it knowing what we are doing, but this does not involve any observational knowledge of our actions, as might be involved if we were to suppose that we had to stand back from ourselves in order to have the knowledge. I think that the basic premise in all this is correct — the knowledge involved in doing something intentionally, the knowledge of what we are doing, is not a knowledge gained from observation of ourselves, nor one that is in any way like that. One might wonder, however, why in that case it has anything to do with self-knowledge. I think that the mediating link in Hampshire's theory is provided by the belief that the knowledge must be conscious and to that extent displayed to ourselves, as it were, even if it is, as he puts it, non-propositional.

It is not clear to me that the non-theoretical character of the knowledge entails that it is non-propositional. The knowledge might be expressible in propositional form even if it were not in fact so expressed. As far as concerns the point about consciousness, it might be argued that when we act with full consciousness of what we are up to there must be a kind of reflexiveness about that consciousness; we are not only conscious of what we are engaged in, we are conscious of *that* and what it involves as well. I am not sure that this is in fact true, since it would imply that the deliberation must take in not only the immediate circumstances of the action but also its large significance for our lives and its place in our conception of ourselves. While this may sometimes be true it is by no means clear that it must always be true. Even so, if what I have said about self-deception is right, it cannot be said that intentional action in general always involves such a consciousness of what we are up to; for knowledge of what we are doing does not necessarily imply consciousness of what we are doing.[4] Thus, although it may be true that someone who does something intentionally does it knowingly and is in some sense responsible for what he does, there need be no implication that he is aware or conscious of what he is up to, let alone that his knowledge brings with it anything that deserves the title 'self-knowledge'. And if in making himself increasingly aware of what he is up to someone thereby increases the control that he has over his actions, his self-knowledge may nevertheless remain very limited. This has large implications for psychoanalysis.

My final point in this connection is that a concentration on the knowledge involved in intentional action, whether or not as a key to self-knowledge, ignores the whole passive side of our mental life. The Spinozistic tradition, within which Hampshire to some extent operates, associates passivity with irrationality and with ignorance or confused consciousness. But the ideal of a rationality that goes with an activity of mind which can transcend the confusedness of passivity has little to do with anything human. Our emotional life, for example, which has to do with the passivity in question, is not just an area of irrationality which increasing awareness can diminish. We are dependent on it in all sorts of ways, and a theory of self-knowledge must take that into account. The supposal that one could be alive to what one is by bringing more and more of one's activities under intention is a likely recipe for self-deception; it would certainly entail an abstention from being oneself — something which, as it seems to me, is a necessary condition of self-knowledge.

What I have said is, I admit, excessively dogmatic, and in taking Hampshire as my target for criticism I may have seriously misunderstood what he has to say. There may, however, be general morals to be abstracted from it all. What it suggests is the extent to which genuine self-knowledge presupposes that we must *be* ourselves and not be in the position of standing back from ourselves in any way. We shall be in that position either if we insist on regarding ourselves theoretically all the time or if, under the influence of a theory, we concentrate our consciousness and attention on one part of ourselves. This does not mean that for self-knowledge we have no need to know all sorts of facts about ourselves, any more than that the thesis which I defended on the last occasion of this kind − that knowing other people presupposes standing in certain relations to them − entails that we do not need to know all sorts of facts about them. No matter what the object of knowledge is, knowledge of it of course involves knowledge of many things about it; the point is simply that it does not involve *just* that. It is obvious enough that there are many attitudes which one can take up towards oneself that will prevent self-knowledge − and this may be so even if one knows a great many things about oneself. This can certainly happen if, as I indicated earlier, the knowledge is strictly theoretical in the sense that it gets no real purchase in practice. Similarly, I suppose, we might know many things in theory about another person without this knowledge getting any purchase in our practical dealings with them. Yet I have argued in connection with other people that genuine knowledge of this kind is not properly to be construed merely as a practical know-how in our dealings with them, whether or not that know-how is backed up by knowledge of their character, temperament, personality, etc. For people are not merely objects the handling of which demands knowledge of this kind; so that it is important that we should stand to them in relations which are appropriate to them as people. If it is less clear what this means in connection with knowledge of oneself, it is at all events evident that certain kinds of knowledge will not be sufficient, given that the knowledge that has to be explained thereby is knowledge of a *self*. In addition there is the important point that the knowledge in question is knowledge of *oneself* and not another self; for this eliminates the possibility of genuine self-knowledge where there is any tendency to stand back from oneself in such a way as to regard oneself, in part at least, as another person. One must be involved in oneself.

## 'KNOW THYSELF'

I wish finally to return to the Delphic saying and Socrates's use of it, and then to try to sum up the implications of it all for our present purposes. I suspect (though I can hardly claim to know) that when Socrates invoked the saying he wanted people to make their own decisions about the conduct of their lives and not simply go by rules however derived. To make those decisions people would have to have some insight into their own position, and their capabilities and limitations, in respect of the situation in which they found themselves, a situation which would inevitably involve other people. If in such a situation you were to obey his instruction you would not simply go by any kind of rote or rule; you would have to think out for yourself what you should do. Some of the factors in that decision might well depend on how you *felt* about certain things, so that you could not necessarily present them as considerations that must appeal to all men irrespective of circumstances. There is in all this a demand for a certain kind of integrity (the parallel of which in Kierkegaard, who admired Socrates so much, is purity of heart and freedom from 'double-mindedness'). I am not entirely sure that this must have the ethical consequences that these thinkers demanded; there is a kind of integrity combined with insight which is quite compatible with an evil disposition. The case of Eichmann has sometimes been invoked in this context. It might also be said that as a moral point of view it pays insufficient attention to social considerations. These are arguable points. Nothing in any case can make moral decision easy in *all* circumstances; nothing can ensure that such decisions are always right. The important thing for present purposes, however, is the reference to *decision*, a point on which I remarked earlier in the paper.

For one of the paradoxes about self-knowledge is that it can be mediated by decision; perhaps indeed it must be in the end.[5] We and our lives are constantly changing. Whether or not it is right to think of this as a development,[6] the changes that take place build on what is past. A decision about the future conduct of our life can alter the whole perspective from which we view ourselves and give a new or different sense to what we have been. That new sense may involve the taking up of things that we did or which happened to us and which seemed only marginally to do with us, so that they become genuinely ours. That is presumably what some moral philosophers have been getting at when they have spoken of giving sense to our lives as a whole and of a kind of self-deception that may pervade a whole life.[7] I think, however, that it has to be said that it can work quite the other way round or perhaps even in some intervening way; things that seemed of vital concern to us can come to be viewed as merely incidental. Once again there is no recipe for how it has to be. The important point for present purposes is the point that an important decision for the future can utterly change our view of ourselves in relation to our past. A person is not a static thing. If there are some constant things about us (there *is* such a thing as personal identity, and some constants about us may be genetically determined), we are also changing entities with both a history and a possible future. For this reason alone there can be no complete story about what has to be known for adequate self-knowledge. Indeed it might be said that a central fact about self-knowledge is that there is no *thing* to be known.

Is not the same true, however, of knowledge of others? Yes, in a sense. Other people are creatures with a past and a possible future. Yet there is an asymmetry; for in a sense what I am is my own past and future, and I must therefore be involved in this in a way and to a degree different from my involvement in those of others. This affects how and what I know in these cases, if I do. The point is really just a corollary of the point, previously mentioned, that my knowledge of anything has as a necessary condition my standing in relations to it of the kind appropriate to things of that kind (Hamlyn, in T. Mischel, 1974). I cannot therefore construe my knowledge of myself, to the extent that it exists, as parallel to that of others, let alone to that of other kinds of thing. We can decide to some extent what our futures shall be (even if to a limited extent only) in a way that we cannot decide on the futures of others. That is vital to any view of self-knowledge that we can form.

## CONCLUSION

All this may seem poles apart from anything that psychologists normally have to do with; and so it is. Yet what I have said must have some implications for the understanding of oneself. There are many respects in which to understand ourselves we may have to view ourselves in ways that are parallel to those which enable us to understand others. But the asymmetry remains even here; and *one* way of coming to understand ourselves — perhaps an all-important way — may be to have to make the kind of decision about our future that I have mentioned, a decision that may bring with it other views of ourselves. That feature, however, need not be taken as undermining the point that within that framework the ways in which we understand others can to some extent be applied to ourselves. We should nevertheless be conscious of the limits involved in this.

I noted near the beginning that most psychological investigations in this area have to do with what are in effect people's beliefs about themselves, under which heading I include how they see themselves, the picture that they have of themselves, all that is included under the notion of the self-concept. To the extent that all this can indeed be put in terms of people's beliefs about themselves, it is feasible to think of the acquisition of such beliefs in terms of getting information; for such beliefs may be acquired in the process of social learning. It is clear that the part played by social factors in a person's forming a picture of himself and in the acquisition of various beliefs about himself should not be underestimated. Our beliefs about ourselves, just as with our beliefs about others, may be founded on stereotypes or they may have a foundation in reality. Part of that reality may be social relationships; for what a person is to others is an important part of what he has to get to know about himself. But self-knowledge as such is, as I have tried to show, quite another thing.

## NOTES

1 See e.g. S.N. Hampshire, 1959, p. 255.
2 See P. Alexander, 1962 and the reply by T. Mischel, 1965.
3 See Hamlyn, 1973. A more extended account of the matter is to be found in my *Experience and the Growth of Understanding*, London, Routledge & Kegan Paul, 1978.
4 See Hamlyn, 1971a, 1971b.
5 I think that I owe much in what follows to Richard Campbell.
6 For which see Hamlyn, 'The concept of development' *Proc. of the Phil. of Ed. Soc. of Gt. Britain*, vol. ix (1975), pp. 26-39 (this volume pp. 149-61).
7 Cf. I. Dilman and D.Z. Phillips, 1971, although I would not myself go along with much of the discussion in that book.

# REFERENCES

Alexander, P. 'Rational behaviour and psychoanalytic explanation', *Mind*, LXXI, 1972, pp. 326-41.

Anscombe, G.E.M. *Intention*, Oxford, Blackwell, 1951.

Dilman, I. & Phillips, D.Z. *Sense and Illusion*, London, Routledge & Kegan Paul, 1971.

Freud, S. *Introductory Lectures on Psychoanalysis* (1916-17), S.E. Vols. XV and XVI, London, Hogarth Press, 1953.

Freud, S. *Inhibitions, Symptoms and Anxiety*, S.E. Vol. XII, London, Hogarth Press, 1953.

Hamlyn, D.W. *The Theory of Knowledge*, New York, Doubleday, 1970, (also London, Macmillan, 1971).

Hamlyn, D.W. 'Unconscious intentions', *Philosophy*, XLVI, 1971a, pp. 12-22 (this volume pp. 181-93).

Hamlyn, D.W. 'Self-deception', *Proceedings of the Aristotelian Society*, Supp. Vol. XLV, 1971b, pp. 45-60 (this volume, pp. 194-207).

Hamlyn, D.W. 'Human learning in *The Philosophy of Psychology* (ed. S.C. Brown), London, Macmillan, 1973, pp. 139-57 (also in *The Philosophy of Education*, ed. R.S. Peters, Oxford University Press, 1973, 178-94, this volume, pp. 132-48).

Hamlyn, D.W. 'Person-perception and our understanding of others' in T. Mischel (ed.), 1973 (this volume, pp. 208-38).

Hampshire, S.N. *Thought and Action*, London, Chatto and Windus, 1959.

Hegel, G.F. *Phenomenology of Mind* (trans. J.B. Baillie), London, Allen and Unwin, 1910.

Hegel, G.F. *Hegel's Philosophy of Mind* (trans. W. Wallace, ed. J.N. Findlay), Oxford, Clarendon Press, 1971.

Laing, D. *The Divided Self*, Harmondsworth, Penguin, 1965.

Mead, G.H. *Mind, Self and Society*, Chicago University Press, 1934.

Mischel, T. 'Concerning rational behaviour and psychoanalytic explanation', *Mind*, LXXIV, 1965, pp. 71-8.

Mischel, T. (ed.), *Understanding Other Persons*, Oxford, Blackwell, 1974.

Ryle, G. *The Concept of Mind*, London, Hutchinson, 1949.

Sartre, J.P. *Being and Nothingness* (trans. H.E. Barnes), London, Methuen, 1957.

Shoemaker, S. *Self-knowledge and Self-identity*, Ithaca, Cornell University Press, 1963.

Wittgenstein, L. *Philosophical Investigations*, Oxford, Blackwell, 1953.

# 15

# THE PHENOMENA OF
# LOVE AND HATE

There has been a good deal of interest in recent years in what Franz
Brentano had to say about the notion of 'intentional objects' and about
intentionality as a criterion of the mental. There has been less interest
in his classification of mental phenomena. In his *Psychology from an
Empirical Standpoint* Brentano asserts and argues for the thesis that
mental phenomena can be classified in terms of three kinds of mental
act or activity, all of which are directed towards an immanent object.
These are, respectively, presentation, judgment and what he calls the
phenomena of love and hate. Once again, less interest has been shown
in what he has to say about the last of these three than in what he says
about the others. I wish to take Brentano's views as the point of departure for a discussion of love and hate, since these notions seem to me to
have a good deal of philosophical interest, for at least two main reasons.
First, I have recently had some concern with the part that personal
relations play in our understanding of others and of ourselves, and love
and hate seem to be very important elements in such relations. Second,
love and hate have long seemed to me to provide important counter-
examples to some prevalent philosophical theories about the emotions.
I shall take this issue first.

It would not be a plausible move to defend any theory of the emotions to which love and hate seemed exceptions by saying that love and
hate are after all not emotions. I have heard this said, but it does seem
to me a desperate move to make. If love and hate are not emotions
what are? Brentano himself adopts a position which is even further
away from that reaction by saying that all emotions involve love and
hate. In considering the third of his classifications of mental phen-

omena he argues that the class includes both feeling and will, but in such a way that they constitute a unity. Feeling, he wants to say, is not merely something passive that happens to us. Even feelings such as those of pleasure and pain involve desires and wants on our part — the willing of the phenomenon to go on in the one case or the willing of it to stop in the other. Hence there are no such things as mere feelings which do not involve some aspect of the will. On the other hand the willing of a phenomenon involves some definite kind of feeling towards it, the sort of feeling that is involved in a desire or an aversion. Brentano concludes, therefore, that feeling and will are united into a single fundamental class, and he argues against other philosopher-psychologists of his time who denied this. He thinks that what unites the phenomena of this class is precisely the role of love and hate in providing the focus for whatever else that is involved. Love is in that respect a kind of positive feeling towards an object which is *ipso facto* through the desire that it involves an aspect of the will. This converse is true of hate. If there are other features in any given emotion one or other of love and hate provides a focus for that emotion. So far, then, from love and hate not being emotions, they are the central core of all emotions; or at least one or the other is.

It might be said that this account stretches our ordinary understanding of the concepts of love and hate, and Brentano faces up to that objection himself (op. cit., London: Routledge & Kegan Paul, 1973, p. 199). I do not wish to approach that issue head on, although considerations that are relevant to it will emerge later. But what of the relation of love and hate to the other classifications of mental phenomena? These classifications are made in terms of 'the different ways in which they refer to their content' (ibid., p. 197). In presentation something is presented to consciousness, and this can be one of a considerable range of things from sensations to thoughts. In judgment, by contrast, there is involved acceptance as true or rejection as false, while in the third category there are the attitudes of love and hate. Brentano believes that in any complete act of consciousness all three of these elements will be included. There is no logical necessity for this to be so, however, and we can conceive of presentation without judgment or feeling, and we can conceive of judgment without any attitude of love or hate. There is nevertheless a logical ordering in the other direction. We cannot conceive, he thinks, of judgment taking place without presentation, nor of love or hate taking place without both presentation and judgment. So he says (ibid., p. 267):

It is certainly not necessary that someone believe that a thing exists or is even capable of existing, in order for him to love it, but nonetheless, every act of love is loving the existence of something. And one love would never arouse another, one thing would never be loved for the sake of another, unless there were a belief in certain connections between the one and the other which played some part. An act of love will be one of joy on some occasions, sorrow on others, or hope or fear or any number of other forms, depending upon what judgment is made concerning the existence or nonexistence, probability or improbability of the object loved. In fact, then, it seems inconceivable that a being should be endowed with the capacity for love and hate without possessing that of judgment.

Brentano's conclusion is weaker than one might have expected from the earlier part of this passage. For he concludes, not that every case of love and hate involves a belief, but that any being that can love and hate must be capable of judgment. That conclusion is, I think, true, although the considerations that he brings forward in its favour are scarcely compelling; for they seem to suggest only that *some* forms of love and hate and *some* phenomena connected with them presuppose judgment. However, if an argument *can* be brought forward for the thesis that only a creature that can have judgment or beliefs can love and hate, it will have to be a much more complex argument than the one that Brentano actually adduces. Such a thesis is nevertheless very different from the thesis that love and hate themselves necessarily involve belief or judgment. It is a thesis of this latter kind about the emotions in general that has become something of the current orthodoxy, even if there are some exceptions to this. In modern times the thesis goes back at least to Errol Bedford's well-known paper on the 'Emotions' (*PAS* 1956/57, pp. 281ff., and reprinted many times), but it is a thesis that was maintained in ancient times by the Stoics, who held, for example, that greed was a false belief in the importance of money.

Let me give a general description of this thesis about the emotions – a description which is, I hope, not a caricature. It is possible to begin with a consideration that is close to something that Brentano has to say, and which is a cardinal feature of most recent philosophical accounts of the emotions – that the emotions take objects and that the range of possible objects of this kind must be restricted in some way. Emotions take objects not just in the sense that there is some actual ject on to which the emotion is directed; indeed this need not be so all since the person concerned may be under a delusion on this point. ere must nevertheless be (with qualifications to be made directly) mething which the person takes as such, something that is *for him* an ject of his emotion. This is what Brentano was getting at in speaking the necessity for an immanent object in this case. Thus if we experi-ce pride it must be pride *in* something, in something that is the object the pride for us whether or not it actually exists. Analogously, we nnot be said to experience envy unless we are envious *of* something nd normally perhaps *for* something). We cannot be said just to be oud or envious except in the sense of those words in which we indi-te a character-trait; and the connection of character-traits with notions in the straightforward sense is a complex matter which need ot concern us now.

It is not necessary that the object be explicit to us in that the person oncerned must be capable of spelling it out. I can be envious of some-hing without being able to say explicitly what it is that I am envious f. The fact that I cannot do this, however, does not in itself preclude vhatever I am in fact envious of being an object of envy for me. There an be other forms of consciousness apart from the explicit conscious-ess which is involved in the ability to spell things out. But there must e something which is for me the object of my envy, the object of my onsciousness in this connection in some way or other. Indeed some philosophers have made this a criterion for distinguishing between emotions and moods; in the latter case we may be in an analogous state of mind, but this need not be directed on to anything explicit, even if it may be caused by something explicit. At the best it may be possible to say of a mood that its object is 'anything or nothing', or perhaps 'everything'. There are however some emotional states, if I may call them that, which are ambiguous in this respect, e.g. joy, happiness and depression. We may take joy in something, be happy about some-thing, or be depressed at or about something, but it is not necessary that this reference to an object should be there; we can be simply joyous, happy or depressed, in a way that is characteristic of moods.

I have been speaking of the sense in which it is true that emotions must take objects, to the extent that they must. As I suggested earlier, these objects must be restricted in some way. One cannot, for example, take pride in *anything*. There is a sense in which this is true, but one needs to be careful over it. If it were said that one cannot *fear* any-thing, it might well be replied that there are surely no bounds to human irrationality, or that if there are they are certainly very wide. We might say of some object that no rational person could be afraid of it. If this were true, it would not follow that it was also true that no *human being* could be afraid of it, let alone that there is some logical or conceptual impossibility in being afraid of it. People have irrational fears about many sorts of object that others cannot understand their being afraid of; that however does not amount to its being unintelligible that one should speak of such fears. What is taken as unintelligible is that *they* should feel the fear; it is not that speaking of the fear is logically absurd. If there are things which it is humanly impossible to fear, to speak of someone fearing them involves a *kind* of absurdity, but not a logical absurdity in the strict sense.

However that may be, it remains the case that even in the case of irrational fears the people concerned must find something about the object to be afraid of, even if they cannot say what this is. The position is perhaps even clearer with pride. I cannot take pride in something if it has nothing to do with me. A person can be proud of his achievements, of his children's achievements, or of his country's achievements. It would be odd for him to be proud of his failures or the failures of others who have some connection with him. To justify the intelligibility of that a very special explanation would be required, although one cannot exclude the possibility that one of that kind may be forthcoming; people do sometimes want to fail. What, however, if I have no connection with the object in a way that would make it intelligible for me to have such concerns with it in one way or the other? Can I, to use an example used by others, be proud of the sea? One might at first blush feel like saying 'No', but that answer would presuppose that the sea has nothing to do with me, not only in the sense that I have in fact nothing to do with *it*, but also in the sense that I do not even *believe* that I have anything to do with it. If someone irrationally believes that he has some responsibility for the sea being as it is, nothing prevents its being said of him that he is proud of it. We should feel that his pride was quite irrational, but that is because the supporting belief is irrational; and without that we might not even understand the attribution of pride at all. This reference to belief brings us back to Brentano.

It brings us back to Brentano because the position arrived at seems to agree with his remarks concerning the extent to which an emotion presupposes some kind of supporting belief. On reflection, however, it may seem that 'belief' is too strong a word to use here. Those who have an irrational fear of mice may in one sense have all the right beliefs about mice. They may know that mice are too small and too harmless in any direct way to be frightening, and whatever view one has about the relation between knowledge and belief it seems right to say that they believe this too – in an intellectual way at least. It may remain true, however, that whatever their intellectual beliefs about mice may be, they cannot help seeing them in practice as frightening little creatures. There is a conflict between their full-blooded rational beliefs about mice and how they see them and cannot help seeing them in concrete circumstances. It might be said that in such a case there is simply a conflict of beliefs, but to insist on this would be misleading. How one sees things may be a function of one's beliefs in a variety of ways; it may, however, be a function of other things, and it is certainly not true that whenever one sees something as such and such one has *ipso facto* a belief to that effect. There are perceptual illusions, e.g. the Müller-Lyer illusion, where one sees things in a certain way whatever one's beliefs about them may be; one's seeing them in that way *may* in some cases at least, be explicable in terms of beliefs that one has, and it may be that one would not be able to see them in that way if one did not have beliefs, but that does not mean that when one sees them in that way one does have beliefs to the same effect. There is what has been called non-epistemic seeing in that way at least. The same applies to seeing mice as frightening. That may be a function of beliefs, but the seeing need not be believing.

It might be replied that the seeing does in this case have consequences both in action and in feeling. There need be no such consequences when one is subject to the Müller-Lyer illusion, so that there is a difference. That seems true. In view of the consequences of the seeing in this case it may be right to say that whether or not one actually believes that mice are frightening when one is frightened by them one certainly has an inclination to believe this. Yet it remains true that to have a given emotional attitude to an object, or at least an emotional attitude of the kind so far surveyed, one has either to have a certain sort of belief about that object or to see it in the corresponding way, whether or not that belief or way of seeing it is in fact justified. If we cannot say simply that a person cannot feel pride in something that has nothing to do with him, we must say that he cannot feel pride in it if he does not have the corresponding belief or at least see it in that light. If none of this is true, then whatever he feels about the object it is not pride.

272

## The phenomena of love and hate

The question that now arises – which brings me to my main topic – is about the extent to which this applies also to love and hate. Like Brentano I shall for convenience apply myself mainly to love, although most if not all of what I have to say applies equally to hate. (I shall introduce some qualifications to this later.) Love and hate are to that extent parallel emotions. They are also both positive attitudes, not simply such that one is the negation of the other. Brentano rightly emphasizes that point, and, more arguably, goes on to contrast the phenomena of love and hate with, e.g. judgment, in the case of which he thinks of rejection simply as the negation of affirmation; this is arguable in the light of the possibility of simple withholding of belief. However, no one could plausibly say that hate was simply the withholding of love. Hence if any theory about love carries over to hate it is not because the one is simply the negation or privation of the other, but because the two really do constitute parallel attitudes for these purposes.

The first thing to note about love is that it is, as one might put it, a very 'catholic' emotion; it takes many forms and takes many kinds of object, and it would be a mistake to ignore or underestimate that fact. It may be that reason alone which makes Brentano give love and hate such pre-eminent importance among the emotions. Let us take first the forms that love can take. At one extreme it is almost a mood; I mean by this to refer to the state of being in love. It is of course true that when someone is in love they are normally in love with someone or something. Cynics might say however that in some cases where someone is in love the object is, as it were, found or invented for the state rather than the other way round, and that this is often a precondition for what we call infatuation. Such a view is not just cynicism; there is the state of readiness for an infatuation. Whether one is prepared to dignify it itself with the title of love is a matter for argument. That is why I say that at this extreme love is *almost* a mood; it is simply that in this state *what* the object is may be of less importance than that there should be one to match the state.

At the other extreme love may at least approximate to an attitude which we can adopt pretty much at will. This seems to be implied by the fact that we may sometimes be instructed to love someone or something, and that loving someone or something may be set up as a principle of action, as it is in the command that we should love our neighbour. Such love is near to simple benevolence, to wishing someone well, and if we cannot adopt such an attitude quite at will, we can certainly take measures to get ourselves into the position of doing so. Brentano associates love with willing something as good, and I take it that he has this kind of love in mind. His way of putting it also has one advantage over a reference to benevolence or wishing someone well. This is that these latter terms may be taken, and often *are* taken, as referring to an attitude of mind which need have no implications for action. When we are told to love our neighbour we are not told simply to have nice and perhaps comfortable thoughts about him or her — as might indeed be implied by the reference to *wishing*; the principle is supposed to be a principle for action and conduct (though what action is notoriously difficult to determine in many cases — a principle like that of 'Love thy neighbour' does not, if adopted, obviate the necessity for difficult moral decisions). If the state of being in love is merely *near* to being a mood and not simply identical with one, the positive attitude of love is *near* to willing some course of action and not simply identical with it. It remains true that these two things represent extremes which are separated from each other by a considerable distance, and this fact about love is worthy of note and must not be ignored in any theory about it.

The other point about love that I was going to mention is about the range of possible objects that it can take. I have spoken of loving someone *or something*. I did so quite deliberately. To emphasize that there can be different forms of love between people would be to underline a cliché. It perhaps requires a little more emphasis that there can be love of objects too. It is obvious enough that people can love beautiful objects, particularly works of art; but they can also love quite ordinary things which have no pretensions to aesthetic value, e.g. possessions. Moreover there does not have to be any very close relation between the lover and what is loved, whether that be a person or a thing. Love at a distance is certainly possible, although it is less and less possible to the extent that the person or object is or must be out of mind. It might be objected that all this simply serves to show that the word 'love' is just ambiguous, and that it means something different as applied to people and as applied to things. I am not sure that I know how exactly to reply to such an objection, except to point to the considerations about love that I shall bring forward in the sequel. It can be said now, however, that if the objection held exactly the same thing would have to apply to various forms of love between persons (sexual love as opposed to parental love and so on), since there are differences between these which are as large as those between love of persons and love of things. In the history of thought many distinctions between forms of love have been made (*eros*, *philia* and *agape*; Aphrodite Urania and Aphrodite Pandemos; sacred and profane love, etc.), but these differences have not usually been thought of as constituting an ambiguity in the word 'love'. That there are differences between forms of love and that the nature of the object may affect the possibility of given forms of love in relation to it remains obviously true.

Given all this, the question that I now wish to raise is this: if one does love X, what beliefs must one have about X, and how must one see or regard X if it is really to be love? For, if love is to be parallel to emotions like pride and fear, it follows from what I have said earlier about those emotions that there must be an analogous answer to this question in its case. The lover must value the beloved in some way, but in what way? In particular, must the lover love the beloved *for* anything (for if so it seems to follow that he must have a belief about the object in that respect or at least see the beloved in that way)? There are no doubt some things about which it might be felt that they could be loved *only* for some specific reason. But this would again be a point about human nature and not a point of logic. W.B. Yeats' poem 'For Anne Gregory', for example, presents the case of someone who, the poet says, could not be loved by human beings except for the colour of her hair, even though the woman wants to be loved 'for herself alone'. (In the first of the three stanzas the 'poet' says:

> Never shall a young man,
> Thrown into despair
> By those great honey-coloured
> Ramparts at your ear,
> Love you for yourself alone
> And not your yellow hair.

The woman replies in the second stanza by saying in effect that she can dye her hair and then they may love her for herself alone and not her yellow hair. But the last verse reads:

> I heard an old religious man
> But yesterday declare
> That he had found a text to prove
> That only God, my dear,
> Could love you for yourself alone
> And not your yellow hair.

There seem to me, incidentally, to be certain defects in the argument, which I shall not go into, but I do not hold them against the poem as such!) If it were true that she could not be loved except for the colour of her hair, this would have to be, once again, a fact of human nature, not a point of logic. It does not seem logically absurd that she should be loved full-stop. (This may not be what the woman in the poem wants when she speaks of being loved for herself alone, but there is a good deal of difficulty in that idea in any case. What I shall say later may have some bearing on it.)

To be loved full-stop is simply to be loved without there being anything that the love is for. In such a situation there is likely to be some explanation why the love came into being, and it is possible with some objects of love for one to love them for the fact that and because of the circumstances in which the love came into being; but there seems to me no necessity that it should be like that — the circumstances may explain the continuance of the love but they may not be what the love is for. I suggest that love is possible where there is nothing that the love is for — or at any rate that nothing logically prevents that possibility. I confess that I have not yet *shown* that it is a possibility. I wish to move in that direction by a consideration of the range of possible attitudes to the object of love that are compatible with that love. That will at least show what beliefs if any are necessary to love.

What I have to say may seem somewhat dogmatic, but I mean to appeal simply to common convictions on the matter, and if the convictions are not shared further argument will inevitably be called for. It seems to me that loving someone or something is not incompatible with, for example, having no respect for them, finding them in many ways distasteful, or recognizing in them a whole series of bad qualities which are not overridden by good qualities. Love, one might say, is to some extent at least a contingent thing; one cannot always explain why and where it falls. It might be objected that it must at least be true that the lover desires the beloved, wants to be with him/her/it, or something of that kind. I am not sure that even this *has* to be true. Suppose that someone has got to the point of recognizing the absolutely disastrous character of a relationship. It is possible for them to renounce it and any desire for its continuance while still loving the person concerned. Some indeed (including, I suspect, Kierkegaard) have made a virtue of this, although it is no part of the phenomenon that it must have that character.

In the face of all this it is very difficult to think of any particular

276

belief that the lover *must* have about the beloved, or any way in which the lover must see the beloved. It might be objected that even if no single particular belief is necessary one or more of some disjunction of beliefs may be, and that if there were not so love and hate could not be differentiated. I am not sure how to reply to the first part of this objection, except to say that considerations similar to those which rule out the necessity for particular beliefs will in the end rule out the suggestion about a disjunction of beliefs. In any case, it is not necessary to resort to this suggestion because of the need to differentiate love and hate, since they may be differentiated by factors other than beliefs. Moreover, it has often been pointed out that while love and hate are opposed for the most part they may in their extreme forms and in their most primitive manifestations be very close together. Passionate love may turn easily into hate without any beliefs changing at the same time and without the change being due to any newly acquired beliefs, however much different beliefs may follow in due course. If love and hate are not differentiated by beliefs they need not be determined by them either.

I suggest, then, that no particular belief or disjunction of beliefs about the beloved is necessary on the part of the lover, nor any particular ways of seeing the beloved. There is of course what might be looked on as a possible exception to this rule − the trivial fact that he or she must see the beloved as an object for love. Brentano said that 'it is certainly not necessary that someone believe that a thing exists or is even capable of existing, in order for him to love it, but, none the less, every act of love is loving the existence of something.' I take it that what he means by 'loving the existence of something' is what I was trying to get at in speaking of seeing the beloved as an object for love. If this is a belief it is not one that provides any answer to the question what the lover loves the beloved for. It is as a belief a merely formal condition of the possibility of love − that the love must have an object. But this presupposes the other point which I believe to be true in what Brentano says − that love is possible only for a believer, or at least only for one who is capable of seeing something *as* something, i.e. in this case as an object of love. (I shall for the sake of convenience ignore the distinction between belief and seeing-as in what follows, as indeed I may have done already; where the distinction is relevant it can be read into my discussion.) Given all this, it might be argued that if I have shown anything it is that no particular kind of belief *about* the object is necessary for love or hate, but not that belief is unnecessary altogether.

277

That would be fair comment, but the conclusion is enough for my purposes.

It is enough because that conclusion by no means entails that love and hate necessarily have particular beliefs as constituents which determine that they are love or hate, let alone that they must be founded on beliefs. As Brentano points out, one *may* love one thing for the sake of another, and in that case the love is certainly founded on the belief that this thing is connected appropriately with that. But it is not always like that. With pride and envy, on the other hand, belief (or seeing-as) *is* a constituent of the emotion in the sense in question, since to experience them one must not only see the thing in question merely as an object for the emotion, one must see it in a way that is appropriate to the emotion. With love the difficulty is to find anything of this kind which is uniquely appropriate to love. My thesis is that there is nothing of this kind that *must* be so, and that this differentiates it and hate from the other emotions. One might indeed argue, as Brentano does, that the other emotions presuppose love or hate in some way. If this is true (and it may well be so) love and hate would best be characterized as 'feelings towards', and would be the primary forms of these. As such feelings they are not just passive states that are produced in us, as pains may be, but something that also involves an attitude, a directedness towards an object, as Brentano suggested.

There is a tendency within the philosophy of mind, which may be a residual legacy of Cartesianism and reactions to it, to divide the phenomena of the human mind into two classes — the first being the class of mental states that more or less occur to us and have a certain passivity, the second being the manifestations of our capacity for judgment and other intellectual activity. Thus we have a constrast between feeling and cognition. But in this sense, feeling remains something that just happens to us. Even in Descartes, of course, feelings were thought of as modifications of thought in the sense that the capacity for feeling, which involves the body, is dependent on the existence of the capacity for thinking, which involves the soul. This dependence is a function of the quasi-substantial union between soul and body, of which Descartes thought no account could be given. This general picture has been undermined in all sorts of ways, largely through the writings of Wittgenstein, which has produced for obvious reasons an emphasis on the philosophy of action and its relevance for the philosophy of mind in general. It has thus come to be seen, for example, that the notion of intention does not fit easily into that original position, even if it is intimately connected with the notion of action. In the case of the emotions, however, there is a less obvious connection with forms of actions, even if we expect them to find some overt expression in many cases. Thus, given this last recognition together with the recognition that feelings as passive states do not provide a sufficient basis for differentiation between different emotions, recourse has been had to judgment or belief for this purpose, this being the remaining factor in our legacy.

Brentano's 'intentionality' thesis, that mentality involves an intention of the mind, a directedness towards certain objects, constitutes a departure from that legacy to some extent. Even here, however, more attention has been given perhaps to the nature of those objects (their 'inexistence') than to the idea involved in the reference to directedness. Thus one interpretation of or gloss on the Brentano thesis, that all mental phenomena involve a thought (cf. R.A. Wollheim, *PAS*, 1967/68, pp. 1-24), in a way goes back towards the Cartesian position; it certainly leaves out the suggestion that feeling, *qua* feeling, may be directed towards an object. What I have said about love and hate amounts to the suggestion that these be considered as feeling towards objects in just this sense. Moreover it seems to me that it is logically possible at least for these 'feelings towards' to exist without any intimate connections between these feelings and any beliefs on the part of the person concerned of the sort that certainly seem requisite for many emotions. If, however, the objects of these feelings are to be objects in anything more than a purely formal sense, those objects must be identifiable in some way; and that certainly presupposes beliefs on the part of the person concerned. Hence, nothing that could be identified as such a feeling could take place in a creature that did not have beliefs. That, however, does not entail that the feelings necessarily involve beliefs as constituents or as the basis for the feelings.

I said that I had two reasons for being concerned with the subject — one of them being the relation of love and hate to other emotions and the implications that this has generally for philosophical theories in this area. My conclusion on this lies in what I have said about 'feelings towards'. I do not know whether it is right to say, as Brentano did, that the other emotions involve love and hate; a more acceptable thesis would be that they all involve 'feelings towards', and that love and hate are particularly pure versions of these because of their possible detachment from particular beliefs. One might therefore say that they constitute the paradigm cases of such feelings, and have an importance for that reason, if for no other. The other reason that I gave for being concerned with the subject was the part that love and hate play in personal relations, especially given the part that these in turn play in our understanding of others and of ourselves. I wish now to say something about this second issue, in so far as what I have already said affects it.

My main point can be put as follows: I have paid some attention to the possibility of love being independent of reasons (whether or not there is a reason for it in the sense of a cause). This seems to me a logical possibility and even a human possibility in the sense that it is intelligible in human beings at any rate as an isolated phenomenon. But it would be odd if it were always like that. Personal relations no doubt involve feeling, but they are not just a matter of one person having feelings of some kind towards another, to which that other responds in kind. There is not enough that is human in that, and it may well be true that that description is satisfied by animals or some of them. Where it is a thing that is the object of love, there may have been reasons in the first place why the person concerned had a love for it, reasons that may have ceased to apply and which are now not even up for consideration. Nevertheless, the fondness for it may remain without the person knowing why, let alone being able to say why (at the bottom, so to speak, the love may remain out of habit, but I am not suggesting that this is necessarily the case). Others may feel that there is a certain touching irrationality in this, and it may even be irritating to those with whom he or she lives. But it need have no consequences beyond that. The same could not be said of a similar love for a person, and the person loved would have the right to demand more.

Why is this? In the case of a loved thing, it can remain simply an object of contemplation, something that the person likes to handle, or perhaps use as a tool when other instruments would do the job as well or better. If this were true of the loved person he or she would rightly feel used. The love in this case must have more consequences and implications than that. The reason for this lies in what it is to be a person and in what, *given that*, it is for a person to be an appropriate object of another person's love.

It may be useful at this point to revert to a consideration of hate. A person's hatred of an object may sometimes be set down as a mere quirk, at any rate if that hatred does not impinge on more human concerns. In that case the only place to look for an explanation of the hate, if one is required, is in something about the person himself, not in any general significance that the object may have that makes hate appropriate. An animal's hatred of something or of another animal may be like this more generally; what can only be described as an attitude of hate may be called out quite generally by an object of a certain type, e.g. another animal in its territory. In that case an explanation of the phenomenon must make reference to the nature of the animal, its genetic make-up and the function that the attitude of this kind has for the preservation of the species; it is not a matter of the precise significance that this particular thing has for the animal in question. It would thus be out of place to speak of the animal's reasons for hating whatever it is. When this happens as an isolated phenomenon in human beings we tend, as I have said, to set it down as a mere quirk. When it happens quite generally and in an extreme way in human beings we tend to reach for the category of the psychopath; for it is part of the psychology of such a person that such emotional attitudes as he has are unrelated to any range of appropriate objects. If there is any relationship between object and attitude it is causal only, and to that extent, although to that extent alone, the situation is like that which holds good over the animals that I have mentioned. There are, however, differences in at least two respects; (a) the causal connection is without evolutionary significance, and (b) intellectual functioning remains even if detached from emotion.

In normal human cases neither of these things is true in that way, and if we find the hatred intelligible it is because it is directed to an object which falls within the range of objects appropriate to that attitude. I do not use the word 'appropriate' here in any moral sense. It is not that there are certain things that we ought to hate and others that we ought not. It is rather that we should have no clear understanding of what hatred was in a normal human being if we did not know something of what sort of thing is normally an object of hatred for such a being. In consequence, if we think of some range of objects as appropriate kinds of object for hatred it is because this fits in with our conception of the place that hatred has in a human life. What hatred is is not something that could be learnt simply from the consideration of a set of behavioural manifestations; we have to understand its wider significance for normal human beings, and we attribute hatred to animals to the extent that they approximate to what holds good of human beings (there are clearly some animals in the case of which speaking of hatred makes no sense). Hence while hatred of something without reason or anything that would count as such is possible in a human being, we should have a very different conception of human beings were it always or even generally like that; such beings would not be human beings as we understand them. Our concept here brings with it a set of normal expectations, so that to fall short of the norm is progressively to manifest a case where our concept has no sensible application. Hatred without reason or anything that might count as such is something that can occur in human beings as an isolated phenomenon, but where it manifests itself frequently the word 'inhuman' progressively comes to mind. In that event we tend to look for the explanation of the hatred elsewhere than in the place that the hatred and its object have in the person's life.

Similar things apply to love except that while hatred without reason (and therefore without the beliefs involved in having a reason) may, if persistent, have dire consequences, we may expect love without reason, even if persistent, to be little more than irritating, if that. Even this need not be so; the case of someone being dragged down to some ill fate by someone else's infatuation is not *that* uncommon. Nevertheless, it is reasonable to expect hatred to have, as a rule, more obvious bad consequences than love can have, simply because of the obvious behavioural connections that hatred may have, even if they do not follow of necessity. Correspondingly, it is perhaps more difficult to think of a love as being inhuman than so to think of hatred; even so I do not think that the idea can be ruled out as senseless. Conversely, while we speak of falling in love, there is no similar expression in common usage which signifies falling in hate. It may be that this is because the possibility is not one that we like to think of because of its possible consequences. It is similarly difficult to think of hatred as the basis of a personal relationship, although it would be wrong not to admit the possibility. These asymmetries exist between love and hate. It remains true that, in a way parallel to that which holds good over hatred, where the love is unrelated to any of those objects that we feel to be appropriate in a human being, or where it has no constancy in that regard, we look for the explanation elsewhere than in the sense that the love has within the person's life. In its extreme form we feel perhaps some of this in connection with falling in love, except that, as I said earlier, there is a tendency for people to *find* objects for their love in some such cases. Nevertheless, if a person discovers that he is the object of someone else's love in *that* way he may reasonably feel that he can object — unless of course he has some other reason for accepting the situation. For, he or she may declare, the person in question has not *learnt* to see them with love. It has either come about causally or come about by a chance of fate given a background of such causality. I mean by this that the explanation of the state of being in love will be causal, and that the explanation of their being the object of the love will either be similarly causal or come about by chance.

The idea of learning to love that I have invoked here is important, although it needs careful handling. I was recently involved as a juror in a case in which it was said of the defendant by a medical witness that he had not learnt to love. Yet it was also said of him (and it was clear that it was *truly* said of him) that his whole life was directed towards others; he lived *through* others. At the same time and at the other extreme he had an excessive passion for certain things beyond what most people would probably feel reasonable. 'He had not learnt to love' — but it was clear that his feelings towards certain things and certain people were very strong indeed (the judge said that he was possessive). The point of saying that he had not learnt to love was presumably that he had not learnt to love things and people in such a way that his life had a coherent sense in relation to them. And part of that sense was a matter of what he was to others as well as what they were to him; for the sense of a life is not determined simply by what holds good solely of the person whose life it is. Learning to love is a matter of learning to see objects in appropriate ways, i.e. ways that are appropriate to that love, and when those objects are other people that involves seeing how you are to them as well as how they are to you. It involves seeing them as other persons in the relation and not *just* as objects.

It might be thought that a failure to do this is just what is suggested in speaking of someone as possessive (as the judge did of the defendant); that is to say that it might be thought that in being possessive a person treats another simply as an object which he owns and can therefore treat as he wishes. That may sometimes be the case, but it is by no means always or necessarily so. It may simply be the case that the person concerned sees the other as closer to him than they actually are. This may indeed involve error, but error of a different order from that involved where someone treats another as an object that he owns; and it is not incompatible with a kind of love, while the other case, it might be argued, is. There is a connected point about jealousy, which is often thought to be incompatible with love and to involve possessive-ness. I am not here concerned with whether jealousy is ever justified, since I have not been concerned with the justification of attitudes, but

283

rather with the conditions for their intelligibility. I *do* in fact think that jealousy is sometimes justified, but the question whether one is ever justified in being jealous is quite different from the question whether being jealous is compatible with love proper. As far as concerns this second question the answer seems to me that it *can* be so compatible, in so far as love for a person by no means implies seeing that person as someone who can be quite independent of the relationship. But if someone has learnt to love in the full sense he will have learnt what the relationship is.

Hence, it is likely that if someone has not learnt to love he will not be able to form, except by chance, stable relationships. And one, though only one, reason for this may be a failure to see what it is for both himself and others to be appropriate parties to such a relationship. If the love has no connection with anything else, with a way of seeing others and oneself that fits coherently with that love, it is likely to be an inadequate foundation for a relationship. What I am trying to get at here is not possessiveness, but something that may be described as a lack of coherence in attitudes. Perhaps 'coherence' is not the best word to use. What I mean is this: a person who has not learnt to love is not one who has simply not developed 'feelings towards', but rather one who has not learnt to have feelings towards the sort of objects and in the sort of way that human life involves if it is to have a sense for those living it. This involves the person not seeing himself and others in the kind of relationships that will promote those 'feelings towards' and encourage their persistence in a way that has sense for those concerned.

None of this need apply to love of mere objects (although it has some application on the other hand to hatred of people – one *can* learn to hate some people, and, conceivably, rightly). I do not mean that there is no place for speaking of learning to love certain objects, e.g. works of art. Rather this does not have the same implications for the conduct and course of our lives. Once again, this shows why, while someone might build his life on feelings towards objects of certain kinds without feeling the need to explain to others or to himself why he has those feelings, this would not be *generally* possible with other people as the objects of those feelings.

Finally, let me say again that I have not been concerned in this with the question of the justifiability of the attitudes or emotions of love and hate. What I have said does not rule out the possibility of such justification, but neither does it speak for it. Certainly love and hate can be considered rational when their objects have certain appropriate qualities, and to that extent they can be considered justified; but if such qualities do not exist in their objects love and hate are not necessarily and for that reason to be considered irrational, even if they are, so to speak, non-rational. My concern has been rather with the limits to the intelligibility of speaking of love and hate where beliefs about their objects are missing. My conclusion is that while love and hate need not involve any beliefs − and may thus be non-epistemic − human love and hate could not universally be like that. There is a certain parallel here with the case of perception. As numerous philosophers, e.g. Dretske, have urged, there is such a thing as non-epistemic perception, cases where to perceive something does not entail believing anything about it. But perception could not be uniformly non-epistemic, or it could not conceivably provide any foundation for our beliefs about and knowledge of the world. Our understanding of the concept of perception presupposes for this reason an understanding of the place that perception has in our life in relation to the world in which we live, and thus an understanding of the relation of perception to our general beliefs about the world. There is a similar point about love and hate. I concluded earlier that 'feelings towards' were possible only for believers even if they did not involve beliefs themselves. In the sequel I have tried to say something about the ways in which love and hate relate to beliefs about or ways of seeing their objects if they are to have sense for those involved. It is only against this background that non-epistemic love and hate, as they might be called, can, as with non-epistemic perception, be given intelligibility.

# 16

# LEARNING TO LOVE

It is clear that not all emotions have the same place or importance for every individual in every society. Compassion, for example, has not been given the same weight in all cultures, and there may be some cultures in which the Schopenhauerian suggestion that compassion is the basis of morality would seem ludicrous. It is not by any means immediately obvious that compassion is a totally natural response on the part of one human being to another when that other is in desperate straits. Moreover, there are certainly human beings who are not moved by compassion at all in circumstances in which others are moved indeed. That last point does not, of course, directly show that it would be wrong to say that compassion is a natural emotion in general; for some individuals may be naturally lacking in what others may possess to abundance, and of course vice versa. Yet, the point about cultures and cultural influences may suggest that differences between people in this respect may not always and necessarily depend on natural and in-born differences between them.

Moreover, some have talked of the education of the emotions in a way that suggests that in the case of at least some emotions these have to be inculcated rather than expected to appear naturally. Roger Scruton, for example,[1] speaks of honest parents seeing that their offspring acquire what he calls the proper feelings — sympathy, pride, remorse and affection; and he suggests that there should be nothing puzzling in that. But there surely *is* something puzzling in that. It is one thing, it might be thought, to teach children what are regarded as the proper or suitable objects for certain emotions, quite another to teach them the emotions themselves. One can imagine parents telling children that they ought to feel for, say, people who are worse off than themselves. But how does the child learn what it is to feel for other people at all, and how in general does what they are told get a purchase? Is it that parents have to build upon what is natural to the child, simply directing the feelings towards the right objects, so to speak? It cannot, surely, be as simple as that, since the feelings are feelings *for* people, and while children may have to learn that some people, or some kinds of people, are more deserving of and more appropriate objects for such feelings, it is still a problem how feelings for people can come about in the first instance. Those feelings cannot be construed as mere occurrences; they have objects, they are feelings *for*. For these reasons is there not something puzzling after all in the idea that such feelings may be taught or brought about by some process of education? It is at all events necessary to explain how it is even possible.

One feasible suggestion here is that what we are interested in in the emotional education of our children is that they should not only be brought to have the right sort of feelings to what we regard as the right sort of objects but also be brought to have a consciousness of what is involved in that. They should be brought, so to speak, to have those feelings towards those objects under the appropriate description, so that, along with and in a sense as part of having those feelings, the child sees the feelings as of a certain kind and the objects as appropriate objects for such feelings. On that view, we should teach children what, say, compassion is, what it is to feel compassion to another and in what circumstances, and why such feelings are called for in those circumstances. Such a view of the education of the emotions would not be implausible, since if it is *education* that is at stake we might well expect of it more than, as a result, a certain tendency towards certain feelings — but in addition a degree of insight into what is involved and why. It is obviously desirable that, as a matter of education, children should acquire something of such an insight. Education is not merely a matter of inculcating good habits, even habits in the way of feeling; it involves also the bringing about of an understanding of what is involved in that, an appreciation of the appropriate sorts of object for such feelings, and some sense of why they are so.

All that, however, depends heavily on the weight contributed by the term 'education'. Whether or not parents have to teach their offspring sympathy, pride, remorse and affection as part of their education in this way, it is not clear that the insight in question is necessarily involved in learning *simpliciter*. In other words the emphasis on education brings with it an emphasis on the acquisition of insight into the emotions through learning and teaching; that says nothing in itself either for or against the thesis that the emotions themselves have to be learned. Children might just come to feel sympathy in certain circumstances; the education of their emotions would consist in that case in the acquisition of an understanding of what is involved in that, what is an appropriate object of sympathy, and so on. We have yet to see whether speaking of learning to feel sympathy itself makes sense. Coming to feel sympathy does not necessarily imply learning to feel sympathy.

It is indeed one thing to say that children have to come to feel sympathy, etc.; it is quite another to say that they have to learn to have such feelings. One may come to have certain feelings as a result perhaps of certain merely causal processes. To learn to have them would involve more than that. It is my belief, indeed, that where learning is involved knowledge has to come into the picture in some way, and indeed that what is learned comes about on the basis of knowledge.[2] To put the matter at its crudest, in learning to feel sympathy there would be presupposed a knowledge or at any rate a seeing of things as being such and such. One would come to feel sympathy in this way on the basis of the knowledge that things are of a certain kind with another and perhaps on the basis of a knowledge of what it is to be affected in that sort of way. It is not easy to set out what sort of course such learning would have to take. Schopenhauer's claim that one comes to feel sympathy with others because of a faint sensitivity to the 'fact' that there is in reality no real difference between oneself and others may have more than a touch of implausibility, even absurdity, about it; but in a sense it is on the right lines. Learning to feel sympathy would on that account be a matter of coming to feel that way on the basis of a real appreciation of the true state of others, an appreciation which is made easy by the metaphysical truth of one's underlying identity with others. Such an account is on the right lines to the extent that, but of course only to the extent that, it founds the acquisition of the emotion on a form of knowledge. It does not do that alone, however, and rightly, since such a knowledge would not guarantee sympathy any more than putting oneself in other people's position does. If learning to feel sympathy is to be possible it must involve more than a reliance on such knowledge, and it is noteworthy that Schopenhauer's account uses the knowledge to connect the feeling for others with a feeling for oneself. Whether or not that is right as a theory, it does indicate the need for a more intimate connection between knowledge and feeling in an account of learning to feel sympathy than we have yet reached.

I have concentrated so far on sympathy. One may get a similar point of view by considering pride, for example. There are people of whom we say that they have no pride. Perhaps they have never learnt to have it. Whatever feelings they may have towards things in relation to themselves it is not pride. I say 'in relation to themselves' in this case because a crucial aspect of pride is that to have or feel pride one must see the putative object of pride as having a peculiar relation to oneself; one must see it as having an importance which reflects back on oneself because of one's part in whatever brings it about. A person who has not learnt to feel pride has certainly failed, for whatever reason, to see things in that way. The feeling has that way of seeing things as a con- stituent part and the person who has not learnt to feel pride must have failed to learn to see things in that way or even to contemplate it as a possibility. And that is in some sense a failure of knowledge. Once again, however, it is not just that, since the feeling and the knowledge (the seeing-as) have to be seen in an intimate relation of which we have not yet arrived at a clear account.

Nevertheless, all this is, in a way, a preliminary to the concern that is reflected in my title — that of what is involved in the idea, if it is a genuine one, of learning to love. When I broached that idea on a previous occasion,[3] I did so in relation to what was said by a medical witness at a trial in which I served as a juror. Let me say a little more about the case. The trial was one for murder, as against manslaughter (it was not disputed that the defendant has killed the person who died). The defendant was a man who had been born illegitimate (and the only reason for remarking on that fact was that it mattered very much to him). He had had an extremely deprived upbringing in nearly every way. He had, however, come to make something of a way in the world, and he had married and had had two children. About two or three years previously his wife had left him and taken the children with her. Despite being given access to the children he had, during that period, tried to see them only once, and even that was late at night, when it was clearly impossible. (There had been some sort of row in consequence and he had broken a radiator in the process.) Neverthe- less, he kept photographs of the children (by the time of the trial rather out of date ones) and performed a kind of ritual towards them of carrying them around with him in the house where he lived and putting a rosary around them.

The house in which he was then living belonged to a woman who was in fact a 'wall of death rider'. She was, as might be expected, something of a 'toughie', but she had been ill-treated and reduced to a poor specimen of humanity by the man who was subsequently killed, who had lived with her. The defendant had moved in in his place and had devoted himself to pulling the woman together – something in which he appeared to have been remarkably successful. Later, when he was in prison on remand, he had behaved similarly to other prisoners, particularly those in a disturbed state. Yet even in the woman's case it was arguable that what was important to him was seeing himself as standing in a relation to her, just as he saw himself, with apparently less reality, as standing in a relation to his children. (It was also important to him that his children were legitimate and on that fact one of the crucial aspects of the case turned.) If I were to give you a complete account of the case I should have to recount the events during the week-end that led up to the killing – a good deal of which was spent by all concerned in a state of blind drunkenness. However, they do not matter for our purposes. What is important for our purposes is that a medical witness described him as someone who had not learnt to love, despite abundant evidence that he had a propensity to devote himself to other people.

Of course the statement by the medical witness does not have to be true. Our concern should be with whether it even makes sense, and if so what sense. I believe that it did have a certain sense, and part of that sense should have been evident in what I have already said. As I have indicated, one thing that seemed very important to the man was his conception of himself as standing in certain relationships to others. At the trial he kept referring to the woman as 'My . . .'. That led the judge to speak of him as possessive, whereas, to my mind, it was much more of an indication of the importance for him of his conception of their relationship. It *might* be said in consequence that there was a sense in which, despite the fact that he had strong feelings towards certain other people – the woman, his children, and perhaps his fellow-prisoners – those feelings were not quite genuine.

What could be meant by that? Perhaps that there was too much self-consciousness about them, so that an unsympathetic critic might say that they were 'assumed'. If that were to mean that the feelings reduced themselves to a deliberate policy of behaving as if he had them, I personally would think the judgment much too unsympathetic. In any case, the dichotomy 'either natural, genuine feelings or a deliberate policy of behaving as if . . .' is far too sharp, and I would like to explore some of the other possibilities to see what light, if any, they cast on the idea of learning to love (it being accepted for the sake of argument that the suggestion that the man had not learnt to love is at least one that makes sense). It would be similarly wrong and unsympathetic to say of the man that his concern was simply for the *idea* of a relationship between himself and the woman or his children, though in the latter case in particular it must often have looked like that. His feelings were not directed simply towards a fantasy, so that the people concerned in fact received none of them. That was certainly not the case with the woman. Hence that is not one of the possibilities that is relevant. It may have been the case, however, that his feelings towards the woman were always, as it were, under the description 'My . . .', so that for that reason there was always a kind of reference back to himself. Hence the self-consciousness. It *is* possible to fail to learn to see things as having a real independence from oneself. Moreover, in so far as the feelings are not directed towards a person as their object in such a way as to be directed towards something which has to any extent that kind of independence from oneself, to that extent it would be reasonable to say that they do not amount to love proper.

In saying that I do not mean to go along with the idea that love is straightforwardly opposed to possessiveness. The invocation of the description 'My . . .', even when this is done consistently with regard to a certain object, does not in any case necessarily signify possessiveness. There are many things which one thinks of as one's own without that entailing a possessiveness on one's part towards them. Possessiveness involves not allowing the person or thing involved a life of its own or even a life for others. To see something consistently under the description 'My . . .' does not necessarily involve that. Nevertheless, if someone does constantly refer to another person as 'My . . .', that may well suggest that what is important for him or her is that the relationship to himself or herself exists.

In certain cases of this, although not necessarily in all, there may be involved a kind of self-deception which itself makes the feelings 'false' or 'not genuine'. Hence this is a possibility that must be considered in this context. Maudlin sentimentality presents a case of false feelings of that kind, and offers at least an analogy to the case where the constant use of 'My . . .' involves self-deception and 'false' feeling. In maudlin sentimentality what is important for the person concerned is the feelings rather than their object, despite the overt impression given that the object in question is such that feeling is called for in its connection. The emotion is 'false' because the person concerned does not have that kind or degree of feeling for that object even if he or she has some feeling without doubt — and knows it! It is that addendum 'and knows it' which makes the case one of self-deception, it being in my opinion a necessary feature of self-deception that the self-deceiver knows in some sense what he is up to. Hence if I say that in the case of maudlin sentimentality the person concerned does not have that kind or degree of feeling for that object even if he or she has some feeling — *and knows it* — it is to indicate that that person is not simply mistaken about him- or herself. On the other hand the feeling is not deliberately assumed; it is not straightforward pretence. There may indeed be a motivation for hanging on, so to speak, to the feelings even when they are inappropriate to the object. Such a motivation may amount to enjoyment, although it may on occasion be much more 'mixed' in its nature. Certainly part of what is involved is likely to be that the person concerned sees himself and his relationship to the object in a way that makes the feeling an easy one. That indeed is one of the things that one is likely to think about maudlin sentimentality — that the feelings manifested are too easy and thus ill-fitted to the circumstances. The feelings exhibited in the constant use of 'My . . .' may strike one in the same way.

I have said, therefore, that when someone constantly refers to another person as 'My . . .' it may well suggest that what is important for him or her is the relationship that the object is taken to have to him- or herself, over and above the person who is ostensibly the object of the feeling. I have also suggested that in *some* cases if we think that the feelings are 'false' in that respect it may be because we feel that something like self-deception is involved. In such cases, however, while we cannot attribute to the person concerned the same kind of self-consciousness as must be involved if the feelings are 'assumed', too much of self and too much knowingness is involved to make it an appropriate case to be identified as one in which the person has not learnt to love. For in that case there must be a sense in which the person does not know what love is or at least does not know how to love. All in all, therefore, I do not think that anything like self-deception is a plausible explanation of what I am after.

In saying that there must be a sense in which the person does not know what love is or at least does not know how to love I do not mean to imply that there is any real distinction. As with other forms of

292

knowing how, there is a considerable difference between not knowing how to love and simply not being able to, and knowing how to love must presuppose knowing what love is. Not being able to love might be due to some physiological defect; that could not be true of not knowing how to love. In general, when one knows how to $\phi$ there is implied some knowledge, to some degree or other, of what $\phi$-ing is and involves. In what way, therefore, could someone, such as the man in the case described, not know what love is and fail to love for that reason, whatever else he was and was capable of? It would not be enough to suggest something that I mentioned earlier — that whatever attitude he had to the other persons involved it was not under the description 'love'. As far as he was concerned, it might very well have been the case that that description was utterly appropriate; the question at issue is whether that would be right.

If the notion of learning to love is to have any purchase, then if the answer to that last question is 'No' it cannot be because there is some mistake involved; it might have been love but it just wasn't. It must be the case that love is not in question at all. It is not in question because of what is in some sense an ignorance, a failure to understand what love is. That failure will result in turn in an inability to see objects in appropriate ways. However much someone in that position may use the word 'love' or use the words of love, others may say that he does not know what love is. It is, however, important to be clear about what that means. Knowing what love is in this sense is not a matter merely of knowing the phenomena of love — the forms that love can take. Hence one cannot learn what love is in this sense simply by, so to speak, reading the right (or even the 'wrong') books. If such a knowledge or a knowledge obtained in that way could enable one to see people in the appropriate way that would be a contingent matter at best.

There is, as I implied earlier, no real puzzle about learning to love certain objects once given an ability to love, any more than there is a real puzzle about learning to see things in certain ways once given an ability to see things in ways at all, once given an ability for 'seeing-as'. That indeed is what the growth of experience is all about — the acquisition of ways of seeing things through experience on the basis of other forms of knowledge and other ways of seeing things that can be connected in some way with the new ways of seeing things.[4] Just as taste can be educated so that one learns to see and value things that one did not previously see in that way, so one can learn to love things to which one was previously neutral or which one even abhorred.[5] It is a matter of learning to see those things in ways that make them for you a suitable object of one emotion rather than another. One cannot always make that come about, but it *can* come about all the same, and in a way that makes 'learn' rather than 'come to' the appropriate verb to precede that expressing the emotional attitude in question. All that presupposes knowing what the emotional attitude in question is in general, and one of my concerns is with how that can be learnt. There is at the same time a practical aspect to it so that what one acquires is not merely a theoretical knowledge of the emotion but a knowledge of what it is, in some sense, to feel that way to some kind or kinds of object. That surely presupposes a similar kind of knowledge of what it is to feel that way at all.

To anyone who has read my *Experience and the Growth of Understanding* it will be evident that I am proceeding in relation to love in the same way that I proceeded there in relation to the growth of experience and ways of seeing things in general. Indeed the idea of 'learning to love someone' was an idea that I mentioned in chapter 9 of that book.[6] In that book and elsewhere I have argued and tried to show that one cannot understand the emergence of knowledge in the individual without taking due account of the part played by feelings that that individual may have towards and from others, as a necessary constituent or condition of the individual's recognition of others and thereby of the ideas of correctness and truth that they mediate — something that is surely presupposed by knowledge.[7] But if love involves knowing what love is and what is for the individual an appropriate object of love, it would appear that love cannot be one of the feelings, the natural feelings with a natural expression, which have to exist to provide the basis for the acquisition and growth of knowledge in general. But that of course is really what we should expect. Love and hate, let alone other emotions, are not, or are not in general, primitive emotions, feelings or attitudes; they have a certain refinement about them. I say 'in general' because it is not to be denied that love and hate, in a way that is not so typical of other emotions, can verge on the primitive; but I think that such cases constitute secondary cases. I argued in my 'The phenomena of love and hate' that love and hate can be non-epistemic, involving no beliefs or other epistemic states, in a way that is not the case with other emotions, but that they could not always be like that. If that account is correct, love in the full-blooded sense is something that *may have* to be learnt, even if there exists in some cases something to which we may want to give the name 'love' of which that is not true.[8]

If that is the case then there may be natural feelings that exist in human beings to which we *could*, perhaps if pressed, give the names 'love' and 'hate', which could provide the basis, given epistemic factors and the conditions that make them possible, for learning to love and hate proper. (Whether that would justify the claim that where non-epistemic forms of love and hate exist in adults they constitute a regression to something more primitive is a question that I would like to leave on one side; if it were true it would not make them less fundamental or perhaps less important for life.) The natural feelings to which I have referred need nurturing, however, not only in the sense that they need to be directed towards appropriate objects (whatever 'appropriate' means in this context), but in the sense, perhaps a connected sense, that they need to be made less contingent than they might otherwise be. What I mean by that is the following. If a feeling has no connection with any epistemic factors, any beliefs or the like about its object, it is likely to be dependent on merely causal factors, and given the complexities of our lives these in turn are likely to be subject to the vagaries that circumstances turn up. There is not likely, therefore, to be any consistency or permanence in such feelings. Learning to love in the fuller sense is, among other things, to acquire something of a consistency and relative permanence in one's attitudes to a variety of things; and that consistency and relative permanence will come about through the sense that those things will have for our lives.[9] It is the organization of our attitudes and feelings by that sort of thing that removes what might otherwise be a contingency in their manifestation and expression. Another thing that might have been said to be wrong with the man involved in the trial that I attended was that he was subject to just that kind of contingency in the direction of his attitudes and feelings.

Yet one could not learn to love in this sense if one did not have any feelings to be organized by epistemic considerations about their objects actual or possible. I said earlier that we might, if pressed, give the names 'love' and 'hate' to those feelings from which love and hate proper are derived. The situation here is very similar to what holds good of the epistemic states which, together with feelings, make possible our seeing of objects as suitable objects for such feelings. As I have argued elsewhere,[10] there is nothing that constitutes, or at any rate nothing that can be identified as, the first item of knowledge in an individual. The possession of knowledge is in any case a matter of degree, in that one's knowledge of any given thing may be more or less determinate, more or less detailed, and the like. Hence, even if a firm judgment on whether a person, a child say, has a certain form of know-ledge may be possible only after a certain time in his or her life, it does not follow that that person has no knowledge of any kind or to any degree before that. Moreover, if knowledge in the full sense is ascrib-able only when certain conditions are satisfied, conditions that may not be satisfiable, properly speaking, at a very young age, something must nevertheless hold good of the child at that time which makes it possible to speak of knowledge later when those conditions *are* satisfied. If we were to say that what so holds good is epistemic, we should be saying no more than what I have just said. It is in the same sense that I say that the natural feelings that provide the basis for later, more developed, feelings and emotions (and also, I think, for knowledge proper) can be called by the same name as the later feelings.

It would not, of course, be plausible to say that with respect to all emotions. It would not be plausible to speak of, say, pride or jealousy with respect to a child a few weeks, let alone days, old. It is that very fact that makes it plausible in turn to say that emotions of that kind are in some sense secondary; they depend on other, more basic, feel-ings. I do not think that the same is true of love and hate, and it may be for that reason, among others, that some have refused to call love and hate emotions, referring to them as sentiments or something of that kind. Brentano, as I noted in my 'The phenomena of love and hate' thought that love and hate provide a focus for all the other emotions, however they are to be thought of in themselves. If pride and jealousy, for example, presuppose certain conceptions of their object in the relation that that has to the person who has the emotions, that is not true of love and hate. Indeed, if what I said earlier about the defendant at the trial having too strong a sense of his relation to the woman con-cerned is true, that would be one reason why one might hesitate to speak of love in his case. But, at the other extreme, a spontaneous, welcoming reaction to what is itself an expression of love might well be called 'love' itself, even if the reaction is transitory and has nothing of the consistency and relative permanence about it that I said was a characteristic of mature love. To learn to love is to learn to give such feelings and attitudes a coherence in terms of ways of seeing the world and particular objects in it.

It is the difficulty of seeing just how that works out that may pro-voke a resistance to speaking of learning to love where the idea of learning to feel pride, for example, may provoke no such resistance. We do, after all, say of some people that they have no pride, and to add that they have never learnt to feel pride is not, as far as I can see, a very great step to take. (If we do feel a reluctance to speak of someone having or not having learnt to feel jealousy, it is, I suspect, for a different reason — that we feel that jealousy is an emotion we ought not to have any way. Whether or not that feeling is justified, it is still the case, as Stuart Brown has pointed out,[11] that we can be said to learn things we do not approve of — bad habits, for example.) If we are to give an account of learning to feel pride, we have to say something about the person concerned learning to see certain things not only as having a value but as having one that reflects on himself. There are of course people who, for whatever reason, never come to see themselves as having any significant role to play in relation to things; perhaps for some reason they refuse to do that or are brought to do so by the facts of their upbringing. Such people are good examples of people who have not learnt to feel pride. It is different with learning to love, since, as I argued in 'The phenomena of love and hate', there is nothing that we *have* to mention about how they must see things if they are to love them. For that reason it does not begin to be plausible to attempt to spell out the steps that have to be taken if love is to result. It is in this case more a matter, as I have suggested, of organizing the feelings that already exist so that they are directed in a consistent and stable way towards certain objects; *which* objects may be a highly contingent matter, which is not to say that as things go on certain considerations do not become relevant for the person concerned. Coming to see such considerations as relevant, the linking up of natural feeling with epistemic factors, is certainly a major element in learning to love and indeed in the education of such emotions.

I should like, in the light of this, to go back to the observations made by Roger Scruton that I quoted at the beginning of this paper. If parents see that their children acquire what he calls the proper feelings, such as sympathy, pride, remorse and affection, they must surely do so (at least in the case of the first three) as part and parcel of getting them to see certain things as the proper objects of such emotions. The children learn what it is to feel sympathy in the course of being taught what is a proper object of sympathy in the context of the inculcation of certain practical attitudes. It is not just that the parents so direct feelings which are natural any way. There may be feelings that *are* natural any way, but it is only in the context and course of the complex process of learning and education that I have mentioned that such feelings become transmuted into emotions such as sympathy proper. It is hard to think of love being learnt in quite that way. It is no doubt true that parents encourage children to express love in certain directions, but that is possible only because something like love and its expression is a natural reaction any way, particularly as a response to love received. Hence, in this case getting children to be loving is not something that parents do as part and parcel of getting them to see certain things as proper objects of that emotion. Indeed, I suspect that most parents take love as felt towards those near to them as something to be taken for granted in their children, rather than as something to be acquired — and rightly so.

They do so rightly, as I see it, for two sorts of reasons. The first is a practical sort of reason — that spontaneous feelings of affection (welcoming feelings, one might say) need to be taken at their face-value and built upon, not only if the capacity for real love is to be developed in the child so that the child can genuinely be said to have learnt to love, but also if the child is to acquire a real sense of personhood. I shall not say more about the latter here, although it is to be noted that some psychologists (notably perhaps John Shotter[12]) have insisted that newborn babies become persons by being treated as persons. As far as concerns the former consideration — the development of a capacity for real love — it might be noted that the defendant at the trial was someone who, because of the circumstances of his birth and upbringing, had not had much of a chance to satisfy the conditions that I have mentioned as necessary for that end to be achieved. These, however, are both practical considerations, and their relevance and validity as such are not matters over which I have any particular expertise. The other sort of reason that I had in mind in saying that parents are right in taking for granted the existence of love on the part of their children towards those near to them is that unless that *could* be taken for granted there would be no possibility of its even making sense to think of love proper coming about. That is a conceptual point, not just a practical one.

Someone might react to that claim with a certain scepticism on the grounds that my argument for that conclusion has been based on the premise that if love proper does come about it must have been learned. Did I not after all accept earlier a distinction between learning to $\phi$ and coming to $\phi$, and could it not be the case that children come to love proper provided only that whatever causal conditions are necessary are satisfied (conditions about which I have said nothing), without this being dependent on learning? I can reply to such an objection only by reverting to the points that love proper, as I have construed it, involves epistemic factors, and that such factors are indeed the only thing that can give love proper the sort of stability that we expect of it, even if only in a relative way. That is to say that while the early feelings on which, as I claim, love proper is based need involve no conception of their object (they are in a literal sense reactions), such a conception of the object is an integral part of love proper. Hence it is that although learning to love is not the same as learning what it is for something to be, as far as oneself is concerned, an object for love it is to be expected that the two go hand in hand and *pari passu*, so to speak. None of that could be achieved by merely causal factors, without reference to epistemic ones, except *per accidens*.

Let me, to finish, emphasize these points in connection with something that I said earlier, and in doing so, I hope, pull the strands of my discussion together. I said, earlier, although only in brief, that the coming about of knowledge in the individual presupposes that that individual is not just an epistemic thing but something that is capable of feeling also. The point that I mentioned was that the possession of knowledge presupposes an appreciation of the force of the notion of truth and that that in turn presupposes the individual's standing in relations to others as a condition of the appreciation of that force coming about. A knowing creature must therefore be one that is capable of the sorts of feeling that make personal relations, or something approximating to them, possible.

The same sort of conclusion emerges from another, non-developmental, consideration that I have also adduced elsewhere:[13] that someone cannot be said to know or believe something unless he also has certain, not strictly intellectual, attitudes to what he knows or believes. There would, for example, be an extreme oddity about saying of someone that he believed something but had no attitude whatever to it as an object of belief (that he did not care one way or the other about it, for example; such a thing might be possible occasionally, but not in general). Hence, once again, believing (and knowing too) is possible only in a creature that has feelings. Given that context, knowledge can come about in the individual through learning only as a result of a complex interaction between epistemic and non-epistemic factors of that kind — the exact course of which it may be impossible to spell out in detail. As far as the epistemic factors are concerned, however, there must exist initially at least a capacity for states that one might call, if only by courtesy, 'seeing-as', even when the conditions for seeing-as proper are not present. (It is in this spirit too, I believe, that we sometimes attribute to certain animals seeing-as, belief or knowledge, when the conditions on which I have insisted are not satisfied. There is, however, all the difference in the world between saying of a being who will eventually acquire knowledge proper that it 'knows' even when the conditions for knowledge proper are not present, and saying the same of a creature in which the conditions will never be present or satisfied. That ought to affect our serious theorizing about the creatures in question.)

The same sort of thing applies in reverse as far as feeling and emotion are concerned. Certain emotions require for their proper manifestation rather specific epistemic states, rather specific beliefs. That is by now philosophically commonplace. It is much less obvious that love (or hate) requires such specific epistemic states, but in so far as the idea of learning to love has a place, as I have suggested that it does, then love in the sense that that results in must involve *some* epistemic conditions (although the range of beliefs that are compatible with love is very wide). Once again, however, such love could never come about, could never be learned, unless there were originally present in the child feelings by way of reaction to things, which are natural and which because a matter of reaction in a relatively straightforward sense involve no epistemic conditions. We can speak of some such feelings as ones of love if we wish (and for the reasons that I have mentioned it is perhaps well that we should do so in practice), but strictly speaking that is by courtesy only, and such an attribution has a reality only where the proper emotion is capable of being developed on its basis.

Thus there is a sense in which we all have to learn to love and thus have any chance of stable emotional attitudes. But we can do that only if conditions having to do with both basic 'reactive' feeling and basic 'reactive' (if I can use that term here too) epistemic states are satisfied. If we fail to learn to love it may be because such conditions are not satisfied or because they are not satisfied in the right way or at the right time and place. Somewhere among all that is to be found the reason why the man at the trial which I attended had not learnt to love — if of course it is true that he had not.

300

## NOTES

1  R.V. Scruton, 'Emotion, practical knowledge and common culture' in *Explaining Emotions*, ed. Amelie Oksenberg Rorty, Berkeley, Los Angeles and London, University of California Press, 1980, pp. 519-36, esp. p. 525. See also R.S. Peters, 'The education of the emotions' in his *Psychology and Ethical Development*, London, Allen and Unwin, 1974, and J. Wilson, *Preface to the Philosophy of Education*, London, Routledge & Kegan Paul, 1979, ch. 7.
2  See my 'Human Learning' in *The Philosophy of Psychology*, ed. S.C. Brown, London, Macmillan, 1973, reprinted in *The Philosophy of Education*, ed. R.S. Peters, London, OUP, 1973, and this volume pp. 132-48, and my *Experience and the Growth of Understanding*, London, Routledge & Kegan Paul, 1978.
3  'The phenomena of love and hate', *Philosophy* 53, 1978, pp. 5-20, esp. pp. 18-19 (this volume pp. 283-4).
4  See e.g. ch. 9, 'Later learning' in my *Experience and the Growth of Understanding*.
5  I myself, to revert to a piece of autobiography, have learned at least to like, and perhaps in some cases to love, pieces of music that I once loathed.
6  I have in addition tried elsewhere to say something about the part played by agency in it all — the practical aspects to which I have referred. See my 'Perception and agency' *Monist* 61, 1978, pp. 536-47 (this volume pp. 43-56).
7  That is a very summary account of what I have been up to. I am tempted to ape Strawson and say that it should not be taken as a substitute for what it summarizes.
8  I argued in that paper that there so exist such cases.
9  Cf. 'The phenomena of love and hate', pp. 283-4.
10  In 'What exactly is social about the origins of understanding?' in *Social Cognition*, eds P. Light and G. Butterworth, Brighton, Harvester, 1982, and this volume pp. 162-77.
11  S.C. Brown, 'Learning', *PASS* 46, 1972, pp. 19-39.
12  See e.g. J. Shotter, 'Acquired powers: the transformation of natural into personal powers' in *Personality*, ed. R. Harré, Oxford, Blackwell, 1976, and (with Susan Gregory) 'On first gaining the idea of oneself as a person' in *Life Sentences*, ed. R. Harré, New York, Wiley, 1976.
13  In 'Person-perception and our understanding of others' in *Understanding Other Persons*, ed. T. Mischel, Oxford, Blackwell, 1974 (this volume pp. 208-38).

# EPILOGUE

I said in the Introduction that one of the themes of the foregoing essays, perhaps the central one, is their opposition to the model of information reception and processing for cognitive psychology. It might well be asked what model I put in its place. With respect to the genetic issues which are raised in a number of the essays it might be asked what positive story I wish to tell about the beginnings and subsequent growth of understanding. The information-processing model is in fact one kind of interactionist account which seeks to understand cognition, and its beginning and growth, in terms of an interaction of a causal kind between the organism and the environment. It may seem obvious that there must be such interaction in some form or other. It is less obvious, however, that cognition is to be understood in its terms, or at any rate in terms of that kind which can plausibly be viewed as doing justice to the complexity and nature of the cognitive process itself.

What I mean by that can perhaps be seen by consideration of one of the earliest and simplest accounts of certain fundamental cognitive processes in interactionist terms. I have in mind the model of the wax and the seal that is introduced to explain perceptual recognition and the place of memory in that by Plato in his dialogue *Theaetetus*. Plato invites us there to consider the mind on the analogy of a wax tablet and to view the incoming sense-impressions as impressions on the wax made by a variety of seals. If an impression persists it constitutes a memory-impression, and subsequent recognition of objects is a matter of seeing whether the seal fits the impressions, and if so which. That account of the matter is interactionist in that it tries to account for the cognitive processes involved in terms of a causal interaction between the environment (the seal) and the mind (the wax tablet). Such an account is likely to seem grossly over-simple. Yet many modern models that are accepted by cognitive psychologists are simply elaborations of the same basic apparatus. For example, Chomsky's reliance on the notion of a language acquisition device which sorts out the 'corrupt' data available to the child from the environment is a reliance upon something very like a wax tablet with a range of impressions built into it. Any view that presupposes coding of information and some form of analyser of the coded input is similar. What Fodor[1] calls the 'representational view of the mind', with the idea that the brain works on computational principles on data which play the role of representations, involves the same approach. It is generally supposed by such theorists that cognitive processes must be explained in terms simply of an interaction between the brain and what is made available to it by the environment.

This is not the place to examine such views in general, nor to comment upon the seemingly paradoxical conclusions to which they have sometimes been taken to lead.[2] My own view is that they involve far too simple a conception of what interactional processes between organism and environment must be presupposed. An implication of what I have to say is that if we are to identify the causal processes that underlie cognition we must not confine our attention to the more obvious processes of interaction between organism and environment ('obvious' if they are to provide analogues of cognitive processes); we must take the relevant system which is to be investigated to be a much wider one which involves other people, as people, as well as the other things round us. So much is the implication of what I have said about the social basis of understanding. Such a system is clearly an immensely complex one, far too complex to make possible the easy plotting of the causal processes involved. Yet if the concept of human understanding necessarily involves a reference to other people it is such a system which must be taken as the relevant one for an understanding of the processes that are presupposed by cognition. To be content with less and make do with the more obvious interactional relationships between brain and environment is in effect to try to run before we can crawl, as I said in the Introduction.

Do not I at least need to give an account of how knowledge and understanding come about which is more than a statement of the conditions necessary for an achievement of those ends — which is in effect all that I have provided? Yes and no. A psychologist who hoped to tell the story about the emerging of knowledge and understanding in a child would, if I am right, have to take account of the parameters which are laid down in my statement of the conditions necessary for the successful attainment of knowledge and understanding. It is nevertheless important that the story should be told, and in a way such that the factors referred to fit intelligibly into a picture of human life and its growth. The actual course of events that takes place in individual human beings during that growth of knowledge and understanding may be extremely variable, even within those parameters. If that is the case it makes the telling of the story all the more difficult. Moreover, there are obvious difficulties about how the stages of that process are to be described, given the fact that our adult categories are applicable only at the end of the process when the ascription of knowledge is fully justified. What one cannot do is to impose on the complex processes that must go on in the child relatively simple schemata which are derived from our understanding of adult knowledge and understanding. That is what the interactionist accounts which I have been criticizing in effect do.

On the other hand, I have no model of the mind or model of mental processes to put in the place of those which I reject, because I do not think that there is any such model. If we think that there must be one, then I think that we fail to learn the lesson which Wittgenstein tried to teach when he said what he said about the myth of the mental process. As Norman Malcolm, for example, has pointed out,[3] there is absolutely no reason to suppose that there is one single kind of process involved in all the cases where we speak of someone remembering something. The same applies to other mental phenomena. What the philosopher can do is to provide a more meticulous description of different mental phenomena and work out what is implied in the concepts presupposed in our categorization of such phenomena. If I am right, what is implied in the phenomena with which I have been concerned, if construed properly (all of which presuppose knowledge in one way or another), is such as to make the models of which I have been talking all quite untenable. If that makes the relation between psychology and the study of neural and other physiological processes a more remote and indirect one than many people today hope and suppose, so much the worse for those hopes and suppositions. I am inclined to think — indeed more than inclined to think — that those hopes and suppositions are illusion. Psychology can, fortunately, proceed without them. A philosopher will have done a worthwhile job if he can establish the parameters involved and make clear what has to be brought to bear on the situation if we are to have a proper understanding of what are, probably misguidedly, called 'cognitive processes'. In this respect, in relation to the issues with which I have been concerned, it is reasonable to assert that philosophy of mind presupposes epistemology; and that in turn, as I have sought to make clear, presupposes in the end other things about people and the self. Such is the complexity of the situation and the issues which arise from it. It will have been something at least to draw attention to that complexity.

## NOTES

1  See J. Fodor, *Representations*, Cambridge, Mass., M.I.T. Press, 1981.
2  I have in mind Daniel Dennett's implied view in various papers in his *Brainstorms*, Brighton, Harvester, 1978, that intentionality is at best a heuristic notion without a realist foundation, and Fodor's declared view (*ibid.*) that learning is possible only if all concepts are innate.
3  Norman Malcolm, *Memory and Mind*, Ithaca, Cornell U.P., 1977.

# INDEX

# Index

Campbell, R., 265
Cartesianism, 137, 211, 239, 240, 278, 279
causality, 51-3, 108
causal processes, 13, 15, 16, 45, 46, 85
character, 245, 270
Chisholm, R., 21
Chomsky, N., 135-8, 140, 145-6, 147, 148, 209, 235, 238, 303
chreods, 153
cognition, 6, 7, 142, 170, 302
Cohen, J.M., 147, 207
colour, 11, 54, 126; colour contrast, 12, 13, 17ff., 23
compassion, 286-7
complexity, 77-9, 88
Compton-Burnett, I., 194
concept, 3, 4, 15, 37, 38, 39, 40, 45, 57, 58, 64, 67, 72, 83-4, 85, 86, 110-16, 120, 122, 124, 126ff., 257
conditioning, 3, 91-106
consciousness, 8, 57, 65, 102, 190ff., 197, 202-5, 211, 235, 249, 250, 253, 268
conservation, 50, 80, 113ff.
constancy hypothesis, 11-13, 16, 18, 19, 31, 48
constancy, perceptual, 33, 36
Cook, J., 238
correction, 123, 144, 164-6, 169
cortex, 11, 12
creativity, 159-60

data, 136-7
decentration, 34, 44, 118-19, 123, 124
deception, 6, 195ff.
decision, 251, 263
Democritus, 63
Dennett, D., 8, 305
development, 82, 88, 90, 109, 115, 119, 125, 127, 128, 139, 149-61
Dilman, I., 265, 266
distance perception, 35, 46, 47ff., 54

double-mindedness, 206-7, 263
Dretske, F., 21, 38, 119, 131, 285

ecological optics, 34, 36, 38, 39
education, 55, 72, 76, 83, 90, 129, 139, 149, 156, 160, 287-8, 298
effect, law of, 97
Elliott, R.K., 150, 151, 156, 159, 235
emotion, 7, 115, 176, 208, 230, 235, 257, 261, 267, 268, 269ff., 284, 286ff., 300; false emotion, 291-2
empiricism, 15, 43, 45, 46, 48, 84, 107, 119, 120, 132ff., 135, 140, 141, 173, 209
epigenesis, 153
epistemic/non-epistemic factors, 2, 5, 6, 7, 20, 27, 51, 59, 66-7, 119, 272, 285, 294, 299
epistemology, 4, 6, 27, 32, 79, 125, 130, 174, 305; genetic epistemology, 3, 4, 55, 107, 109, 116ff., 129, 130, 170, 171ff., 176
ethology, 133, 143
exercise, law of, 97
experience, 4, 12, 16, 23, 24, 25, 31, 34, 35, 41, 45, 49, 57, 59, 72, 87, 102, 103, 119, 120, 122, 127, 129, 133-4, 218ff.
exploration, 44, 47
external world, 137-8

feeling, 5, 6, 26, 27, 64, 65, 66, 115, 198, 235, 257, 268, 279, 284, 287, 289, 294-300
figures, ambiguous, 22, 64
filiation, 123
Fingarette, H., 197, 198, 199, 200, 204, 207
Flew, A.G.N., 182
Fodor, J., 28, 305
forms of life, 111, 121-2, 128, 142, 230, 237, 257
foundations of knowledge, 15-16
freedom, 253, 255

307

# Index

knowing-how, 72, 254, 262
knowledge, 1, 2, 3, 5, 6, 7, 15, 16,
  22, 23, 27, 41, 54, 56, 57, 58,
  72, 79, 84, 86, 87, 107, 117,
  122, 129, 133, 134, 138, 139,
  140, 141, 147, 163ff., 174,
  189, 190, 191, 194ff., 202ff.,
  209, 210, 211-12, 212-26,
  227, 231, 233, 244, 257, 262,
  288, 292, 294, 295-6, 300,
  303; practical knowledge, 260-1

Laing, D., 243, 260, 266
Langford, S.G., 150
language, 121, 136-7, 145-6
learning, 3, 4, 7, 8, 31, 37, 40, 50,
  51, 53, 71-90, 102, 103, 127,
  129, 132-48, 157, 283-4,
  286-301; rote learning, 75
light, 17, 35, 36
Locke, J., 49, 107, 131
love, 7, 146, 176, 229, 230,
  267-85, 286-301

Malcolm, N., 304, 305
manipulation, 50, 54
master-slave relation, 255, 256
Mead, G.H., 241-2, 258-9, 266
medium, 60-1
memory, 37, 154, 302, 304
Merleau-Ponty, M., 56
Michotte, A., 51-2, 56
Mischel, T., 110, 131, 265, 266
Moore, F.C.T., 55
motives, 182-4, 210
Müller, J., 12
Murray, D., 56

Nagel, E., 155
Nammour, J., 176, 177
Neisser, U., 44, 55, 57, 68
nerve endings, 12, 14, 57, 61, 93
normality, 78, 88-9, 129
norms, 142, 164, 175, 176

objectivity, 86, 117, 119, 130,
  138
occlusion, perceptual, 41

ontogeny, 110, 130
operants, 98ff., 101
operations, concrete and abstract,
  87, 127, 154

pain, 14, 234, 257
passivity, 43, 44, 46, 49, 51, 53,
  54, 261
Pavlov, I.P., 91-3, 94-5, 97, 98,
  103, 105
perception, 1, 2, 3, 5, 7, 8, 11-29,
  30-42, 43-56, 57-68, 285
personality, 31, 245
personal relations, 5, 144, 196,
  198, 207, 213ff., 216, 221,
  222ff., 227, 229, 230, 231,
  237, 258, 262, 299
persons, 7, 49, 143, 164-5, 208ff.,
  217, 230, 231, 233, 235, 236,
  280
Peters, R.S., 155, 156, 161, 182,
  301
phenomenology, 23, 25, 31, 46,
  51, 96
Phillips, D.Z., 265, 266
philosophy, 15, 108-10, 117-18,
  125, 130, 162, 305
photographs, 31
physics, 50, 80, 87
physiology, 1, 3, 7, 8, 23, 39, 85,
  93-4, 95, 96
Piaget, J., 2, 3, 4, 5, 7, 21, 34, 35,
  43, 44, 45, 50, 55, 74, 79, 80,
  81, 85, 86, 87, 88, 89, 107ff.,
  113, 114-15, 116-25, 127, 128,
  129, 130, 131, 134, 135, 136,
  139, 141, 142, 146, 153, 161,
  163, 173, 174, 177, 228
Plato, 140, 204, 302
possessiveness, 283, 290-1
pride, 271, 272, 287, 297
principles, 72, 73-4, 83, 86, 87,
  144
priorities, epistemological, 89,
  125-9
privacy, 213
psychoanalysis, 7, 184, 188, 201,
  254, 261

309

# Index

psychology, 15, 71, 73, 76, 77, 79, 82, 85, 89, 107, 108-10, 139, 241, 302: cognitive psychology, 1, 2, 6, 7, 128, 303; developmental psychology, 4, 128, 173; social psychology, 7
psychophysics, 31, 32, 48

rationalism, 107, 120, 132, 134, 135, 140, 141
rationality, 199-200, 261, 284-5
realism, 32
reflex, 92-3, 95, 96, 98, 104, 105
Reid, T., 37, 38
reinforcement, 92, 100
relationships, social, 7; see 'personal relations'
retina, 11, 12, 23, 30, 31, 47, 48, 49, 61
roles, 223, 225, 237-8, 258
Roxbee-Cox, J.W., 29
Russell, B., 154, 161
Russell, J., 176, 177
Ryle, G., 240, 266

Sartre, J.-P., 199, 202-3, 211, 238, 240, 266
schema, 57, 63
Schopenhauer, A., 286, 288
Scruton, R.V., 286, 297, 301
Seabourne, A.E., 147
seeing-as, 2, 25, 41, 232, 272, 278, 293, 300
selective mechanisms, 64-5
self, 7, 8, 53, 243ff.; self-consciousness, 242, 243, 260, 290-1; self-deception, 6, 188-9, 192, 193, 194-207, 248-52, 291-2; self-knowledge, 6, 7, 201, 239-65
sensation, 13, 14, 16, 18, 19, 20, 24, 25, 26, 27, 28, 31, 32, 33, 36, 37, 40, 41, 46, 48, 59, 60, 66, 121, 239, 257
sense-data, 14, 35, 36, 43, 45, 59, 120
sense-impressions, 14, 15, 41

sense-organ, 12, 14, 15, 34, 59, 94
set-theory, 75-6
Shoemaker, S., 239, 266
Shotter, J., 298, 301
Sibley, F., 29
sign, 95, 104, 105
situation, 96, 97
skill, 19, 24, 77, 106, 140, 186-7, 231
Skinner, B.F., 3, 91, 97, 98, 101, 102, 103, 106
social factors, 5, 6, 81, 86, 87, 115, 129, 162, 166, 167, 174, 259, 303
Socrates, 206, 242, 243, 263
Spinoza, B., 253, 261
stimulation/stimulus, 11, 14, 15, 16, 31, 32, 33, 34, 38, 40, 47, 48, 57, 61, 62, 63, 66, 67, 92, 95, 99, 105, 118, 228-9; stimulus generalization, 96-7
Stoics, 253
Strawson, P.F., 23, 25, 301
structure, 5, 8, 63, 64, 113-15, 119
subjects, 73ff., 81, 82, 125
sympathy, 288-9, 297, 298
systems, perceptual, 32, 34, 36, 37, 38, 39, 40, 43, 58, 59

Taylor, C., 94, 106, 132, 147, 151, 156, 160, 161
teaching, 89, 129, 144, 286-7
teleology, 151, 155
Thorndike, E.L., 97
Tinbergen, N., 143
Tolman, E.C., 144
touch, 25ff., 36, 46, 47, 59ff.
Toulmin, S., 110-16, 126, 127, 131
Treisman, A.M., 64
truth, 45, 138, 158, 163-4, 167, 175, 224, 256, 294

understanding, 3, 4, 6, 7, 15, 22, 23, 25, 45, 72, 84, 87, 110, 112ff., 122, 126ff., 138, 139, 160, 162-77, 209, 210, 211-12,